MW01194850

Weapons of Mass Distraction

Soft Power and American Empire

Weapons of Mass Distraction

Soft Power and American Empire

Matthew Fraser

KEY PORTER  BOOKS

National Library of Canada Cataloguing in Publication Data

Fraser, Matthew, 1958–
    Weapons of mass distraction: soft power and American empire / Matthew Fraser.

Includes index.
ISBN 1-55263-250-4

    1. Popular culture—United States. 2. United States—Cultural policy. 3. United States—Relations—Foreign countries. I. Title.

E744.5.F73 2003   303.48'273   C2003-903353-8

THE CANADA COUNCIL | LE CONSEIL DES ARTS
FOR THE ARTS | DU CANADA
SINCE 1957 | DEPUIS 1957

ONTARIO ARTS COUNCIL
CONSEIL DES ARTS DE L'ONTARIO

The publisher gratefully acknowledges the support of the Canada Council for the Arts and the Ontario Arts Council for its publishing program.

We acknowledge the financial support of the Government of Canada through the Book Publishing Industry Development Program (BPIDP) for our publishing activities.

We acknowledge the support of the Government of Ontario through the Ontario Media Development Corporation's Ontario Book Initiative.

Key Porter Books Limited
70 The Esplanade
Toronto, Ontario
Canada
M5E 1R2

www.keyporter.com

Design: Peter Maher
Electronic formatting: Heidy Lawrance Associates
Printed and bound in Canada

03 04 05 06 07 5 4 3 2 1

For Rebecca

Contents

Preface

THIS BOOK IS about American power—its sources, its influence, and the deeply paradoxical reactions it provokes.

If this book can claim any originality, it resides in its specific analysis of American "soft" power as a strategic resource in international affairs. We are not primarily concerned here with the Pentagon's military firepower, but rather with the instrumental role of American *pop culture* in U.S. foreign policy. The novelty of this book is its elevation of Hollywood, Disneyland, CNN, MTV, Madonna, Big Macs, and Coca-Cola to a higher status in the complex dynamics of global geopolitics.

The central thesis in the pages that follow may seem outlandish, controversial, and provocative. It will be argued here that, while U.S. military and economic power is indispensable to America's superpower status, soft power historically has been a key strategic resource in U.S. foreign policy. During the First World War, one of America's most powerful ambassadors was Charlie Chaplin. When the Second World War broke out two decades later, Mickey Mouse and Donald Duck conducted Disneyland diplomacy to spread American values throughout the world. Today, in the Information Age of the Internet, soft power has become increasingly instrumental in the emerging world order dominated by an American Empire.

The notion of "empire" is admittedly contentious, even among American leaders. President George W. Bush declared: "America has no empire to extend or utopia to establish." And yet, when President Bush demonstrated the awesome force of American hard power against despicable regimes in

Afghanistan and Iraq, it suddenly became fashionable to discuss, even if disapprovingly, America's imperialist ambitions. When U.S. bombs obliterated targeted sections of Baghdad, the United States was referred to as a "smart-bomb imperium." Despite claims that America is a reluctant hegemon, the new global reality of a Pax Americana is a fact that cannot easily be contradicted.

Today, no nation disputes America's status as the planet's sole superpower. Recognition of America as a "hyperpower" is usually based on material facts—specifically, the superiority of American hard power. Yet America's global domination has been achieved largely through non-military means—in short, through the extension, assertion, and influence of its soft power. If hard power, by definition, is based on *facts*, soft power is based on *values*. American hard power is necessary to maintain global stability. American soft power—movies, pop music, television, fast food, fashions, theme parks—spreads, validates, and reinforces common norms, values, beliefs, and lifestyles. Hard power threatens; soft power seduces. Hard power dissuades; soft power persuades.

Ironically, many Americans are only vaguely aware of the global impact of U.S. soft power. Yet America's adversaries have never underestimated its effects. Mao Zedong once warned that American pop cultural products were "candy-coated bullets." He was wrong on only one point: their impact is much more powerful. One can only imagine how Mao would react today upon learning that one of his successors, Jiang Zemin, succumbed to the allures of American soft power. In 1998, the Chinese leader confessed he'd seen, and enjoyed, the Hollywood movie *Titanic*. Jiang Zemin even recommended the movie to members of his communist Politburo.

Today, American pop culture is ubiquitous. Pop diva Madonna is a superstar in India. In the Middle East, youths dance to the pulsing videos of MTV, while their political leaders watch CNN. Teenagers in Brazil wear Nike sneakers, T-shirts, and baseball caps. American basketball superstar Michael Jordan is hero-worshipped in China, where Kentucky Fried Chicken opened an outlet next to Tiananmen Square and Starbucks opened a store in the Forbidden City. In the West, a Disneyland theme park was built just outside Paris, where café intellectuals drink Coca-Cola while railing against American "cultural imperialism." American television shows—from soap operas to prime-time sitcoms—are watched daily in virtually every corner of the earth where TV sets can be found. American soft power is inescapable, spreading its underlying values and its commitment to free markets and liberal democracy. → real threat

Reactions to American soft power are diverse and ambiguous. Soft power incites awe and envy, but also provokes resentment and hostility. reactions Anti-globalization protestors condemn the United States as a cultural juggernaut driven by the commercial values of "Brand America." Hostile passions are easily inflamed against American cultural symbols, which are associated with a cosmopolitanism that incites deep-seated anxieties. In France, Hollywood and McDonald's are bitterly resented among élites— who denounce "Coca-colonization"—despite profound historical affinities with America as an enlightened republic founded on the same universal values. Even in Canada, the most American nation outside the United States itself, local patriotism is tinged with deep-seated anti-American Canada sentiments. In the non-Western world, American cultural icons and U.S. corporate brands—from MTV to McDonald's—are resented precisely because they are so seductive. If American-style cultural globalization is considered subversive, it's because its powerful messages are so efficiently transmitted and readily received. When Islamic ayatollahs invoked the Koran to ban MTV from their local television screens, their interdictions were symbolic declarations of war against America. Some countries, like Saudi Arabia, benefit from the protection of American hard power, yet banish the symbols of American soft power—despite a predilection among their élites for Cadillacs and Gulfstreams. In North Korea, communist dictator Kim Jong-il idolizes Michael Jordan and is a fan of Hollywood movies, and yet his regime provokes America with the threat of nuclear arms.

These intense and contradictory reactions to American soft power pose a serious challenge to America's overwhelming presence in the world. US Traditionally, U.S. foreign policy has been torn between the cold calcula- foreign tions of self-interested realism and the high-minded mission of moral policy idealism. As Franklin Roosevelt once declared: "Our chief purpose to humanity rests on our combining power with high purpose." Today, in the early years of the 21st century, U.S. foreign policy appears to be inspired by a more assertive unilateralism—or what has been called the Bush Doctrine.

The Bush Doctrine was born on September 11, 2001, when the entire planet watched in horrified disbelief as New York's gleaming World Trade

Center collapsed into a colossal heap of twisted metal onto lower Manhattan. Osama bin Laden's space-age barbarians perpetrated their terrorist violence not against the United States, but against an entire system of values and beliefs. The Islamic terrorists had no specific demands. Their cause professed greater ambitions: the destruction of Western civilization. And the West's leader was the Great Satan: America.

really a "global" act?

When the United States retaliated against the Taliban regime, which was harbouring bin Laden's Al Qaeda operation, U.S. military strikes in Afghanistan immediately provoked violent counter reprisals throughout the Islamic world. America's fanatical enemies, powerless to counter American hard power, targeted the usual symbols of American soft power: McDonald's, Coca-Cola, Pizza Hut, KFC, and Burger King. No American pop cultural icon was safe from hysterical acts of fundamentalist vandalism. The impact of these spontaneous outbursts was immediately felt around the world. International tourism ground to a panic-stricken halt. Major airlines were driven close to bankruptcy. Stock markets plummeted, wiping out billions in wealth. The Walt Disney Company, fearing more terrorist attacks, closed its Disneyland theme parks. Mickey Mouse, it seemed, was hastily retreating to a Disney bunker to escape the wrath of Allah.

targeting of soft power

It did not take long, however, for the U.S. military to retaliate and reassert American power. When President Bush declared that America would embark on a full-scale "crusade" to rid the world of evil, his word choice—denounced by critics—evoked medieval Christian expeditions to recapture the Holy Land from the heathens. Ominous predictions about a looming "clash of civilizations" seemed prescient. America's decimation of bin Laden's terrorist regime in Afghanistan was the first demonstration of the Bush Doctrine's broad reach. The overthrow of Iraqi dictator Saddam Hussein sent an even more powerful message to the world that America was prepared, even unilaterally, to impose its will on the world. Yet once again, the assertion of U.S. hard power met with fierce reactions against symbols of American soft power. The Golden Arches, in particular, became the target of anti-American violence from Buenos Aires and Quito to Seoul and Manila. For America's adversaries, McDonald's has become a preferred substitute for U.S. embassies.

concluding remarks

Make no mistake, America's global domination is based mainly on the superiority of U.S. hard power. But the influence, prestige, and legitimacy of the emerging American Empire will depend on the effectiveness of its soft power. No empire—Greek, Roman, French, Ottoman, British—has been indifferent to the effects of its soft-power resources. The endurance of the American Empire, too, will depend on the effectiveness of its soft power.

This book provides a detailed analysis—historical and contemporary—of the complex role played by soft power in the emergence of an American Empire. Divided into four main sections: movies, television, pop music, and fast food—the pages that follow will trace the origins, history, and current role of soft-power resources in U.S. foreign policy. By the end of this book, it will have been demonstrated that America's soft-power arsenal contains awesome weapons of mass distraction. → conclusion

Introduction

ON AN OFFICIAL visit to North Korea in the fall of 2000, U.S. Secretary of State Madeleine Albright was intrigued to discover that even this brutal Stalinist dictatorship was not impervious to the appeal of American pop culture. Secretary Albright had been tipped off that North Korea's enigmatic leader, Kim Jong-il, was an unconditional fan of the American basketball star Michael Jordan.

Albright had an idea. When she arrived in Pyongyang, Albright ceremoniously presented Kim Jong-il with a basketball personally autographed by the Chicago Bulls superstar. The North Korean dictator was thrilled.

"He loves Michael Jordan," Albright later remarked.

Kim Jong-il surprised Albright even further by demonstrating his impressive knowledge of Hollywood movies, which the North Korean dictator evidently watched obsessively on videocassette. "He told me he agreed with the Oscar choices," confided Secretary Albright when she returned to the United States.[1]

Only a few months later, a bizarre diplomatic incident revealed how Kim Jong-il's fascination with American culture ran in the family. In early May 2001, Japanese police at Tokyo's Narita Airport detained a fat, oafish North Korean man accompanied by two young women and a four-year-old boy who had just arrived on a flight from Singapore. All four were travelling with false passports from the Dominican Republic.

At first, the pudgy, bespectacled North Korean gave his name as Pang Xiong, which is Chinese for "fat bear." But Japanese officials were suspicious. They were used to stopping North Korean criminals from entering

Japan with false passports. This chubby, shambling fellow did not look like a drug smuggler, but he was an unusual sight. First of all, Pang Xiong was a highly unlikely name for a citizen of the Dominican Republic. What's more, none of the four—all Asians—could speak Spanish. The corpulent Asian, though dressed in a dull brown vest and black pants, sported a diamond-encrusted Rolex watch and gold rings. What's more, an eye-popping wad of American $100 bills was stuffed into his pant pocket. His female companions, both in their early thirties, were carrying upscale Louis Vuitton bags.

As Japanese police persisted with their interrogation, the strange North Korean decided to come clean. "I am Kim Jong-nam," he declared. "I'm the son of Kim Jong-il. We just want to visit Tokyo Disneyland."

Astounded, Japanese authorities hastily conducted a background check on the detainee making this extraordinary claim. To their amazement, he did indeed appear to be Kim Jong-nam, the 29-year-old eldest son and political heir to North Korea's communist dictator.

News of Kim Jong-nam's illegal entry into Japan was immediately communicated to Japan's prime minister, Junichiro Koizumi. The Japanese prime minister hastily convened high-level meetings to deal with this delicate—if somewhat ludicrous—diplomatic crisis. Japan had grounds to throw Kim Jong-nam in jail for his effrontery. But such a gesture would almost certainly provoke an international crisis, especially since Japan and North Korea had no formal diplomatic relations. North Korea's communist propaganda machine had long been virulently anti-Japanese. Recently, state-controlled *Pyongyang Times* had asserted that "the intellectual level of Japan equals that of beasts."

Why had Kim Jong-nam been so determined to visit Tokyo's Disneyland? A possible explanation resides in the bizarre, dysfunctional family that has been ruling North Korea's brutal, Stalinist dictatorship for decades. The "hermit kingdom" of North Korea is, by any measure, the most baffling nation on the planet—a despicable ideological paradox that has managed to reconcile an official policy of animosity and isolation vis-à-vis the West and unofficial fascination by its élites for all things Western—including Disneyland.

Kim Jong-nam—nicknamed the "Little General"—is even more of an enigma than his father. Kim *père* inherited North Korea's communist throne from his father, Kim Il Sung, the so-called "Great Leader." Thus,

North Korea is the world's only communist dictatorship whose leadership was following the succession principles of hereditary monarchy. Kim Jong-il, well-known as a vain and capricious womanizer before succeeding his father in the mid-1990s, is an eccentric figure who sports a permed hairdo and wears high-heeled boots to compensate for his small height. By most accounts, he fathered three children, each with a different wife. The mother of Kim Jong-nam was the Dear Leader's second wife, Song Hae Rim, a film actress who had left her first husband in the 1960s to take up with North Korea's playboy communist heir. Kim Jong-nam was born in 1971, but his mother was forced into gilded exile—first in Moscow, then in South Korea—after being supplanted by an even younger beauty.

When the pudgy Kim Jong-nam was growing up in his father's Stalinist regime, he was virtually isolated from the outside world. He was sent to school in Switzerland, but he shunned his studies and preferred to drive about in sports cars. Though he and his father were distant, Kim Jong-il decided to groom his ill-equipped eldest son as his chosen successor. As a young man, Kim Jong-nam was interested mainly in computers and girlfriends. He developed a predilection for sloshing around in the infamous bathhouses of Tokyo's Yoshiwara district, where he was tended to by lovely young women. The frequency of his visits to Tokyo soaplands was such that he became recognizable for the tattoo of a dragon on his back.

On this particular visit to Tokyo, however, Kim Jong-nam appeared to be on his way to Disneyland. The four-year-old boy with him was believed to be his own offspring. Tokyo Disneyland, less than an hour's drive from Narita Airport, is a replica of the original Disneyland theme park built in California in the 1950s. Kim Jong-nam's fascination with Mickey Mouse and Donald Duck was intriguing, to say the least. News of his arrest and detention was immediately leaked and quickly spread throughout the international media. *Time* magazine speculated on the purpose of Kim Jong-nam's bizarre visit to Tokyo: "A Mickey Mouse summit? Maybe in Tomorrowland. In the real world, Pyongyang-watchers from Seoul to Washington were left wondering, as is usually the case with North Korean affairs, what's up."

The timing of Kim Jong-nam's Disneyland diplomatic kerfuffle was not propitious. While the ungainly North Korean dauphin and his companions were being detained in Tokyo, his father was in Pyongyang toasting a diplomatic mission from the European Union led by Swedish prime minister

Goran Persson. While the North Korean dictator was announcing a moratorium on missile testing, Japanese authorities were thrown into a quandary about what to do with his son.

After frantic talks between the Japanese and North Korean governments, it was finally decided that Kim Jong-nam would be hastily deported and flown to China, which was North Korea's staunchest ally. At the Tokyo airport, television cameras caught Kim Jong-nam—the first time he'd been photographed publicly since his cloistered boyhood—as he shambled across the tarmac of Narita Airport. He was a short, pudgy, rather comical-looking man. When his flight arrived in Beijing, he was quickly whisked away in a fog of secrecy by a fleet of vans from the North Korean embassy.

Kim Jong-nam's Disneyland debacle was an embarrassment for everybody involved—not least Kim Jong-nam himself. It was not immediately known what his father thought of his son's escapade. Kim Jong-il himself was known for his fascination with Hollywood movies and American sports stars. He could hardly scold his son for liking Mickey Mouse, Donald Duck, Pluto, and Goofy. Attempting to enter Japan with a forged passport was another matter. As the *Asia Times* put it: "Kim Jong-il, we may safely predict, like Queen Victoria is not amused. His prodigal son—who flew home on Tuesday, after giving reporters the slip in Beijing at the weekend—will have got an almighty dressing-down, and won't be meeting Mickey Mouse any time soon." [2]

Kim Jong-nam's misadventures on his way to Disneyland underscored the perverse paradox, and astounding hypocrisy, at the core of North Korea's Communist power elite. Here was a country that, faithful to doctrinaire Stalinism, was driving its suffering population towards famine due to severe food shortages. And yet, at the same time, the hapless heir to North Korea's despicable regime was swanning around capitalist countries in search of idle distractions in the company of Mickey Mouse, Donald Duck, Pluto, and Goofy—to say nothing of his flashy Rolex watch and posh Louis Vuitton bags.

Kim Jong-nam's fascination for the Magic Kingdom, like his father's hero-worship of Michael Jordan, demonstrated the powerful attraction of American soft power. It wasn't sufficient, however, to deter Kim Jong-il from building hard-power weapons of mass destruction. Only eight months after Kim Jong-nam's Disneyland kerfuffle, President Bush lashed out at North Korea as part of the "axis of evil" threatening global stability. By mid-2003, America and North Korea were heading towards a direct confrontation. Not even a direct intervention by Mickey Mouse could likely defuse this crisis.

Soft Power

This book's subtitle is *Soft Power and American Empire*, which invites a rigorous definition of terms.

Let's begin with *soft power*. The term has been championed by Joseph S. Nye, a Harvard professor who served as Assistant Secretary of Defense under President Bill Clinton. Nye has defined soft power as "the ability to achieve desired outcomes in international affairs through attraction rather than coercion." Nye argues, more specifically, that America's global influence cannot depend solely on its economic strength, military muscle, and coercive capacities. Yes, hard power is needed as an implied threat, and should be used when necessary—as was demonstrated in Afghanistan and Iraq. But American leadership in the world must depend on the assertion of soft power—namely, the global appeal of American lifestyles, culture, forms of distraction, norms, and values. In short, American leadership is more effective when it is *morally* based.[3]

Soft power has the advantage of being much less violent than brute force. It can claim, moreover, the not inconsequential virtue of being much less costly. Why keep the peace with ground troops, aircraft carriers, and inter-continental missiles when Big Macs, Coca-Cola, and Hollywood blockbusters can help achieve the same long-term goals? Soft power also includes artistic expression and institutional arrangements—such as travelling exhibitions and scholarly exchange programs—that help export American models. When foreign students undertake studies in the United States, they return to their home countries immersed in American values, attitudes, and modes of thinking.

The attraction of American culture has been analyzed and debated for many decades. Many have been highly critical of the effects of so-called American "cultural imperialism." As Madeleine Albright observed at a White House conference shortly before leaving office in late 2000: "There are some who describe our country as hegemonic, equate globalization with Americanization, and say unkind things about our hamburgers." Albright's quip about Big Macs doubtless would be taken seriously by French intellectuals who rail against America's global "McDomination." Hostility towards American soft power is frequently a negative symptom of its effectiveness.

The first chorus of ideological protest against American soft power came not from Parisian café culture, but from within the United States itself. The historical backdrop for this groundswell of cultural self-indictment was the turbulent 1960s and student radicalism on many American campuses. In 1969, Herbert Schiller published *Mass Communications and American Empire*, in which he argued that the U.S. State Department was sponsoring an "electronic invasion" of the world—led by U.S. media giants such as CBS, RCA, and NBC—to promote the interests of American capitalism. In the 1960s, like-minded critics of U.S. imperialism regarded American mass culture with deep suspicion as an intoxicating instrument of worldwide domination. Some claimed America was exploiting its superpower influence to manipulate the agendas of international regimes regulating global telecommunications, satellites, postal systems, and intellectual property.

By the 1970s, criticism of American cultural imperialism had become a received truth in the mainstream. Some anti-American polemicists developed elaborate theories about the noxious effects of U.S. pop logos and icons. It was argued, for example, that the exploits of Donald Duck and Mickey Mouse were comic-book expressions of American capitalist ideology. In the 1980s, the action hero Rambo was interpreted as a Hollywood-fabricated warrior symbolizing U.S. global domination. Donald Duck, Mickey Mouse, and Rambo were thus archetypal bad guys—pop-cultural Ugly Americans.

Critics of American cultural domination could at least be credited with conceptual coherence: They regarded the United States not as a country, but as an imperial power. This notion was embedded, in fact, in the semantics of the emotionally charged term, cultural *imperialism*. By definition, imperialism suggests domination by a powerful centre of a submissive periphery. Critics of American cultural imperialism located the centre as the United States and the periphery as the non-Western world. In the 1970s, when America was extricating itself from the Vietnam War, this schism—between the West and non-West—galvanized a global anti-imperialist movement that was deeply hostile to the United States. The movement found institutional expression through the United Nations Economic, Scientific, and Cultural Organization (UNESCO), whose political agenda had become captured by newly decolonized Third World countries on the non-Western periphery. UNESCO's famous MacBride Report, published in 1980, openly accused the United States and its Western allies of monopolizing the world's cultural flows. The target of UNESCO's anti-American diatribe was the so-called "Free Flow Doctrine," which advocated the free transmission and exchange of information, ideas, and cultural products without restriction or censorship. UNESCO's proposed antidote to the Free Flow Doctrine was the creation of a "New World Information and Communications Order," which would end the West's alleged monopoly on information flows.

Against this backdrop, some industrialized nations—notably France—broke with traditional alliances to join attacks against U.S. cultural imperialism. In 1981, France's flamboyant minister of culture, Jack Lang, provoked a diplomatic incident while attending a UNESCO conference in Mexico. Lang lashed out against the noxious cultural influence of American television shows, such as *Dallas,* and railed against the United States as a "vast empire of profit" that was "no longer appropriating only territories but peoples' trains of thought, ways of life." When Lang's anti-imperialist call-to-arms was reported in the French press, he was cheered by Parisian intellectuals who had long denounced American "Coca-colonization." They were joined by critics in the United States, where the movement of political correctness found a natural ally in tirades against U.S. cultural imperialism. In 1986, students at Stanford University protested against a course in Western civilization by chanting: *"Hey hey, ho ho, Western culture's gotta go!"* Some anti-Western critics, notably Edward Said, claimed that great works of art—from Jane Austen novels to Verdi operas such as *Aida*—were propagandistic expressions of the West's cultural domination. Denounced for its moral absolutism, the West was rejected, *holus bolus,* in favour of value-free relativism. There were no longer any moral absolutes. The new creed was: Do your own thing, anything goes.[4]

In this climate, it became fashionable to be anti-American during the 1980s, when the presence of Ronald Reagan in the White House divided Americans and provoked ridicule abroad. President Reagan, while revered by American conservatives, was mocked on U.S. campuses as a B-movie leading man who once cavorted on screen with a chimpanzee in *Bedtime for Bonzo*. Hollywood, it seemed, had captured the White House. President Reagan indeed turned to Hollywood for his most powerful metaphors, *metaphor* including "Star Wars" for his anti-Soviet defence system. Hollywood was also producing movies such as *Wall Street* and *Bonfire of the Vanities*, which reflected a pervasive mood in the United States that America was being eroded from within by its own moral corruption. "Greed is good" was now a respectable credo. Gang violence was turning American cities into urban war zones. Some portrayed the United States as ancient Rome, rotting at its core, a global superpower going through a death-rattle phase of inexorable decline. America had emerged from the Second World War as the undisputed leader of the free world, but only four decades later the United States seemed like a spent force. It seemed the vaunted "American Century" was coming to a turbulent end.

Prophets of doom marshalled seemingly unimpeachable evidence to support their claims that America was terminally ill. They observed that U.S. share of world manufacturing output had severely eroded since 1950. Foreign competitors were now hammering America in strategic sectors such as consumer electronics, steel, automobiles, semiconductors, computers, and media. The signs of America's decline were everywhere— especially in Asia, where Japan's economic star was rising. Jacques Attali, chief advisor to François Mitterrand in the Elysée Palace, dismissed America as "Japan's granary." At the end of the 1980s, when the Japanese electronics giant Sony bought a Hollywood studio, Columbia Pictures, the takeover was splashed ominously on the cover of *Time* and *Newsweek*. Many Americans feared that the Japanese—the perpetrators of Pearl Harbor—were deploying their strong currency to buy the "soul" of America. The bias of global power seemed to be shifting inexorably from the Atlantic-oriented Old World towards the Pacific Rim dominated by Asian tigers.

Debate about America's decline was particularly animated in the United States. MIT economist Lester Thurow observed: "Rome lasted a thousand years, the British Empire about 200. Why are we slipping in about 50 years?" The most highly publicized voice of the so-called "Declinist" school was Paul Kennedy, a Yale professor whose 1988 book, *The Rise and Fall of the Great Powers*, became an international bestseller. Kennedy argued that the United States was the latest example of a great power whose decline could be attributed to "imperial overstretch." America was suffering from an overextended strategic commitment to foreign domination, yet had diminishing economic means to maintain its global military presence. The prognosis: the United States, with weakening industrial and agricultural output relative to other nations, was destined to become just one of several powers in an emerging multipolar world. Hollywood's Rambo, it seemed, had merely been a compensatory expression of American insecurity. [5]

US may not fall, but won't remain in power

But the Declinists were dead wrong. Kennedy's thesis, while fascinating, was quickly repudiated by watershed events he had failed to predict. Only a year later, the Soviet Union collapsed, the Berlin Wall came crashing down, and America re-emerged triumphantly as the planet's sole superpower in the post-Cold War era. The Declinists, reduced to embarrassed silence, were suddenly out of favour. Their "Revivalist" adversaries, once dismissed as American jingoists, were now vindicated by the reassertion of American power. The American Century wasn't over after all. A glorious epoch of American power and prestige promised to extend well into the next millennium.

The Revivalists wasted no time in trumpeting their victory. In 1990, Henry Nau published *The Myth of America's Decline*—a theme that found comfort in Francis Fukuyama's famous essay, "The End of History," which asserted that liberal democracy had finally triumphed over socialism and other adversaries. The most articulate Revivalist was Joseph Nye, whose book *Bound to Lead* was an eloquent manifesto for American leadership into the 21st century. The United States, argued Nye, should not retreat into isolationism. America should assume its role as the world's pre-eminent

not isolation

superpower and make the necessary investments to meet its commitment to provide global leadership. [6]

Nye correctly understood that the Declinists—whose claims were based on measures of industrial output and military spending—had failed to grasp the critical importance of intangible dimensions of U.S. influence. In the past, imperial powers like France depended on agriculture and a large population to assert their domination, and later Britain exploited its superior industrial and naval strength to become a global empire. In the future, American power could not be based solely on military capability or economic domination. America would also have to lead by example. And to do so,

America's most persuasive weapons were its values, way of life, and culture. In other words, American soft power. *↳ establishing a new super power weapon of preservation*

Empire & Globalization

Many Americans would bristle at the suggestion their country has imperial ambitions. America is a republic, they would say—not an empire.

Yet long before the Declaration of Independence, great republics had expanded into great empires. Ancient Rome began as a republic, and ended up a vast empire. In the 21st century, it might be asked: Has America—whose national capital pays architectural tribute to classical antiquity—followed the same inexorable trajectory towards imperial power? And if so, is an imperial America good for the world?

Empires, more than other political constructs, depend on soft power. Indeed, empires are unique because they are essentially *cultural* constructions. True, empires are built on material resources, driven by wealth accumulation, and require political organization, institutions, and efficient infrastructures. Empires, formally speaking, impose some form of domination over the territories they control. But empires are not merely commercial or military enterprises. Empires also impose informal forms of domination through soft power. Empires encompass shared beliefs and values. Race, ethnicity, and class are not criteria for inclusion; adhesion is acknowledged through common cultural bonds. Minorities are not excluded, but embraced so long as they make no specific territorial claims. Empires may contain a multitude of ethnic groups within their bosom, but they assume an overarching cultural identity.

Empires thus can be contrasted with city-states, feudal orders, and nation-states. City-states are commercially driven. Feudalism is a moral order whose cohesion is assured through a power structure founded on personal fealty. The logic of nation-states is based on power and territory. Nations are turned inward, confer exclusive citizenship rights, and exercise a monopoly of legitimate violence over demarcated territories. States impose border controls. In short, nations are concerned principally with the logic of territory and legitimacy.

Empires, by contrast, are socially inclusive and geographically expansive. Most empires have vaguely established frontiers, which the ancient

Romans called *limes*—a term whose semantics can still be found in the notion of *limits*. If the nation-state is preoccupied by the dictates of space, the empire is concerned with the challenge of endurance. In a word, empires are situated in time. Empires, above all, tend to be founded on universalist pretensions, which provide moral justification for their expansive ambitions. Hence the vital role of soft power. Throughout the entire course of history, few empires—Greek, Roman, Ottoman, Austro-Hungarian, French, British—have prospered without exploiting the advantages of their soft power. [7]

like US

The Roman Empire was driven by the pretension of *dominium mundi*. Rome's world domination was assured largely through military coercion. Rome dealt with the challenge of centralized administration through a complex system of military force, administrative organization, tribute taking, and infrastructure building. But if physical constraints and political subordination were indispensable facts of life in the Roman Empire, neither was perceived as coercive because a common culture of values forged a bond among those, especially élites, who were subject to imperial coercion. Rome's symbolic coercion—or soft power—was achieved through the spreading of Roman civilization.

Rome's soft power policy was highly successful. Edward Gibbon, in his monumental *The Decline and Fall of the Roman Empire*, observed: "The Roman name was revered among the most remote nations of the earth. The fiercest barbarians frequently submitted their differences to the arbitration of the emperor." The Romans, added Gibbon, were acutely conscious of the necessity to combine military domination with cultural pre-eminence: "So sensible were the Romans of the influence of their language over national manners, that it was their most serious care to extend, with the progress of their arms, the use of the Latin tongue." The desired result was pervasive cultural assimilation throughout the Roman Empire, which Gibbon estimated counted some 120 million souls. "Domestic peace and union were the natural consequences of the moderate and comprehensive policy embraced by the Romans," he noted. "Obedience of the Roman world was uniform, voluntary, and permanent. The vanquished nations, blended into one great people, resigned the hope, nay the wish, of resuming their independence, and scarcely considered their own existence as distinct from the existence of Rome." [8]

Only the Greeks, while acknowledging Roman supremacy, remained disdainful of Roman culture. "The situation of the Greeks was very different from that of the barbarians," noted Gibbon. "The former had been long since civilized and corrupted. They had too much taste to relinquish their language, and too much vanity to adopt any foreign institutions. Still preserving the prejudices, after they had lost the virtues, of their ancestors, they affected to despise the unpolished manners of the Roman conquerors, whilst they were compelled to respect their superior wisdom and power." Many centuries later, modern Americans would confront this form of cultural snobbery when encountering the Old World pretensions of Europeans, especially their British cousins. As British prime minister Harold MacMillan once remarked: "These Americans represent the new Roman Empire and we Britons, like the Greeks of old, must teach them how to make it go." *[strategic US/Brit bond]*

After the fall of Rome circa A.D. 476, the Roman world order collapsed into a prolonged state of chaos and violence commonly known as the Dark Ages. Several centuries later, the Holy Roman Empire—which Voltaire remarked was "neither holy, nor Roman, nor an empire"—provided a classic example of a cultural construction of imperial ambition and scope. It contained some 243 micro-states and had no definite territorial shape. Though secular rule was exercised by local potentates, the common cultural bond stretching across Europe was Christian faith, which was transmitted by a trans-regional cultural élite whose members spoke and wrote in Latin. *[commonality in culture]* Monastic and knightly orders also served as trans-regional institutions that helped spread Christianity—or "defend the Faith"—during the bloody Crusades. Despite the Holy Roman Empire's pretensions to recreate Rome's centralized administration and revive its cultural glory, Europe stubbornly remained a patchwork of overlapping dukedoms and principalities. The Church's dominion was a non-territorial sphere whose supreme ruler, the Pope, found himself in constant conflict with territorial-based potentates, called kings.

The long overdue collapse of the Holy Roman Empire in 1648—with the Treaty of Westphalia—is often cited as the end of feudalism and the birth of the international order of nation-states. [9] The so-called "Westphalian" system of state diplomacy, based on international law and territorial sovereignty, dominated international affairs until the end of the Second World War and beyond. Still, feudalism did not die in 1648. Modern nation-states, as we know them today, didn't crystallize until the 19th century. What's more, quasi-feudal empires endured well into the 20th century. It took the First World War to put an end to the world's major empires: Russian, Austro-Hungarian, and Ottoman. The British and French empires would soon follow, collapsing after the Second World War when the United States and Soviet Union emerged as the world's two superpowers. This historical dynamic was not marked by sharp ruptures, but characterized by a complex overlapping of old and new political orders. Generally speaking, however, during the 300-year period from Westphalia till the Second World War, the world remained dominated by Old World empires that deployed a combination of hard and soft power to assert their supremacy and expand their global reach. Throughout this period, the imperial ambitions of France, Britain, Spain, Portugal, Holland, Belgium, and other European countries came into conflict as each scrambled to find, explore, seize, control, and exploit overseas territories. In many respects, their imperial rivalry triggered a precursor of what today we call *globalization.*

At the outset of the 20th century, America benefited from tremendous historical good luck. After many decades languishing on the margins of Euro-centric geopolitics, the United States was emerging as a powerful nation with a rightful place at the high table of international diplomacy. A combination of technological changes, shifting demographic realities, and cataclysmic wars provided America with powerful economic, military, and cultural advantages vis-à-vis Europe and the rest of the world. Above all, America was the beneficiary of the first modern wave of globalization at the end of the 19th century. During the *belle époque*—from the 1890s to the outbreak of the Great War in 1914—globalization in trade, information flows, and migratory movements was even more intense than similar patterns today. In the mid-19th century, the push for free trade, linkage of capital markets, building of railways, laying of submarine telegraph cables, and trans-Atlantic migrations of people had set the stage for a great burst of globalization toward the end of the century. The importance of submarine cables and telegraphy as an electronic conduit—not unlike the Internet more than a century later—cannot be overstated. In the late 1850s, cables were stretched across the Atlantic Ocean to link Britain and North America. Soon underwater cables were linking Europe with the Middle East and India and other colonial outposts. Messages from the imperial centres of

Europe could now be transmitted in a matter of seconds to colonial possessions throughout the world, improving the efficiency of both commerce and military operations. These new technologies not only reinforced the dominance of imperial powers over their colonies, but also strengthened their strategic position regarding other imperial rivals. If transmission wasn't as simultaneous as today's satellite or Internet technology, news travelled with astonishing rapidity thanks to the telegraph. When the *Titanic* sank in the early morning hours of April 15, 1912, people on several continents woke up the same morning to the tragic news.

These historical facts are significant because they demonstrate how 19th century globalization shifted power from Europe to America. The United States had the good fortune to be emerging as a strong and populous nation at precisely this time in history. Previously, worldwide cultural fascination with the United States had been mainly folkloric, especially through tales about the "Wild West." In the 1890s, Buffalo Bill enthralled audiences throughout the world with his famous rodeo show, thus reinforcing the popular image of America as being populated by rough-and-tumble cowboys. But even while Buffalo Bill was spreading these stereotypes throughout Europe, America was emerging as a powerful industrial nation.[10]

When Theodore Roosevelt entered the White House in 1901, he declared: "Our people are neither craven nor weaklings, and we face the future high of heart and confident of soul eager to do the great work of a great world power." Even in Britain, whose empire was at the apogee of its glory, it was obvious the young American republic was emerging as a global power. In 1901, the British journalist William Stead wrote a book with the prescient title, *The Americanization of the World*. More than a century later, fulminators against American "brand bullies" doubtless would be intrigued to learn that, circa 1900, there were similarly paranoid declarations that American brands—Kodak cameras, Otis elevators, Heinz ketchup, Colgate tooth powder, Borden condensed milk, Williams soap, Waterbury pocket watches, and Quaker oats—were dominating the world. In 1901, Englishman Fred McKenzie wrote *The American Invaders*, in which he observed: "These newcomers have acquired control of almost every new industry created during the past fifteen years." [11]

Following the First World War, President Woodrow Wilson played a key role in the post-war treaty negotiations at Versailles Palace. While Old

World empires were either collapsing or retreating, America was emerging triumphantly as a great power. The sphere of American influence had already expanded well beyond its own geographical backyard. America's most powerful ambassador was Hollywood. In the early 20th century, the emergence of motion pictures as a mass audience form of entertainment provided the United States with a tremendous soft-power advantage, as "silent" American movies captivated audiences throughout the world. At the end of the Second World War, America was the undisputed master of the free world. American hard power had established U.S. military superiority beyond any doubt. Now American soft power—already spreading globally in the world's movie theatres—found reinforcement with jazz music, television, fashion, rock music, chewing gum, and American cigarettes. America's only adversary in the post-war era was communism. During the Cold War, the U.S. government supported, and even financed, the spread of American soft power through state-owned broadcaster Voice of America and the State Department's United States Information Agency. At the same time, the CIA covertly sponsored cultural activities as part of its anti-Soviet operations. The CIA-financed Congress for Cultural Freedom, for example, financed publications, exhibitions, conferences and other events that attracted numerous intellectual and artistic figures such as Hugh Trevor-Roper, Arthur Koestler, Raymond Aron, and Bertrand Russell. These "Atlanticists" were mobilized by the CIA to counter the influence of equally prominent intellectuals—Albert Einstein, Leonard Bernstein, Arthur Miller, Aaron Copeland—who clustered around so-called "peace" conferences that scarcely concealed a communist-inspired agenda.

By the 1960s, new communications technologies like satellites made Cold War espionage more efficient. Satellites, which facilitated the global transmission of television images, set the stage for round-the-clock all-news channels such as CNN. Jet travel, meanwhile, made it possible for millions of people to visit exotic locations, which helped spread American lifestyles and values. The sights, sounds, images, and tastes of American pop culture—Big Macs, Coca-Cola, Disney theme parks, Hollywood movies, rock music—were globally omnipresent. By the 1980s, the term *globalization* had become entrenched in the vocabulary of international affairs. Geopolitical experts analyzed the impact of cultural flows, financial exchanges, migratory patterns, multinational corporations, and even criminal organizations. And international agencies like UNESCO likewise analyzed information flows to support their own ideological agendas.

Today, globalization is no longer a disputed term, but there is considerable disagreement about its intensity, impact, and long-term consequences.

Neo-liberals—or "Hyper-globalists"—subscribe to a largely economic theory of globalization, arguing that new forms of social, cultural, and political organization are emerging in a borderless, cosmopolitan world where states are no longer all-powerful actors. They associate globalization not only with free market forces, but also with the triumph of liberal democracy and the emergence of a global civil society. In the opposing camp, so-called "Realists" argue that globalization has not diminished the powers of states, which remain the privileged units of international diplomacy and sole instruments of legitimate constraint in the enforcement of laws and treaties. Realists claim, moreover, that states—contrary to exaggerated predictions of their imminent demise—have been the main beneficiaries of globalization. States, they argue, can impose their agendas on the global order by leveraging their power through transnational organizations such as the United Nations and World Trade Organization. Adherents of the Realist school maintain that neo-liberals have seized on globalization as a catch-phrase to legitimize a transparent political agenda in favour of market-based economic solutions to social problems.[12]

Others argue that globalization is synonymous with "Americanization"—or U.S. imperialism. Proponents of this view include the youthful protestors who have taken up the anti-American cause of their Marxist forbears and brought their slogans to the streets of Seattle, Davos, Prague, Quebec, and Genoa. They have failed to grasp, however, a critical distinction between *imperialism* and *globalization*. The first is a deliberate project of a center extending its influence and control over a periphery. The second describes the infinitely subtler and more complex interplay among many interconnecting cultures and economies.

A more recently developed analysis has attempted to strike a balance between the Hyper-globalist and Realist positions: Globalization is perceived as a complex process that nonetheless is profoundly transforming the nature of political communities, modes of social interaction, and structure of cultural identities. This assessment of globalization is not incompatible with what is sometimes referred to as *glocalization*—namely, that the world is moving toward an era in which there is no longer any clear distinction between local and global, between centre and periphery, between internal and external, between domestic and foreign. A constant tension exists between the two levels, even within patterns of cultural identity. The influences of soft power operate naturally in this sphere: American culture may extend far beyond the borders of the United States, but it is also penetrated and influenced by the influences of innumerable other cultures.

This analysis of globalization is not incompatible with the theory known as "New Feudalism," which associates globalization with the absence of centralized systems of power, the disappearance of sovereign territories, the emergence of overlapping spheres of influence, fluctuating frontiers, and diffuse, flexible, and shifting cultural identities with multiple loyalties.[13] Zbigniew Brzezinski, in his book *The Grand Chessboard*, evoked the image of America as a neo-medieval Holy Roman Empire when describing America's allies as "vassals and tributaries." According to Brzezinski, a top White House advisor in the 1970s under President Jimmy Carter, American imperial geostrategy would seek to "prevent collusion and maintain security dependence among vassals, to keep tributaries pliant and protected, and to keep the barbarians from coming together." The evocation of the Middle Ages, if not the Roman Empire, could not be more explicit.[14]

A more accessible metaphor for Americanized global culture has been evoked by Benjamin Barber, whose vision of "McWorld" describes a bleak Disneyland civilization where values are transmitted by MTV, Macintosh, Microsoft, and Big Macs. McWorld symbolizes the triumph of market forces and consumer reflexes. McWorld may be materially successful, but it risks degenerating into a vast global shopping mall populated by a universal tribe of soulless consumers. Barber's central argument is this: Neo-liberal globalization's victory is essentially Phyrric because market forces and unbridled consumerism do not necessarily produce liberal democracy. [15]

McWorld's fiercest adversary is the violent, bloody, and fanatical world of "Jihad," a term that evokes Osama bin Laden and Iran's mad mullahs. McWorld and Jihad paradoxically depend on each other to affirm their own values. Ayatollahs need the metaphorical imagery of America as the "Great Satan" to reinforce their moral authority, and America exploits the demonic personas of Saddam Hussein and Osama bin Laden to justify strategic U.S. military strikes and troop movements.

It is possible to share Barber's pessimism and still feel confidant that good will triumph over evil. Samuel Huntington, for example, has amplified on Barber's McWorld vs. Jihad vision with a more ambitious—and more provocative—theory known as "clash of civilizations." Huntington argues that, in the post–Cold War world, the most significant cleavages in world affairs are no longer ideological, political, or economic, but *cultural*.

"The distribution of cultures in the world reflects the distribution of power," observes Huntington. "Trade may or may not follow the flag, but culture almost always follows power. Throughout history the expansion of the power of a civilization has usually occurred simultaneously with the flowering of its culture, and has almost always involved its using that power to extend its values, practices, and institutions to other societies."

Huntington asserts that, in the post–Cold War world, the main fault line in geopolitics is no longer between the United States and Soviet Union, or between capitalism and communism—but rather between *civilizations*. Thus, in the future, the deepest conflicts in international affairs will not break out between nations within a single civilization—as occurred during European conflicts from the Renaissance to the Second World War—but between civilizations themselves. More to the point, it's the West's universalist pretensions that is bringing McWorld into conflict with other civilizations—notably Islam. [16]

The spectre of a violent clash of civilizations—no longer an unthinkable catastrophe after the events of September 11, 2001—comports with Barber's vision of a capitalist McWorld confronted by bloody Jihad cultures. But Huntington remains optimistic about America's role as the beacon of Western civilization. Huntington concedes that the West, like all previous civilizations, will inevitably decline and perish. He even admits that American society is showing classic symptoms associated with moral decline: family breakdown, crime, violence, hedonism, lack of civic spirit, and poor scholastic achievement. Yet Huntington affirms the strategic importance of soft power as a key resource for American influence and the spreading of Western values.

"The futures of the United States and of the West," he says, "depend on Americans reaffirming their commitment to Western civilization."

The Geopolitics of Popular Culture

This book's main argument—that soft power is a key strategic resource for America's global domination—is based on two central postulates about the origins, nature, transmission, impact, and potential long-term consequences of soft power.

First, while American soft power was deployed throughout the 20th century to promote the national interests of the United States, the global extension of American soft power was never strictly a trade issue, as economic interests were invariably linked with an ideological mission to disseminate American values in the face of geopolitical threats, especially Communism. In the post-Cold War era, however, soft power has become a key strategic resource for the American Empire. America has emerged as an undisputed imperial power whose soft-power umbrella overarches the entire world. Its legitimacy is acknowledged in liberal democracies that share cultural values and strategic interests with America, and meets resistance in regions where those values are not shared.

Second, American soft power is historically unprecedented due to the scope, velocity, and intensity of cultural globalization. The global transmission of American soft power is virtually simultaneous thanks to communications technologies such as satellites and the Internet. Foreign cultures are no longer protected by the ramparts of time, space, and barriers such as high tariffs and distribution costs. The precise effects of American soft power, and reactions it provokes, can be debated, but the reach of American soft power is indisputably global. Few corners of the world have not been touched by its influence. The global ubiquity of American soft power has made it more difficult to resist in regions where élites are hostile to liberal democracy and free-market capitalism.

And yet animosity toward American soft power persists, even in the West. But as we shall see, hostility toward American soft power in Western countries is not based, despite political rhetoric, on a rejection of American values in the name of national "cultural sovereignty." Rather, anti-American cultural resistance in Western countries is the expression of an institutionalized complicity between national political élites and domestic commercial players seeking to protect their mutual interests. Cultural trade skirmishes between America and its Western allies are little more than family feuds characterized by rhetorical posturing by governments that, in most cases, deliberately blur distinctions between commercial self-interest and cultural protectionism.

Hostile reactions to American soft power in non-Western cultures, on the contrary, reveal more obviously demarcated fault lines drawn by deeply entrenched religious, moral, and ideological differences. This cultural divide, though increasingly porous, poses serious geopolitical challenges to the American Empire. If multilateral trade disputes within the WTO are essentially family feuds among industrialized Western nations, American soft power faces serious opposition from cultures whose religious doctrine, political ideology, and underlying value systems are hostile to the American way of life.

The global triumph of an American Empire should invite debate about the long-term role and impact of soft power in the new world order. Under a Pax Americana, what will happen to the definition of political communities, the structure of cultural identities, and the forging of individual loyalties? Some believe individuals will increasingly feel disconnected from the state-based authority of territorially defined nations, that cultural identities will be more flexible, shifting between local roots and wider spheres defined by broad common values. At the same time, the dictates of geopolitics could shift from state-centred diplomacy dominated by nations to soft-power geopolitics dominated by an American Empire possessing not only the strategic advantages of overwhelming military and economic superiority, but also a decisive leading edge in a global Information Age.[17]

It has famously been asserted, and often repeated, that communications technologies are shrinking the world into a "global village." This book asserts that, in fact, soft power is expanding the world into a global empire.

one
Movies
The Power and the Glamour

PLANET HOLLYWOOD. The name says it all: Hollywood going global, ubiquitous Tinseltown, promoting the American way of life through an extravagant network of gastronomical theme parks. On the menu: California nosh, movie memorabilia, and the cult of global celebrity.

The first Planet Hollywood restaurant opened in Los Angeles in 1991. Its original investors boasted a clutch of American movie icons including Sylvester Stallone and Arnold Schwarzenegger. What better Hollywood symbols—Rambo and Terminator—to spearhead Planet Hollywood's global expansion. Planet Hollywood restaurants attracted millions of tourists worshipping at the commercial temple of American movie stardom. As new Planet Hollywood restaurants opened around the world, Stallone, Schwarzenegger, Bruce Willis, Whoopi Goldberg, Demi Moore, and other superstars were flown in for movie-premiere-like galas that attracted throngs of adoring fans. By the late 1990s, Planet Hollywood had opened nearly 100 outlets in far-flung locations including Cannes, Munich, Dublin, Dubai, Kuala Lumpur, and Cape Town.

But Planet Hollywood, like other American icons, soon became a victim of its own global success. Its name, logo, and allure of international celebrity culture transformed Planet Hollywood into a neon sign for America itself. And Planet Hollywood quickly discovered how American pop culture and global geopolitics can become dangerously intertwined.

In late August 1998, a terrorist bomb blast devastated the Planet Hollywood outlet in Cape Town. Two people were killed and 25 others were seriously injured. When a group calling itself "Muslims Against Global Oppression" claimed responsibility, the origins and motives of the attack were obvious. The Islamic terrorist group declared that the bombing had been a "fire-against-fire" reprisal against America. A week earlier, the United States had launched cruise missile strikes against suspected Islamic terrorist targets in two countries, Afghanistan and Sudan. The U.S. military strikes had been retaliation for terrorist bombings of the American embassies in Kenya and Tanzania. More than 250 people had been killed in the attacks against the U.S. diplomatic compounds. These bombings had been masterminded, ominously, by Osama bin Laden, who at the time was a little-known, Saudi-born billionaire driven by a deep-seated hatred for America. Bin Laden's terrorist agents had not selected a Planet Hollywood restaurant at random. The word "Hollywood" powerfully evoked America's global cultural domination. Bin Laden had chosen Cape Town because President Clinton had recently visited South Africa.

The U.S. reprisals provoked a groundswell of anti-American hysteria throughout the Moslem world. Its targets included McDonald's restaurants and movie theatres showing Hollywood movies. In the Islamic world, Hollywood was feared not only as a massive commercial juggernaut, but also as a global conveyor of values that threatened regimes whose power was based on political ideologies and religious doctrines profoundly antithetical to American values of individualism, capitalism, secularism, and cosmopolitanism.

For the enemies of the United States, Hollywood and America were interchangeable targets of their wrath.

Motion Pictures and American Power

Hollywood has been a powerful instrument of U.S. foreign policy from the birth of motion pictures. Fortuitously, cinema was born—circa 1900—at precisely the moment America was emerging as a major power on the world stage. And it did not take long for motion pictures to become a myth-making extension of America's global ambitions.

Many believe Thomas Edison, the famous American inventor, invented motion pictures. It is true that, at the end of the 19th century, Edison devised a peephole contraption called the Kinetoscope. But it was France's Lumière brothers who invented the first machine, called a Ciné- matographe, that projected moving pictures onto a screen. Movies were born in France, not America.

paradoxical

After giving their first Cinématographe demonstration in their home- town of Lyons in 1895, the Lumières took their invention to Paris to sponsor a public projection in the French capital. The first showing took place in the basement of the Grand Café on the Place de l'Opéra. Enormous crowds were soon lining up and waiting for hours along the boulevard des Capucines to get a glimpse of the marvels of motion pictures. The conservative-minded Louis Lumière was skeptical about the future of cinema. He called motion pictures "an invention without any commercial future."

The Lumières nonetheless were shrewd enough to take their newfangled contraption to America. On June 29, 1896, the Cinématographe enjoyed a spectacular commercial debut at a New York vaudeville theatre. The *New York Times* ecstatically hyped motion pictures as the "sensation of Europe" and "the greatest marvel of the 19th century."

While New Yorkers were dazzled by motion pictures, the Cinématographe arrived in America at an inauspicious time for commercial relations with France, which in the late 19th century had become tense. France, it was true, had offered America the Statue of Liberty as a fraternal gift in 1886. But the two great republics remained mutually suspicious rivals. The emergence of photography, in particular, had exacerbated U.S.–French trade tensions. In 1890, the McKinley Tariff—named after future president William McKinley—imposed high import duties on French photographic equipment and other products in order to promote America's infant industries.

When the Lumières arrived in America with an invention even more compelling than photography, crafty American businessmen instantly saw the commercial potential of motion pictures. One of them was an associate of Thomas Edison who hastily invented a U.S.-patented projector called the Biograph. Another U.S.-made camera was developed by the Vitagraph company. French ingenuity had created movies, but American commercial savvy would harness their mass-audience appeal.

In its earliest days, the American motion picture industry was grafted directly onto vaudeville theatres to attract working-class audiences seeking popular entertainment. The first American movies were thus shamelessly sensational. When the Spanish–American War broke out in 1898, early motion picture cameras followed the lead of "yellow" newspaper journalism by stirring up patriotic emotions during America's first imperial war. In New York, movie audiences clapped and cheered at brief images of the U.S. battleship *Maine* sailing off for Cuba—where, in fact, it later sank in the Havana harbour. Other early American movies, such as *The Great Train Robbery*, appealed to mass audiences with simple and sensational plots.

Yet, America was a mere colony of the French movie industry in the early years of cinema. In France, pioneers such as Charles Pathé and Léon Gaumont, backed by major French banks, were churning out hundreds of exportable films. In the United States, French movies were sweeping the country by 1905. The most lucrative venues for motion pictures were no longer vaudeville theatres, but storefront screening rooms called "nickelodeons"—so-named because a nickel was the price of admission and "odeon" evoked ancient Greek amphitheatres. Some 3,500 nickelodeons had sprung up all over the United States. Many of Hollywood's future movie moguls—Harry Warner, Marcus Loew, Adolph Zukor—were getting their start as nickelodeon owners importing most of their celluloid product from France.

Since early motion pictures were "silent," there were no linguistic barriers to imported movies. At the time, the United States—with its recent explosion of European immigration—boasted a huge ethnic population with a popular taste for motion pictures. Pathé Frères, the leading producer of French motion pictures, became so successful in the U.S. nickelodeon market that its studio was selling more films than all its American rivals combined. Pathé Frères' so-called "Red Rooster" movies—named after the company's logo—were the driving force behind the so-called "nickel delirium" sweeping through America. In the first few years of the 20th century, if there was cultural imperialism in the movie industry, it was French imperial annexation of America.

But French cultural imperialism wouldn't last on American movie screens. Thomas Edison, determined to end Red Rooster's quasi-monopoly in the U.S. market, came up with an idea that would have a lasting impact on the American movie industry.

"The French are somewhat in advance of us," Edison told *Variety* in 1908, "but they will not long maintain their supremacy."

The same year, Edison banded his American rivals together to form a cartel, which was baptized the Motion Pictures Patents Company. The Edison-led trust's main ambition was to drive foreign competition—especially French motion pictures—from the U.S. market. The Edison cartel was not adverse to dirty tricks. The most effective tactic was a well-orchestrated smear campaign to stir up fear and hostility towards European films as "alien." The scheme proved timely and successful in an era when xenophobia was growing in America as a reaction to massive immigration from European countries. In the trade press, magazines like *Motion Picture World* pointed out that owners of movie theatres were "foreigners who are not citizens." Protestant clergymen referred to the "rapidly increasing Hebrew element" in the burgeoning movie exhibition business. And French films, in particular, were condemned as morally dubious and offensive to American tastes.

The combination of immigrant Jews and French movies was sufficient to evoke strong negative emotions vis-à-vis a perceived alien invasion of America. Yet in truth, home-made American movies—featuring gangsters, hoodlums, and hussies—had little to commend them when judged by the same standards. From the earliest days of motion pictures, working-class audiences in America were attracted to movie theatres by violence, crime, and sex. In Edison's *How They Do Things in the Bowery*, for example, the lead characters were a collection of thieves and loose women. French movies were, by comparison, culturally sophisticated. So-called *films d'art* from France included *Mary Stuart*, based on a Victor Hugo work, and a movie version of the Balzac short story, *La Grande Bretèche*. Other typical European motion picture themes of the era were *Queen Elizabeth*, starring Sarah Bernhardt, as well as Italian movies based on Dante's *Inferno* and Homer's *Odyssey*.

But Edison's anti-Red Rooster campaign proved devastatingly effective. The American trade press, especially *Variety*, vilified French movies as effeminate and immoral while lauding American movies as red-blooded and manly. In 1909, newspapers such the *Mirror* and *World* were calling for movies that featured "Anglo-Saxon" models of youth and "clean, good-looking actors." In 1910, an American movie company called Thanhouser Film took out an advertisement in *Moving Picture World* that confidently claimed: "The American People Prefer American Pictures." The ad was flog-ging Thanhouser's latest release, an "all-American" motion picture called *Her Battle for Existence.*[1]

At the American box office, xenophobia proved lucrative. American motion pictures deliberately exploited patriotic themes that would be certain to appeal to domestic audiences. The "western," in particular, quickly became a classic genre that invariably portrayed the U.S. cavalry heroically putting down violent Indian revolts. Like Indians, Mexicans were usually featured as swarthy villains. The Japanese, too, were portrayed as belligerent, untrustworthy, and anti-American in movies with alarmist titles like *The Japanese Invasion.*

Pathé, now on the defensive, frantically attempted to Americanize its product by releasing its own Wild West movies. By 1910, however, Pathé's domination of the American movie market was coming to an end. A lethal combination of monopoly market practices, American patriotism, and virulent xenophobia had conspired against the once-proud Red Rooster brand. At the apogee of Pathé's glory circa 1905, European films had accounted for 70 percent of the U.S. box office. By 1912, however, roughly 80 percent of new releases in the United States were American movies. In 1915, U.S. anti-trust authorities busted up Edison's Motion Picture Patents Company as a monopolistic cartel. But it was too late for French movies. The Red Rooster's once-alluring plumage had faded forever in America.

The American movie industry got another boost from the First World War. When war broke out in 1914, national film industries throughout Europe ground to a halt and shut down. But in the United States—which was neutral until 1917—movie producers kept churning out motion pictures. Thus, war-ravaged Europe quickly became a captive export market for American movies. As *Moving Picture World* noted: "Within the next year or so the demand for American movies in Europe will be large enough to justify a greater 'invasion' than Europe has ever known before."

It was during the First World War that America's first movie moguls—most of them immigrant Jews from New York—moved to California to build motion picture factories in the Los Angeles suburb of Hollywood. One of the first to arrive was Carl "Lucky" Laemmle, founder of Universal Film Manufacturing Company. Adolph Zukor, the Famous Players boss, merged his production company with the Paramount distribution outfit to integrate the two businesses. Under Zukor—who famously asserted that "the public is never wrong"—Paramount rapidly became a Hollywood giant producing more than 100 motion pictures a year.

Hollywood was becoming a political force, too. American politicians were now taking an interest in the movie mania sweeping the country. In 1915, D.W. Griffith's classic Civil War epic, *The Birth of a Nation,* was screened at the White House for President Woodrow Wilson. The movie had been produced with the assistance of West Point engineers, who served as technical advisors on the Civil War battle scenes. Although President Wilson apparently enjoyed *Birth of a Nation,* he was forced to distance himself from the film due to concerns about its anti-Negro racism and positive portrayal of the Ku Klux Klan. Wilson nonetheless understood that movies could be used for propaganda purposes, especially as America prepared to join the Great War. The National Association of the Motion Picture Industry made this explicit in a memo to the White House: "The motion picture can be the most wonderful system for spreading national propaganda at little or no cost," President Wilson agreed. An idealist, Wilson was convinced Hollywood could serve as a vehicle for American values to take hold throughout the world.

"The film has come to rank as the very highest medium for the dissemination of public intelligence," Wilson declared in a wartime speech. "And since it speaks a universal language, it lends itself importantly to the presentation of America's plans and purposes."

An official partnership between Washington and Hollywood was consummated when President Wilson authorized the creation of a congressional Committee on Public Information. Its mandate was to sell the war at home and spread the "Gospel of Americanism" abroad by promoting American culture and values via motion pictures. Wilson hand-picked well-known journalist George Creel to head the committee, which was quickly dubbed the "Creel Committee." Creel recruited battalions of advertising executives, journalists, filmmakers, and playwrights to promote the Wilsonian vision of world peace and liberal democracy.

President Wilson's global celebrity owed much to the Creel Committee, which feverishly distributed photos and speeches of Wilson in many foreign countries. While criticized in America as a crass propaganda instrument, the Creel Committee successfully spread the image of America as a prosperous and peaceful model for all the nations of the world. To proselytize the gospel of the American Dream, Creel created a government-run wire service, Compub, to relay American "news" stories to foreign publications. Creel also launched a film division that produced a combination of short documentary tributes to the American way of life and feature-length films such as *America's Answer* and *Pershing's Crusade*. The latter was a tribute to the U.S. military hero, General John Pershing, whose name later would become famously associated with U.S. missiles. At the same time, the U.S. government created a Foreign Film Service, whose staffers were dispatched to foreign countries to promote the spread of American movies in local cinemas. In Europe, their mission was to drive German films from local movie houses. In America, the U.S. government hired "Four-Minute Men," so-called because they delivered four-minute patriotic speeches in American movie theatres during projection-room reel changes.

George Creel also exercised tremendous power over Hollywood movies. Through the U.S. War Trade Board, he could approve, or refuse, export licences for all American motion pictures. Empowered to impose export conditions on Hollywood movies, Creel insisted that film shipments contain 20 percent of "educational matter"—namely, propaganda footage. Any movie that portrayed "false" American values, or that conveyed negative impressions of the United States, were banned for export. One film singled out for censorship was *Jesse James*, about the infamous American outlaw. To keep German movies out of international cinemas, Creel threatened to withhold all American films from any foreign movie exhibitor who screened German motion pictures.

Urged by the Creel Committee, Hollywood moguls like Lucky Laemmle, Adolph Zukor, and Marcus Loew enthusiastically embraced their patriotic duty during the war by enlisting their biggest stars to appear in short films promoting the American way of life. The White House, too, encouraged Hollywood's role in U.S. foreign policy. President Wilson summoned Samuel Goldwyn to the White House and urged him to rush as many Hollywood films as possible to France so America could win the hearts of the French. Among Hollywood's anti-German movies of the period were *The Hun Within*, *The Kaiser: The Beast of Berlin*, *The Claws of the Hun*, and Cecil B. deMille's *The Little American*, starring Mary Pickford. Known as "America's sweetheart," Mary Pickford was—along with Douglas Fairbanks and Charlie Chaplin—an international superstar who used her celebrity to promote the sale of wartime U.S. liberty bonds.

When the First World War ended, President Wilson was the most powerful figure among victorious world leaders meeting at Versailles in 1919. The United States had emerged from the Great War as the world's leading creditor nation. A generation earlier in 1900, some $3 billion in American currency had been held in Europe; but in 1919, Europe's leading nations were debtors to the United States. President Wilson, for his part, owed a great debt to Hollywood, whose motion pictures were now a mass cultural extension of America's new-found global power. The White House even declared movies to be an "essential industry."[2]

The international success of American movies during this era was due to a number of convergent factors. First, the Hollywood star system promoted worldwide adulation of a select number of famous actors, such as Charlie Chaplin and Rudolf Valentino. Second, the Hollywood studios increased their competitive advantages by centralizing production and using highly specialized labour. Third, America's large population gave Hollywood a huge domestic market over which the cost of movies could be amortized before being exported at low cost. Finally, since America's population was largely immigrant—especially in large urban centres such as New York and Chicago—Hollywood deliberately appealed to a lowest common denominator with uncomplicated narratives that could be grasped by all audiences, whatever their nationality or level of education. Consequently, Hollywood movies were ideal export products—and spread American tastes and values throughout the world. As Sidney Kent, a top Paramount executive, stated at the time: "Imagine the effect on people who constantly see flashed on the screen American modes of living, American modes of dressing, and American modes of travel."

This was no exaggeration. In Britain, shoe manufacturers protested that they were forced to invest in new machinery to churn out footwear similar to shoes worn by film stars in American motion pictures. Elsewhere in Europe, fashions in belts, collars, and silk hosiery changed to mimic those worn by Hollywood movie stars. In Brazil, American-style bungalow houses and swimming pools were highly coveted thanks to Hollywood's images of America. Soaring automobile sales in foreign countries were also partly due to the influence of American movies.

As Hollywood moguls increasingly saw the entire planet as their market, they began taking a more proactive interest in U.S. trade policy. In 1925, when the *Saturday Evening Post* famously declared that "trade follows the film," it was already the unofficial slogan of the Hollywood moguls. The same year, American movies commanded 95 percent of the British and Canadian cinema markets, took 70 percent of the French market, and captured 80 percent of screen time in South America. Hollywood, now a powerful industrial force, could turn to Wall Street for financial backing. Lehman Brothers, for example, was allied with the Loews theatre chain. Goldman Sachs & Company provided financing for Warner Bros. Paramount was backed by Kuhn Loeb & Company. The Rockefellers had invested in RKO. And J.P. Morgan money was behind several Hollywood studios. Wall Street's support not only gave Hollywood tremendous respectability, it also was a sign that American capital markets believed in movies.

In Washington, the White House remembered its wartime debt to Hollywood. In the 1920s when Douglas Fairbanks and Mary Pickford, now married, travelled the globe as American goodwill ambassadors, their foreign trips were financed by the U.S. State Department. Mary Pickford declared: "The cheering crowds of the Far East were shouting not for me, but for the American motion picture and the American people and for the world of make-believe. Therefore, I hold that, in a large sense, we were ambassadors not only of the motion picture, but of our own country."

It wasn't long, however, before Hollywood's post-war domination of the global movie industry met fierce opposition—even among America's closest Western allies.

Yankee Go Home: Hollywood Imperialism

Canada was the first country whose movie industry fell under Hollywood control. In fact, America's friendly northern neighbour—whose English-speaking citizens are generally indistinguishable from Americans—was simply annexed as part of Hollywood's domestic movie market.

When Paramount's Famous Players movie theatres extended into Canada in the early 1920s, the major Canadian-owned theatre chain was family-owned Allen Theatres. Famous Players, refusing to share the market with a local rival, attempted to force the Allens to sell out. When the proud Allens stubbornly refused, Famous Players threatened to deprive Allen Theatres of all movies made by Paramount. Faced with a Paramount boycott, and eventual bankruptcy, the Allens finally gave in. The addition of the Allen movie houses gave Paramount more than 200 cinemas in Canada. The only serious competition to Famous Players was in Toronto, where another Hollywood major, Loews, also operated movie theatres.

The Americanization of movie theatres in Canada posed no threat to the domestic film industry. Canada, still a British dominion, had no movie industry to speak of. Debate about Hollywood's domination was inspired mainly by loyalty to the British Empire. Some Canadians wondered whether Hollywood films would monopolize movie screens and thus prevent the importation of motion pictures from the United Kingdom. In Canada, the issue was not how to promote a domestic movie industry, but whether the country should be a cinematic colony of London or Los Angeles.

An answer was readily available by looking at the situation in Britain itself. By the early 1920s, the British movie market was almost totally controlled by Hollywood. But unlike Canada, Britain could at least boast some semblance of a domestic movie industry. Although British cinema was still in its infancy, anti-Hollywood attitudes were already finding expression in the U.K., especially among élites. As London's *Morning Post* stated in 1923: "If the United States abolished its diplomatic and consular services, kept its ships in harbour and its tourists at home, and retired from the world's markets, its citizens, its problems, its towns and countryside, its roads, motor cars, country houses and saloons would still be familiar in the uttermost corners of the world … The film is to America what the flag was once to Britain. By its means, Uncle Sam may hope some day, if he be not checked in time, to Americanize the world."[3]

By the mid-1920s, British movie lobbyists were pressuring their government to take action against Hollywood. In 1925, support came from an illustrious group of Britons—including composer Edward Elgar and novelist Thomas Hardy—who lashed out against Hollywood in a petition published in the London newspapers. Sidestepping the issue of Hollywood's commercial threat, their letter emphasized, somewhat haughtily, the negative cultural influence of American movies: "The bulk of the films shown in this country have, to say the least of it, a non-British atmosphere.

These films are shown in our Dominions, Colonies, and Dependencies, and in all the countries of the world outside the British Commonwealth of nations. Many of them are inferior productions, neither healthy nor patriotic in tone, while the psychological influences which they may convey have far-reaching consequences." This pompous plea was taken up by Lord Newton, who rose in the House of Lords and declared: "If we are condemned to watch perpetual rubbish, for heaven's sake let it be British rubbish in preference to American rubbish."

Cultural snobbery aside, these distinguished Britons were proxy spokesmen for a complaint that, in truth, was strictly commercial. British movie producers were angered by the Hollywood practice of "block-booking"—namely, selling to U.K. movie theatres packages of several American films to ensure that every American movie gained maximum exposure on British cinema screens. Many of these films were of B-movie quality. But block-booking nonetheless impeded access to movie screens for British films. British cinema owners, for their part, didn't share élitist concerns about Hollywood domination. They relied on a steady flow of popular Hollywood fare to fill seats in their movie theatres.

The British government was less indifferent to high-minded complaints. In Parliament, Prime Minister Stanley Baldwin warned against the "enormous power which film is developing for propaganda purposes, and the danger to which we in this country, and in our Empire, subject ourselves if we allow that method of propaganda to be entirely in the hands of foreign countries." In truth, propaganda wasn't the danger. It was who controlled cinematic propaganda—and that, clearly, was America. Baldwin was echoing a growing concern among Britain's influential chattering classes about creeping Americanization. As London's *Daily Express* put it: "The bulk of picture-goers are Americanized to an extent that makes them regard the British film as a foreign film. They talk America, think America, dream America. We have several million people, mostly women, who to all intents and purposes are temporary American citizens."

Opposition towards Hollywood among British élites was sufficient to put the issue on Britain's foreign policy agenda. Prior to the Imperial Conference of 1926, the British government circulated a document entitled "Exhibition Within the Empire of Empire Films." The U.K. position paper unmistakably took aim, albeit tacitly, at America: "It is clearly undesirable that so very large a proportion of the films shown throughout the Empire should present modes of life and forms of conduct which are not typically British, and, so far as setting is concerned, tend to leave in the minds of untutored spectators the impression that there are no British settings, whether scenic or social, which are worth presentation." More explicitly, Sir Philip Cunliffe-Lister, Britain's industry minister, argued at the Imperial Conference that the United States was increasing its exports of consumer goods worldwide thanks to the influence of Hollywood movies. Cunliffe-Lister was putting his finger on the real issue: America's rise as a global economic power. Cultural snobbism was merely a pompous expediency that camouflaged the less lofty reality of commercial protectionism.[4]

It was in this climate that, in 1927, the British government passed the *Cinematograph Films Act*, which imposed a relatively modest quota of 5 percent—to be increased to a minimum of 20 percent within ten years—on domestic U.K. movies. Curiously, the quota produced an unintended consequence in colonial Canada. The U.K. quota's definition of a "British" movie included any film shot in the British Empire—including Canada. This loose geographical definition opened up a back-door opportunity for the Hollywood studios. Soon Hollywood was busy shooting so-called "quota quickies" in Canada in order to flood the British market with cheap "British" films. The main goal of the "quota quickies" wasn't to make money in Britain, but rather to demonstrate to the U.K. government that its quotas were laughably unworkable and therefore ineffective. Anti-Hollywood grumbling in Britain, not suprisingly, continued. In 1929, Lord Baden-Powell, founder of the Boy Scouts, told a large gathering of schoolchildren in London that he enjoyed going to the pictures, but that he could not abide "those rotten American films with their silly plots."

Anti-Hollywood sentiments in France were similarly disdainful of America, though the real issue—as in Britain—was commercial protectionism. Despite the decline of Red Rooster films, France continued to be Hollywood's fiercest cinematic adversary. In the 1920s, a French tariff on foreign films had done little to stem massive imports of Hollywood movies, which were taking more than 80 percent of French box-office receipts by 1925. French movie producers lobbied their government to establish a quota system. Specifically, they proposed a trade-off: four American movies would be allowed into France for every French movie exported to the United States. While the ratio seemed to favour American movies, Hollywood threatened to boycott the French market if the quota were implemented. Hollywood's threat produced the desired effect of intimidating owners of French movie theatres, who feared they would lose their supply of popular American movies.

In the end, the French government settled on a watered-down compromise: for every domestic movie produced in France, import permits would be issued for seven foreign films. But the damage had already been done. France's major movie producers—Pathé Frères, Gaumont, Éclair—had ceased making movies and were now concentrating on operating French movie theatres showing American films. In 1929, the French newspaper *Le Matin* observed: "Americans are trying to subject Europe to their ideas and they think, correctly, that motion picture propaganda—which enables putting American propaganda before the eyes of every public—is the best and least costly way of spreading their influence."

In Germany, despite its post-war humiliation, motion pictures enjoyed a tremendous boom in the 1920s. The hyper-inflation that crippled the German economy actually helped the domestic film industry. Movie distributors couldn't afford foreign movies due to the dramatic devaluation of the German currency, but foreign movie distributors could buy German films cheaply. German import restrictions also gave a boost to the domestic movie industry. In 1921, the Weimar Republic imposed a quota limiting the importation of foreign movies to 15 percent of the total number of films screened in Germany. The quota was not rigorously enforced in practice, but German films still commanded about 40 percent of total screen time in the early 1920s.

German cinema owed its success to an American commercial practice: the creation of large, vertically integrated movie companies. Universum Film AG—called "UFA"—was not only Germany's biggest producer of movies, but also controlled a major circuit of movie theatres. Backed by some of Germany's biggest industrial groups, UFA had been created during the war as a propaganda machine. After the war, UFA sponsored the careers of some of German's greatest cinematic talents, including Fritz Lang. One cinematic masterpiece of the era, *The Cabinet of Dr. Caligari*, was a classic of German expressionism, though the film was boycotted in America due to anti-German feelings in the wake of the First World War.

Hollywood eventually conquered the German film market thanks to U.S. economic aid aimed at helping the defeated Germany fight hyper-inflation. With U.S. loans and investments came a flood of Hollywood movies. In the mid-1920s, when UFA was on the verge of bankruptcy, it was rescued by a $4 million loan from two Hollywood studios, Paramount and MGM. By the end of the 1920s, German movies accounted for only 27 percent of the total European market, while Hollywood boasted a European market share of 60 percent.

In the United States, the Hollywood studios had followed the example of Thomas Edison's cartel by forming a powerful trust. Its members included Paramount, Fox, Warner Bros., Loews, and RKO. In 1922, the Motion Picture Producers and Distributors of America—or the MPPDA—was created to represent their joint interests. The five major studios, moreover, were aligned with some 2,400 movie theatres throughout America, thus ensuring that their movies enjoyed guaranteed "first run" access to the domestic U.S. market. The MPPDA also served as a censorship body to help clean up Hollywood's sullied image during the Roaring Twenties. The trend towards looser moral standards had been particularly contentious in Holly-wood, especially after series of highly publicized scandals, including Mary Pickford's divorce. Negative publicity reached a crisis when manslaughter charges were brought against comedian Roscoe "Fatty" Arbuckle following a bizarre sexual incident with a young woman. The Hollywood moguls decided it was time to launch a public relations campaign to keep box-office cash registers ringing throughout Middle America.

The creation of the MPPDA also marked the beginning of what would turn out to be a long and mutually beneficial relationship between Holly-wood and Washington. The MPPDA's first president was Will Hays, a long-time Republican political organizer from Indiana who had managed President Warren Harding's successful election campaign in 1920. When Harding entered the White House, he rewarded Hays with a cabinet post as Postmaster General. Shortly afterwards, Hays left the Harding administra-tion and moved to the MPPDA to take care of Hollywood's interests. While his immediate task was to improve Hollywood's image in America, the MPPDA also monitored American movies destined for export. Cultural sensitivities in international markets had already provoked some foreign governments either to censor or ban outright certain Hollywood movies.

Hays' first major diplomatic challenge was responding to official protests from Mexico, where many cinema-goers felt insulted by Hollywood's stereotypical portrayal of Mexicans as greasy, villainous characters. In 1922, the Mexican government banned the entire output of any Hollywood studio that produced movies considered as a slur against Mexico's national character. Hays, in frantic damage-control mode, personally defused this bilateral crisis through direct negotiation at the highest levels of the Mexican government. China, too, registered protests with the United States against Hollywood movies. In 1929, China banned Harold Lloyd's *Welcome Danger* because it portrayed people in San Francisco's Chinatown as kidnappers, gamblers, hoodlums, and opium smokers. In Japan prudish censors deleted kissing scenes in Hollywood movies. Anti-Hollywood hostility was particularly intense in countries like France, which still boasted a relatively strong domestic movie industry. At a League of Nations meeting in 1928, the French delegation proposed that all countries be allowed to restrict the importation of American movies in defence of their respective "intellectual and moral" traditions.

Despite these kerfuffles, Hollywood movies enjoyed tremendous popularity in most foreign countries. Audiences flooded into cinemas to see American movies whose simple plots and emphasis on emotion and action had widespread cross-cultural appeal. Hollywood nonetheless could not be impervious to diplomatic and commercial pressures, and its xenophobic attitude changed in the post-war years. In 1926, Hollywood complied with an official German protest by altering the plot of *A Woman Disputed* to avoid offending German movie-goers. The film's villain, originally a German, was transformed into a Russian (Hollywood movie exports to the Soviet Union were less lucrative). Hollywood made similar efforts to appease France by refraining from portraying French women as loose, immoral, and adulterous. Some Hollywood movies were custom-made for separate national markets. When *Peter Pan* was produced in 1924, the scene where Peter runs up a flag over Captain Hook's pirate ship was shot several times, showing a different national flag each time. Hollywood's most successful strategy, however, was to focus production on "mythical" and fantastic movies that travelled easily across cultures, at least in Western and Christian countries. Biblical epics like *Ben-Hur* and *King of Kings* became international hits in the 1920s. Another way of appealing to international audiences was to import foreign actors and transform them into Hollywood stars. By the 1930s, Greta Garbo, Charles Laughton, Maurice Chevalier, David Niven, Charles Boyer, Marlene Dietrich, and many others were internationally famous, non-American movie stars.

The most powerful Hollywood mogul of the era was unquestionably Louis B. Mayer. Like Will Hays, he was actively involved in Republican politics and enjoyed close proximity to Washington power circles. Throughout the 1920s, Mayer courted many cabinet ministers in the Harding and Coolidge administrations, including a rising political star named Herbert Hoover. As a member of President Harding's cabinet, Hoover had used his influence to give Mayer and press baron William Randolph Hearst highly coveted frequencies to start commercial radio stations. When Hoover ran for the presidency in 1928, Mayer obligingly lobbied Hearst to put his powerful newspaper empire at the service of Hoover's campaign. Mayer himself was a key player in the presidential candidate's inner circle. Other Hollywood figures—Helen Hayes, Eddie Cantor, Irving Berlin, George Jessel—publicly supported Hoover's Democratic rival, Al Smith. But thanks to Mayer's unquestioned powers of persuasion, Hoover enjoyed tremendous support in Hollywood, including endorsements from Cecil B. DeMille and D.W. Griffith. When Hoover won the 1928 presidential election, his first dinner guests at the White House were Mr. and Mrs. Louis B. Mayer.[5]

Four years later, Mayer again worked tirelessly to get Hoover re-elected. But the Great Depression had changed America. In 1932, Hoover appeared like a bloated, pin-striped capitalist from a heartless era that had produced urban shantytowns known as "Hoovervilles." Hollywood was split over the bitterly fought election campaign, which opposed President Hoover and New York governor Franklin Delano Roosevelt. Moguls Jack and Harry Warner organized a magnificent campaign pageant for FDR at the Los Angeles Coliseum. Another FDR backer was a non-Jewish movie mogul named Joseph Kennedy, father of the future American president. On election day, FDR swept into the White House and immediately began implementing his New Deal policy to pull America out of the Depression. Joe Kennedy was later rewarded with the U.S. ambassadorship to the United Kingdom.

In Hollywood, meanwhile, America's economic collapse had created a deeply divided political climate. Throughout the 1930s, Hollywood was becoming dangerously entangled in radical politics that, to many, seemed antithetical to America's most cherished values.

Hollywood and the Cold War

It is easily forgotten that socialism once had a chance in America. In the 1920 presidential election, Eugene Debs won nearly one million votes as the Socialist Party candidate—even though, during the campaign, he was incarcerated in an Atlanta prison for his anti-war activities.

But socialism, overwhelmed by the ebullient optimism of the Roaring Twenties, would quickly run out of ideological steam. Wall Street, it seemed, was like a Hollywood movie—it always had a happy ending. After the Crash of 1929, however, capitalism appeared to have failed and was no longer regarded as the only economic model for society. Suddenly, socialism became fashionable again in America and other Western countries.

[handwritten margin note: ideology as fashionable]

But the Hollywood moguls would have none of it. They used all their powers—including the choice of movie subjects—to back capitalism against the "red menace." Movies such as *The House of Rothschild* were unmistakable tributes to capitalism. On a more populist note, the home-spun optimism of child star Shirley Temple encouraged Americans to remain faithful to their basic values. But Hollywood movies and Hollywood people were not always synonymous. While Middle America was watching cheery Hollywood versions of the American way of life at their local cinemas, the American movie industry had become a hotbed of radical politics.

Hollywood's first "communist" controversy flared up in 1934, when socialist writer Upton Sinclair announced his candidacy, under the Democratic banner, for the governorship of California. Hollywood moguls were horrified by the prospect of Sinclair in the governor's mansion. Their hostility was not unrelated to his electoral platform in favour of higher taxes on the motion picture industry. Louis B. Mayer and William Randolph Hearst quickly swung into action to rally support for Sinclair's Republican rival, Frank Merriam. Not surprisingly, the long-ruling Republicans in state politics traditionally had shown tremendous fiscal indulgence towards Hollywood. In 1932, for example, the major Hollywood studios had paid only $3,142 in taxes. The moguls wanted to keep it that way.

[handwritten margin note: Conservative side in Hollywood]

Mayer was notorious for strong-arming the Hollywood community into backing Republican candidates in California. His favoured method was taxing Hollywood salaries to generate contributions for Republican campaign coffers. This time, however, there was a revolt. Movie stars James Cagney and Jean Harlow spearheaded an actors' rebellion, while screenwriters mobilized the California Authors League to support Upton Sinclair. Holly-wood writers were especially well-known for their Communist sympa-thies. One was John Howard Lawson, an outspoken Communist who headed the Screen Writers Guild. The U.S. Communist Party had success-fully targeted Hollywood as fertile ideological terrain for radical politics and lucrative fundraising.

[handwritten margin note: a little stereotypical]

But the power of the Hollywood studios was formidable. During the California election pitting Upton Sinclair against Frank Merriam, the moguls arranged for phony newsreels to be shown in cinemas portraying Sinclair supporters as shabby, dissolute characters, while Frank Merriam's Republican supporters appeared as outstanding and wholesome Ameri-cans. At one point, the moguls threatened to pull up stakes and abandon California if Sinclair were elected governor. Mayer's MGM told the *Los Angeles Times* that the studios were prepared for "a hurried exodus" from California. In this climate, few were surprised when Merriam won the elec-tion. One can imagine Louis B. Mayer's sense of betrayal, however, when Frank Merriam, now in office, pushed through Upton Sinclair's dreaded income tax legislation.

Before the Second World War, most Communist sympathizers in Holly-wood positioned their political views in opposition to "fascism." Nazi Germany was on the rise in the 1930s and the Spanish Civil War drew Hollywood writers and actors to the Socialist movement against General Franco. In this climate, many Hollywood figures—Melvyn Douglas, Ring Lardner Jr., Jimmy Cagney, Paul Muni, Olivia de Havilland—were attracted to leftist politics. In the opposing camp, a solid rump of Hollywood stars stood squarely behind conservative American politics. On the political right-wing, an organization called the Motion Picture Alliance for the Preservation of American Ideals won the support of Walt Disney, Gary Cooper, and King Vidor. Showing solidarity with the moguls, this group of Hollywood conservatives issued a statement declaring: "We refuse to permit the efforts of Communism, Fascism, and other totalitarian-minded groups to pervert this powerful medium into an instrument for the dissemination of un-American ideas."

In Washington, when the House Un-American Activities Committee—known as "HUAC"—commenced its hearings in 1938, Hollywood leftists were high on the committee's list of suspects. As HUAC member Martin

Dies, a Democrat from Texas, put it: "All phases of radical and communistic activities are rampant among the studios in Hollywood." In truth, Hollywood Communists were divided among themselves about the Soviet Union—especially after the Kremlin signed a non-aggression pact with Nazi Germany in 1939.

During the Second World War, President Roosevelt ran twice for re-election—in 1940 and 1944—and each time Republicans smeared FDR's Hollywood supporters as Communists. Orson Welles was one target. In 1944, Welles, an outspoken liberal, actively campaigned against FDR's Republican rival, Thomas Dewey. Other FDR supporters included Frank Sinatra, Judy Garland, Humphrey Bogart, Rita Hayworth, Irving Berlin, and Groucho Marx. Dewey, for his part, could count on the support of Hollywood's conservative establishment, including Louis B. Mayer, Cecil B. deMille, Walt Disney, Fred MacMurray, Ginger Rogers, Gary Cooper, Lionel Barrymore, and David O. Selznick. During the 1944 election campaign, Dewey charged that Roosevelt's Democrats had been captured by "the forces of Communism." Dewey nonetheless lost the election.

Despite ideological differences, the Hollywood moguls rallied to FDR's White House when Pearl Harbor provoked America's entry into war in late 1941. The Hollywood studios eagerly agreed to serve as the White House's unofficial propaganda arm. Darryl Zanuck, for example, made a feature film, *Wilson*, under the auspices of the Office of War Information. The movie, pure propaganda, glorified President Woodrow Wilson's crusade to create a new world order under the League of Nations. Warner Bros. meanwhile, pitched in with an anti-German film, *Confessions of a Nazi Spy*. Other wartime anti-Nazi movies included Alfred Hitchcock's 1940 film, *Foreign Correspondent*. Adolf Hitler was said to have been exasperated after treating himself to a private screening of Chaplin's satire, *The Great Dictator*. Germany and its axis allies—Italy and Spain—banned all American movies. Hollywood self-censorship was also a common practice. RKO Studios, pressured by the White House, agreed to put the kibosh on the U.S. release of the Cary Grant movie, *Gunga Din*, which glorified the British Empire. The Hollywood studios also submitted movie scripts to the Bureau of Motion Pictures for prior approval.

While Hollywood's cooperation with the White House was greatly appreciated in Washington, its commercial activities in the domestic U.S.

market were once again coming under scrutiny by U.S. anti-trust officials. The so-called "Big Five" studios—MGM, Warner Bros., RKO, Paramount, and Fox—collectively controlled 70 percent of all first-run movie theatres in the largest 92 cities. The "Little Three" studios—Universal, Columbia, and United Artists—had integrated production and distribution, but owned no movie theatres. A number of obnoxious commercial practices— especially block-booking—were rampant in the movie industry. Block- booking filled movie theatre screens with Hollywood product so that no independent movies could gain access to theatres. Anti-trust officials concluded that the major Hollywood studios were deliberately conspiring against non-Hollywood independents to eliminate competition. Will Hays, still Hollywood's chief lobbyist, warned President Roosevelt that an aggres- sive anti-trust investigation would destroy the American movie industry.

After the Second World War, the climate in America was turning against Hollywood. The baby boom meant many Americans were staying home and listening to radio or watching television instead of going to the movies. Also, post-war prosperity created a market for suburban houses, automo- biles, appliances and other commodities, which competed with the cinema for disposable income. These trends could be readily quantified: immedi- ately after the war, U.S. box-office receipts began declining precipitously. The worst news for Hollywood came on May 3, 1948, when the U.S. Supreme Court—rendering its famous "Paramount Decrees"—ruled that the Holly- wood majors constituted an illegal cartel that was guilty of restraining trade. The U.S. high court forced the Hollywood studios to divest their movie-theatre circuits to curtail block-booking.

The reaction in Hollywood was apocalyptic. "Hollywood is like Egypt, full of crumbling pyramids," lamented mogul David Selznick. "It'll just keep crumbling until finally the wind blows the last studio prop across the sands."

The Paramount Decrees unquestionably dealt a serious blow to the Big Five studios. And yet, ironically, the Hollywood studios responded to their setback in America by becoming even more aggressive in foreign markets. And, in a further irony, they could count on the support of the same U.S. government that had been aggressively prosecuting them on American soil. Indeed, while the Hollywood studios were facing anti-trust investiga- tions at home, they established an export cartel—the Motion Picture Export Association—with total immunity from prosecution in the United

States. The MPEA was perfectly legal in America thanks to 1918 legislation, the *Webb-Pomerene Act*, which had allowed U.S. corporations to organize themselves as cartels for export purposes. In short, the Hollywood cartel was a devil at home, but a saint abroad.

The Allied victory proved to be an enormous boon for American motion pictures internationally. In 1945, the United States welcomed the addition of Hollywood's soft-power arsenal to reinforce its hard-power military triumph. The Marshall Plan—named after U.S. Secretary of State George Marshall—was, in effect, a Mogul Plan. As part of Marshall's two-pronged strategy, economic aid and cultural influence worked in tandem. Accordingly, the Hollywood studios received roughly $10 million in direct subsidies as part of Marshall's European Recovery Plan. One American senator called on Hollywood to contribute to "a worldwide Marshall Plan in the field of ideas." A Hollywood producer put it more succinctly: "Donald Duck as World Diplomat!"[6]

Hollywood's new ambassador was Eric Johnston, who had succeeded Will Hays as head of the Hollywood lobby, now rebaptized as the Motion Picture Association of America. Like Hays, Johnston—former head of the U.S. Chamber of Commerce—was well connected at the White House where he had worked as an emissary for FDR. Now on Hollywood's payroll, Johnston frequently met with President Harry Truman to discuss Hollywood's role in American foreign policy. Besides Johnston, Hollywood's chief lobbyist in Paris, Frank McCarthy, had been General Marshall's military secretary during the war, and later served as assistant Secretary of State. Little wonder that Johnston's MPAA was referred to as the "Little State Department."

The real U.S. State Department, for its part, insisted that exported Hollywood movies promote American values. As one State Department report asserted: "American motion pictures, as ambassadors of good will—at no cost to American taxpayers—interpret the American way of life to all the nations of the world, which may be invaluable from a political, cultural, and commercial point of view." Eric Johnston's own thinking was reliably in line with official State Department policy. He outlined three foreign threats to Hollywood's interests in the post-war era: a hard money crisis, social chaos, and virulent nationalism. The hard money crisis was the most pressing concern, as the Hollywood studios were growing increasingly worried about so-called "frozen coin"—namely, policies in foreign countries that limited the amounts of currency the Hollywood studios could remit to the United States.

Hollywood's post-war diplomatic skills were first put to test in France, which was in a state of ruinous economic collapse. France had disastrously flirted with patriotic fascism under the Vichy regime, and its honour was saved only at the eleventh hour in 1944 when Charles de Gaulle, assisted by Allied troops, liberated Nazi-occupied Paris. During the war the Vichy regime had banned all American movie imports. This meant that the French film industry, with no competition from American movies, actually flourished during the war. Classic films of the period included *Les enfants du paradis*. Following the Liberation, however, the U.S. Army's Psychological Warfare Division flooded the French market with some 400 prints of the latest Hollywood movies in a campaign called "Arsenal of Democracy." The Hollywood movies were immediately popular with French audiences, who were eager to see, for the first time, movies such as *Gone with the Wind*. Even French communist Edgar Morin declared in late 1944: "We need the American cinema like an old friend back from afar." But Charles de Gaulle, whose grandiose patriotism was tinged with anti-American jealousy, quickly restored import restrictions on American movies.

After the French elections of 1945, in which the Socialists and Communists won 50 percent of the popular vote, there was talk of nationalizing the French movie industry. Hollywood, needless to say, was horrified. In an atmosphere of mutual suspicion, the French and U.S. governments hastily instigated bilateral negotiations over motion pictures. In early 1946, Félix Gouin—who had succeeded Charles de Gaulle as head of France's provisional government—called on former French prime minister Léon Blum to strike a deal with the Truman administration. Blum, a left-wing Jewish intellectual who had led the short-lived Front Populaire government in 1936, was a legendary figure in French politics. But when Blum met with U.S. Secretary of State James Byrnes, the Americans had the upper hand. The French desperately needed Marshall Plan economic aid, and they knew it. When the Franco-American accord was finally signed after tense negotiations, the United States agreed to wipe out France's war debt, to provide France with a $318 million loan, and to accord France $650 million in credits from the U.S. Export-Import Bank to help rebuild the collapsed

French economy. The United States insisted on one trade-off as part of the so-called "Blum-Byrnes" accord: France would eliminate its pre-war import restrictions on American movies. In effect, France flung open its doors to American movies.

Blum was immediately denounced in France as a sellout to American interests. The Blum-Byrnes accord gave Parisian intellectuals a timely pretext to rail against the negative effects of Hollywood movies. Maurice Thorez, head of France's Communist Party, warned his compatriots against the noxious cultural influences of American films, which he said "poison the souls of our children, young people, young girls, who are to be turned into the docile slaves of the American multimillionaires, and not into French men and women attached to the moral and intellectual values which have been the grandeur and glory of our nation."

In Britain, the Labour Party led by Clement Atlee had swept into office in 1945 and promptly began constructing the Welfare State. Atlee's socialist government quickly discovered that U.S. loans to Britain had run out and, what's more, the country's balance-of-payments crisis was being exacerbated by revenue drains from imported Hollywood movies and American cigarettes. Hollywood was earning about $60 million annually in the U.K.—about 4 percent of total British consumer expenditures were on American goods. The Labour government had already cut imports of food and other essential goods in order to maintain an acceptable level of hard currency. Now something had to be done about Hollywood's impact on Britain's balance of payments. In 1947, the Atlee government imposed a punitive 75 percent *ad valorem* tax on Hollywood movies. The so-called "Dalton Duty"—named after Hugh Dalton, Britain's Chancellor of the Exchequer—meant, in effect, that the Hollywood studios could retain only 25 percent of their revenues in Britain. For the Hollywood moguls, the Dalton Duty was a declaration of war.

Hollywood had already been nervous about Britain, because British movies like Laurence Olivier's *Henry V* were achieving great commercial successes in the United States. In the late 1940s, it seemed the British movie industry was reawakening. One British film of the era, *Passport to Pimlico*, parodied British post-war fear of American domination. In the movie, a London neighbourhood absurdly declares statehood to assert its own sovereignty during the economically difficult post-war years. The tribulations of the tiny state of Pimlico were, in fact, intended as a caricature of difficulties encountered by small states such as Britain in the new Cold War reality of rival superpowers. Hollywood clearly lacked a British sense of humour. After the Dalton Duty, the Hollywood moguls were determined to show British leaders that, in international diplomacy, the U.K. was not much stronger than the tiny fictional state of Pimlico.

On August 6, 1947—the day after the Dalton Duty was announced—the Hollywood majors threatened a total boycott of British movie screens. To prove they were serious, Hollywood launched a blitzkrieg advertising campaign throughout London for a fictitious American movie. Hollywood posters blanketing the streets of London were deliberately ambiguous, showing only a large bald eagle and the word "Unconquered" emblazoned across the top. It was an aggressive scare tactic that must have struck Britons as typically American. But the Hollywood studios, true to their word, began boycotting British movie theatres in the fall of 1947.

The British government was incensed by Hollywood's hardball tactics. Prime Minister Atlee nonetheless was concerned about the long-term effects of a bitter trade dispute with the United States, especially while the Marshall Plan was rolling out across Europe. That consideration did little to appease hostility towards Hollywood among British élites. One Member of Parliament, Robert Boothby, declared in the House of Commons: "I have a great admiration for the acting of Mr. Humphrey Bogart. Nevertheless, as I am compelled to choose between Bogart and bacon, I am bound to choose bacon at the present time." It was not certain, however, that the British people agreed with this sentiment. As the Atlee government knew only too well, working-class Britons were tremendously fond of going to the "pictures" to see American movies—one of the few luxuries they could afford in a rationed post-war economy.

In an effort to defuse the crisis, Atlee dispatched his industry minister, Harold Wilson—the future Labour prime minister—to negotiate with the Hollywood majors. Lawyer Allen Dulles, who later would be appointed head of the CIA, represented the Hollywood studios. Wilson, who was only 31 years old, was astounded by the hostility he encountered in America during the negotiations. The Hollywood lobby, in an effort to smear Wilson as a socialist menace, had distributed copies of his speeches in American movie theatres. Wilson bit his lip, because he knew his mission was to secure a deal. In Britain, meanwhile, movie theatre owners suffering under the U.S. boycott were forced to screen reruns of old American movies such as *Hellzapoppin'*.

A compromise was finally reached with the signing of an Anglo-American Film Agreement, which came into effect in June 1948. According to the bilateral accord, Hollywood would be allowed to distribute 180 movies in Britain and remit £17 million annually to the United States, with any unremitted sums to be spent in the United Kingdom. In addition, the Hollywood studios would be allowed to remit a sum equal to the earnings of British films in the American market.[7]

Defending his compromise, Harold Wilson observed: "We were paying out not 17 million pounds, but 50 million pounds, for the privilege of seeing *Hellzapoppin'* for the third time and *Ben-Hur* for the twenty-third!" Still, critics in Britain blamed Wilson for caving in to the Americans. As the *Financial Times* put it: "We couldn't have come off worse in the negotiations if we had been represented by the four Marx brothers." In 1949, Wilson saved face by creating the National Film Finance Corporation, which was capitalized at £5 million, to subsidize U.K. movie production. In 1950, the U.K. government took further measures by slapping a tax—called the "Eady Levy" after senior treasury official Sir Wilfrid Eady—on British box-office tickets. Some of the proceeds generated by the Eady Levy were funnelled into a new British Film Production Fund. The Hollywood studios, too, began tapping into the Fund to finance movies they shot in Britain using local talent and technicians.[8]

In Italy, Hollywood encountered a somewhat more complex post-war challenge. Before the war, Italy had boasted a strong domestic cinema industry thanks partly to Hollywood's boycott. Another reason was Mussolini, who for propaganda reasons had been a strong supporter of Italian cinema as an expression of national pride. In 1937, the Italian dictator had personally laid the cornerstone at Rome's Cinecittà studio, where he posed before an enormous sign that read: "Cinema is the Strongest Weapon." Following the war, some U.S. officials believed Italy's cinema industry should be smashed apart due to the emergence of Italian communism as a powerful political force. The CIA, which played a key behind-the-scenes role in post-war Italian politics, worked covertly to ensure that elections were won by the conservative Christian-Democrats.

When the Italian Communists were politically sandbagged, it didn't take long before Hollywood movies began saturating Italian movie screens. By 1946, Italian movies were earning only 13 percent of domestic box-office receipts in their domestic market.

Italy responded to Hollywood's dominance in two ways. First, Italian filmmakers began shooting "neo-realist" films that had little in common with Hollywood's "entertainment" movies. Second, the Italian government encouraged domestic movie production through quotas, tax rebates for exhibitors, and direct subsidies—all of which were allowed under the multilateral GATT trade accord. In the subsequent years, Italian movies began selling throughout the world, especially with the emergence of directors such as Federico Fellini, Vittorio de Sica, and Italian film stars like Sophia Loren. Italian producers who emerged during this era included Dino de Laurentiis and Carlo Ponti. The big breakthrough for Italian movies, however, came in the 1960s with the global success of low-budget "spaghetti westerns." A classic example of this genre was Sergio Leone's *A Fistful of Dollars*, which launched the career of an unknown American actor called Clint Eastwood.

The White House had learned a valuable lesson in Europe. In the wake of Britain's Dalton Duty controversy, the Truman administration took measures in 1948 to assist Hollywood studios in repatriating revenues generated from European markets. The U.S. government created a program, run out of the State Department, called the Informational Media Guaranty—or IMG. Through the IMG, the U.S. government gave Hollywood studios dollars in exchange for soft foreign currencies earned in Europe. There was one proviso: To qualify for the currency conversions, Hollywood studios were obliged to export movies that portrayed American life and values in a positive manner. In effect, the U.S. State Department was subsidizing the distribution of Hollywood movies in foreign countries where local currencies were blocked by foreign-exchange restrictions. The IMG was also a financial instrument used to spread American values throughout Europe during the early Cold War years.

Hollywood's relations with the Soviet Union, needless to say, were virtually non-existent. Under Stalin, movie production in the Soviet Union and its Eastern European satellite states came under strict Kremlin control. The Kremlin was, for obvious reasons, resolutely hostile to the importation of movies from Hollywood and other capitalist countries. The Soviet Union banned not only movies that were judged to be anti-Communist, but also films considered unduly pro-American. The Soviets also banned Hollywood movies featuring stars who had delivered anti-communist testimonies before the U.S. House Un-American Activities Committee, or who were considered to harbour anti-communist views. The Soviet black list included Robert Taylor, Gary Cooper, Robert Montgomery, Ginger Rogers, Greta Garbo, Barbara Stanwyck, and Clark Gable.

Ironically, the Hollywood studios had been producing pro-Soviet movies—such as *Mission to Moscow* and *Song of Russia*—during the Second World War to create good feelings between America and its Russian allies against Hitler. After the war, however, Hollywood promptly joined the anti-Red crusade. True, some Hollywood movies expressed a liberal-minded hostility towards the excesses of McCarthyism. In the 1956 movie, *Storm Center*, Bette Davis played a small-town librarian who courageously defends her right to stock her shelves with so-called "radical" books. More typical, however, was Don Siegel's *Invasion of the Body Snatchers*, which evoked the communist threat in the form of aliens who dehumanized small-town Americans. Other Hollywood movies were much less subtle. In 1950, *I Married a Communist* starred Robert Ryan playing a radical who is blackmailed into working for the Soviets. John Wayne, the macho Hollywood symbol of American patriotism, also jumped on the anti-Communist bandwagon in 1952 by starring in *Big Jim McLain*, in which he played a tough HUAC investigator pursuing communists in Hawaii.

The real HUAC, meanwhile, was stepping up its witch-hunt of suspected Hollywood communists. Some Hollywood liberals, such as Humphrey Bogart and Groucho Marx, attempted to shame the HUAC hearings, but theirs were minority voices. Hollywood moguls were keen to send a message to Washington that the American movie industry was not infiltrated by left-wing subversives. Louis B. Mayer assured Washington lawmakers that he "maintained a relentless vigilance against un-American influences." In November 1947, the Hollywood moguls issued a "Waldorf Statement"—so named because it was drafted at New York's Waldorf Hotel—in which they declared that suspected pro-communist screenwriters would be blackballed. A list of targeted screenwriters—known as the "Hollywood Ten"—saw their reputations tarnished and careers destroyed. The same fate awaited any known communist or anyone who refused to cooperate with the HUAC. McCarthyism was just around the corner.

In this ideological climate, the U.S. State Department shrewdly understood that Hollywood movies were powerful Cold War weapons. In 1954, American journalist Harrison Salisbury returned from the Soviet Union convinced that Hollywood movies should be exported to the Soviet Union. "There is no question that in Russia, as everywhere else," he said, "American pictures are the best and most forceful medium for selling the United States." But the Hollywood moguls resisted the idea. There was some concern that the Soviets would deform Hollywood movies into anti-American propaganda. When *Mr. Smith Goes to Washington* and *Mr. Deeds Goes to Town* were shown in the Soviet Union, for example, the State Department ordered copies to be returned to the United States because the Soviets had drastically edited the movies to disparage life in America. In *Mr. Deeds Goes to Town*, Gary Cooper plays a small-town American who strikes it rich but, after a series of disappointments, ends up giving his $1 million to poor farmers during the Depression. In the re-edited Soviet version, Cooper was shown being hauled off to an insane asylum—thus underscoring the sins of capitalist wealth and the unavoidable fate to which its accumulation inevitably leads. The Eisenhower administration nonetheless agreed that Hollywood movies would be powerful weapons behind the Iron Curtain. U.S. Secretary of State John Foster Dulles—brother of Hollywood lawyer and future CIA boss Allen Dulles—strongly favoured exporting Hollywood movies throughout the Communist world. In the late 1950s, Washington and Moscow finally signed a cultural exchange agreement according to which a limited number of Hollywood movies were allowed into the Soviet bloc. The Soviet Union chose ten American movies for distribution, including *Oklahoma, Roman Holiday, The Old Man and the Sea, 7th Voyage of Sinbad,* and *Man of a Thousand Faces.* Under State Department orders, however, Hollywood refused to sell the Soviets any movie that portrayed America in a negative light, such as *Elmer Gantry* and *Dr. Strangelove.*[9]

The Hollywood moguls may have been genuinely committed to exporting pro-American movies for ideological reasons, but Hollywood's international strategy during the Cold War was largely a response to challenges in the U.S. domestic market—namely, the steady decline in movie attendance throughout the 1950s due to television and other lifestyle changes in America.

The strategy worked. Hollywood's international campaigns throughout the 1950s and 1960s revitalized the fortunes of the major studios.

Jack Valenti and Hollywood Hardball

When John F. Kennedy entered the White House in 1961, the longstanding complicity between Hollywood and Washington could not have been closer. JFK's father had been a Hollywood mogul, and while in Hollywood had conducted a secret extramarital affair with starlet Gloria Swanson. Like his father, JFK was attracted to the glamour—and the women—of Tinseltown. Once in the White House, President Kennedy cavorted with the infamous Hollywood "Rat Pack"—Frank Sinatra, Dean Martin, Sammy Davis Jr., and his brother-in-law Peter Lawford.

On November 22, 1963, the day JFK was assassinated, a little-known Houston advertising man named Jack Valenti was riding in the presidential motorcade through Dallas. Valenti, an ex-Second World War pilot who had earned an MBA at Harvard, was riding six cars behind President Kennedy as part of Vice-President Lyndon Johnson's retinue. Valenti had first met LBJ in 1957 when Johnson, a veteran Texas politician, was Senate majority leader in Congress. Valenti had started dating Johnson's personal secretary, Mary Margaret Wiley, and was frequently a guest at Johnson's ranch in Texas.

After the shots rang out in Dallas, Valenti rushed to the city's Parkland Hospital with Johnson, who became President of the United States the instant JFK was pronounced dead. Valenti flew back to Washington with President Johnson, and was standing at LBJ's side aboard Air Force One as the new president was sworn in. As America and the world mourned, Jack Valenti suddenly, through tragic circumstances, had a new career as a senior White House political assistant.

In Washington, Valenti's close relationship with President Johnson was known everywhere, and the connection quickly made him a powerful figure on Capitol Hill. Valenti was now married to Mary Margaret Wiley, who also was working for LBJ in the White House. Emboldened by his new status as a powerful Washington player, the diminutive and impeccably dressed Valenti quickly became LBJ's indispensable conduit to Congress. When congressmen were looking for presidential favours in exchange for supporting White House initiatives, they went to see "Jack."

While at the White House, Valenti discreetly nurtured a friendship with Hollywood mogul Lew Wasserman, who he knew was a close friend of President Johnson. Wasserman, head of MCA, was a longtime power broker in Democratic politics who, in 1963, had sponsored a lavish fundraising dinner for President Kennedy at the Beverly Hills Hilton. In 1964, President Johnson had offered Wasserman the post of U.S. Commerce Secretary, but the mogul declined in favour of running MCA. Wasserman didn't need a top Washington job to exercise influence at the LBJ White House. Wasserman's friend, United Artists president Arthur Krim, was also among LBJ's most trusted associates. It was Krim who had organized the famous 1962 birthday gala for JFK at Madison Square Garden, where Marilyn Monroe sang "Happy Birthday, Mr. President." It was Krim, too, who had created the President's Club as a national fundraising machine for Democratic politicians, including LBJ. Like Wasserman, Krim had turned down LBJ's offers of a top job in his administration—in his case, U.S. ambassador to the United Nations. Indifference to the perquisites of power must have impressed LBJ. During the five years Johnson was in the White House, Wasserman and Krim were among the President's most influential insiders.

"Wasserman was one of the first to realize that Hollywood could have clout in Washington," recalled Sam Goldwyn Jr. "He said: 'We can be an influence—but don't kid yourself, it means patronage.'"

In 1966, Wasserman and Krim were looking for someone to run the Motion Picture Association of America, which had been leaderless for two years after the death of Eric Johnston. JFK's speechwriter, Ted Sorensen, was considered for the job, but he demurred. Other names, such as former presidential candidate Adlai Stevenson and ex-JFK press secretary Pierre Salinger, were also floated. Wasserman finally fixed his sights on Jack Valenti, LBJ's bright and energetic political assistant. Valenti, though loyal to LBJ, was immediately interested in the high-profile job as Hollywood's spokesman.

"Wasserman convinced me that the presidency of the MPAA would give me spacious opportunity to continue my interest in global politics and international affairs," Valenti recalled.

After less than three years at the White House, Valenti accepted Wasserman's offer in April 1966. President Johnson was reluctant to part with his trusted aide, but finally agreed on the condition that Wasserman "take care" of Valenti. When Valenti left the White House for Hollywood, President Johnson wrote his protégé Jack an affectionate note: "I thank you and love you and am very proud of you."[10]

With Valenti's arrival at the MPAA, the traditionally tight relationship between Hollywood and the White House was cemented again. For Valenti, heading the MPAA was almost like being appointed U.S. Secretary of State. Indeed, he would boast that "the motion picture industry is the only U.S. enterprise that negotiates on its own with foreign governments." Valenti proved highly talented at lobbying foreign governments. His effectiveness undoubtedly depended on the perception that Valenti had a direct line to the White House. This was true, though Valenti did not have the same degree of political clout as Lew Wasserman. In many respects, Valenti was Wasserman's personal envoy, whether abroad or in Washington.

As Hollywood mogul Sid Sheinberg, a longtime Wasserman associate, recalled: "Without detracting from Jack's ability to cater to these people in Washington and build relationships, the truth, to be candid, is that politicians, then and now, tend to like those who enable them to raise money. And had Jack not had the Lew Wassermans of the world—although there was, really, just one Lew Wasserman—Jack would not have been so successful."[11]

By the late 1960s, LBJ had left office and Richard Nixon was installed in the White House. These were difficult years for Valenti. The Republicans had taken over Washington. Valenti's Democratic friends were out of power. What's more, Hollywood suddenly seemed out of touch with turbulent, counter-culture America. The United States was undergoing wrenching social upheaval at a time when the Vietnam War, civil rights movement, sexual liberation, and rock music were at the forefront of the American conscience. Yet Hollywood's image was associated with Rat Pack movies, John Wayne westerns, and Doris Day comedies. In the late 1960s, these films seemed old-fashioned compared with independently produced movies like *Easy Rider*, about two pot-smoking hippies travelling across America on motorcycles to the psychedelic sounds of Jimi Hendrix.

To make things worse, the U.S. economy was suffering a downturn in the early 1970s. As a result, Hollywood box-office receipts began to plummet to the point where the American movie industry accumulated losses of about $100 million. Some studios resorted to desperate measures to raise cash. MGM auctioned off highly treasured memorabilia, including

Judy Garland's famous ruby slippers from *The Wizard of Oz*. At the same time, a new generation of movie directors—Francis Ford Coppola, Martin Scorsese, Brian de Palma—was emerging with a new, gritty brand of American cinema inspired by European films. American society was changing, and it was time for Hollywood to catch up.

Jack Valenti had to change, too. Valenti set about implementing a two-pronged strategy to turn around Hollywood's fortunes. First, he would win concessions in Washington to improve Hollywood's financial position in the domestic U.S. market. Second, he would fight for greater market share for Hollywood products in foreign countries.

Valenti's first lobbying victory came in 1970, when the Federal Communications Commission adopted its famous Financial and Syndication Rules. The so-called "fin-syn" rules barred the U.S. television networks—CBS, NBC, ABC—from broadcasting programs made by their own production affiliates. The fin-syn rules were meant to protect independent producers from the market power of the self-dealing TV networks. To some extent, this worked. But the real winner was Hollywood, whose studios now had regulated access to the prime-time schedules of the major TV networks. Television was no longer Hollywood's enemy, but its best friend. Valenti, meanwhile, was scoring big on Capitol Hill. In 1971, Senator Thomas Kuchel put forward a piece of legislation called the Domestic Film Production Incentive Act. The draft law, which could have been written by Valenti's own pen, proposed a 20 percent tax exemption on the production or export of any film made in the United States. At the same time, Congress held hearings examining the "unemployment problems in the American film industry." Ronald Reagan, the conservative governor of California who had once headed Hollywood's Screen Actors Guild, vigorously supported a taxpayer-subsidized rescue of the Hollywood majors. Reagan's successor at the Guild was movie star Charlton Heston, who argued passionately in Washington that Hollywood was "in desperate need of federal assistance."

The Domestic Film Production Incentive Act never became law, but hardly anyone noticed. Valenti and Wasserman were scoring an even bigger victory with the Nixon White House. In 1971, Valenti and Wasserman fought to include the movie industry as a sector qualifying for 7 percent tax write-offs on investments in machinery and equipment. The tax credits, provided for in the newly drafted *Revenue Act*, originally excluded movie studios. But

Wasserman used his considerable clout in Congress to secure inclusion for Hollywood. Besides the fiscal bonus, Congress also allowed Hollywood studios to create subsidiaries called Domestic International Sales Corporations—or "DISCs"—which could defer paying tax on half of profits earned from exports. An even bigger jackpot was another proposed tax credit that would allow investors to claim a 100 percent tax exemption on investments in American movies. This tax-credit scheme provoked heated debate in Congress. In the U.S. Senate, Ted Kennedy opposed the tax shelter as an "outright tax subsidy" for the profitable Hollywood industry. Other senators argued, however, that the U.S. movie industry was an "American institution" and therefore deserved taxpayer support—particularly as a response to the threat of foreign movies that were also subsidized by their governments. Such was Wasserman's power within Congress that one of his allies, Senator Alan Cranston, called Wasserman from the floor of the Senate to report the good news about the tax credits: "Done!"

The tax shelters gave an enormous boost to Hollywood's fortunes. In 1972, *Variety* reported that 97 percent of Universal's profit increase was directly attributable to the new tax credits. Walt Disney cleverly applied for retroactive tax credits back to 1963, when the fiscal incentives originally had been introduced as part of another law. Thanks to this loophole, Disney and other Hollywood studios won $400 million in back tax credits. Charlton Heston, expressing Hollywood's gratitude for the fiscal boondoggle, said the tax credits had been "of inestimable help in our desperate predicament." While some denounced the tax shelter for encouraging fraud, it nonetheless provided financing for critically acclaimed feature films such as Milos Forman's *One Flew Over the Cuckoo's Nest*, Bob Rafelson's *Five Easy Pieces*, and Martin Scorsese's *Taxi Driver*.[12]

Having secured the home front, Valenti's battles abroad would be even more controversial, especially in the 1980s when the United States was attempting to assert itself internationally to dispel perceptions that America was in decline. Even among American political élites, there was growing concern that the United States was losing its international influence and prestige. Not even the arrival of Ronald Reagan in the White House and the global popularity of Sylvester Stallone on the world's movie screens—as Rocky and Rambo—was sufficient to assuage concerns about America's decline. Determined to reassert American supremacy, Washington began taking a tough, no-nonsense stance on bilateral and multilateral trade issues, especially in the media and entertainment industries. It was especially important to maintain open market access for Hollywood movies. The annual growth rate of U.S. domestic revenues for Hollywood movies was 10 percent, while sales in foreign markets were growing by 22 percent annually. Given these figures, Washington was particularly vigilant about import restrictions on Hollywood films.

In 1984, a subcommittee of Congress issued a report titled *Trade Barriers to U.S. Motion Pictures and Television, Pre-recorded Entertainment, Publishing and Advertising Industries.* Canada was at the top of Washington's list of countries whose trade policies were identified as hostile to American interests. The Reagan administration, largely deaf to Canadian claims about its "cultural sovereignty," was particularly angered by Canada's restrictions on American investment in the media industries. Canada maintained an arsenal of restrictive regulations preventing the importation of American cultural products, even though Canadians were free to own U.S. newspapers, magazines, cable TV companies, and movie studios. Some of these issues were resolved when the United States and Canada began negotiating a Free Trade Agreement in the mid-1980s. Canada's biggest concession to Washington was in the area of Hollywood movies. The Canadian government had been attempting to enact legislation that would limit the dominance of the Hollywood majors in the Canadian market. But when the White House, pressured by Jack Valenti, threatened to scupper the free-trade pact if Canada's anti-Hollywood legislation was passed, the Canadian government hastily retreated.

Hollywood faced more formidable opposition in Europe, whose transformation into a supranational trading bloc posed a much greater threat. As in the past, relations between the United States and France were particularly tense, especially after 1981 when socialist François Mitterrand was elected as France's head of state. President Reagan was astounded when Mitterrand appointed four Communists as ministers in his first government. Mitterrand's flamboyant culture minister, Jack Lang, was not a communist, but he was fiercely anti-American. Shortly after the Socialists took power, Lang called on the nations of the world to embark on a "crusade" against the American entertainment industries, which he denounced as a capitalist campaign of "financial and cultural imperialism that no longer, or rarely, grabs territory but grabs consciousness, ways of thinking, ways of living." The following year, at a UNESCO-sponsored conference in Cancun, Mexico, Lang again lashed out at America, which he said had "no other morality than profit" and inflicted a "uniform culture" on the entire planet.

"Our destiny is not to become the vassals of an immense empire of profit," declared Lang, pointing out that Europe had a massive negative trade balance with the United States in the entertainment industries.

While evoking the rhetoric of cultural sovereignty, Lang inadvertently *just* betrayed the real issue: France's negative balance of payments. Indeed, *economic?* France's main reason for opposing free global trade in movies was strictly economic. By the mid-1980s, Hollywood movies had begun surpassing French movies at the domestic box office. In 1984, French movies took 49.3 percent of box-office receipts, while American movies earned 36.9 percent. By 1987, Hollywood surpassed French films with a 43.7 percent share compared with only 36.2 percent for French-made movies. While lushly produced French movies like *Madame Bovary* found critical success, at the box office Hollywood movies like Steven Spielberg's *Jurassic Park* invariably crushed all local competition. *Jurassic Park* was so popular in France, in fact, that a new French verb—*jurassiquer*—was coined to denote Hollywood domination. When *Jurassic Park* was stomping, dinosaur-like, over the European movie market in the fall of 1993, France's Gaullist culture minister, Jacques Toubon, dismissed the film as "a series of special effects." That didn't stop millions of Europeans from lining up to see the movie. As Carla Hills, President George Bush's special trade envoy, remarked to European filmmakers: "Make films as good as your cheeses and you will sell them!" Even the French government, caught between the competing dictates of domestic and foreign policy, had to acknowledge that many of its citizens immensely enjoyed watching dubbed versions of Hollywood movies. → *of course, how is that weakening their position?*

France's cinematic dilemma was underscored again in the late 1990s when the French movie *Astérix and Obélix against Caesar* was pitted in mortal combat against a Hollywood blockbuster, *Titanic*. In 1998, *Astérix and Obélix against Caesar* was hailed in France as a patriotic metaphor for the country's cultural battles against America. For centuries, French school-children have learned about the legendary Astérix, the plucky Gaul who fought against Roman imperialism. Now Astérix was taking on the American Caesar in France's movie theatres. But at the box-office, *Astérix*—featuring French movie star Gérard Dépardieu—received mixed reviews. Even worse, *Astérix* conceded defeat when *Titanic* smashed all French box-office records. The Romans had defeated Astérix, and now so had Hollywood.

France's hostile attitude towards Hollywood increasingly has been tempered by pragmatism. It became difficult to denounce American cultural imperialism in the early 1990s when a major French bank, Crédit Lyonnais, took effective control of a Hollywood studio, Metro-Goldwyn-Mayer, after backing a short-lived takeover of MGM by Italian businessman Giancarlo Parretti. Crédit Lyonnais also financed the Hollywood ambitions of other non-American producers such as Dino de Laurentiis and Israelis Menahem Golan and partner Yoram Globus. It was thanks to the Crédit Lyonnais that Carolco—which produced *Rambo* and *Terminator 2*—emerged as a major force in Hollywood. Even Jack Lang held out an olive branch by decorating Sylvester Stallone—Rambo himself—with France's prestigious Legion of Honour.

British movies, meanwhile, enjoyed several years of success internationally in the 1980s. The decade had begun with the Academy Awards triumphs of U.K. movies such as *Chariots of Fire* and Richard Attenborough's *Gandhi*, which were both major hits in America. There was even talk in Hollywood about a "British invasion." British producers such as David Puttnam were landing key jobs at the top of Hollywood studios. But the loudly trumpeted British invasion of Hollywood never happened. In 1985, Margaret Thatcher abolished the Eady Levy—a tax on box-office receipts—that had been subsidizing British movies. The immediate consequence was reduced output of British movies: in 1985, more than 50 films were produced, but by 1989 output had plummeted to 30 movies. Some British movies—like *Four Weddings and a Funeral*—scored with audiences at home and abroad. But the British movie industry was in no position to challenge Hollywood's dominance.

By the early 1990s, Jack Valenti's biggest challenge in Europe was the supranational push in favour of a continental strategy to combat Hollywood domination. Washington feared a "Fortress Europe" strategy in multilateral trade negotiations led by the European Commission in Brussels. The EC realized that European cinema would never achieve competitive advantages vis-à-vis Hollywood without harnessing the same

economies of scale available in the domestic U.S. market. And as long as
Hollywood films dominated local cinemas in Europe, most of the proceeds
would continue to flow back to America. The EC solution was to encourage
the pooling of resources in European co-productions, aided by subsidies
and quota restrictions. A notable Euro-production had been *The Name of
the Rose*—a German-French-Italian film starring Sean Connery—which
grossed more than $120 million worldwide. But the movie's success was
undoubtedly due to the fact that, because it was shot in English, it enjoyed
ready access to the American market.

On the diplomatic front, the European Commission was demanding a
"cultural exemption" as part of the Uruguay Round of the GATT negotiations. Jack Valenti, incensed by the EC's effrontery, pressured Washington to
seize on GATT to play hardball with Europe. Valenti worked furiously behind
the scenes to sabotage the European effort to carve out "audiovisual" products
from GATT. He publicly reminded his European detractors that many of
Hollywood's most successful directors—Ridley Scott, Paul Verhoeven, Alan
Parker, Jean-Jacques Annaud—were Europeans, as well as movie stars such as
Arnold Schwarzenegger and Jean-Claude van Damme. Valenti also privately
twisted the arms of Steven Spielberg and Martin Scorsese, who somewhat half-
heartedly made a public statement against "protectionism." European film
directors—including Stephen Frears, Pedro Almodavar, Bernardo Bertolucci,
and Wim Wenders—countered with a public statement saying European
cinema needed to be protected against "complete annihilation." French intellectual Régis Debray seized on more familiar language to denounce Hollywood imperialism: "An American monoculture would inflict a sad future on
the world, one in which the planet is converted to a global supermarket where
people have to choose between the local ayatollah and Coca-Cola."

Valenti's trump card was the White House. He believed he could count
on the support of President Bill Clinton, whose special trade representative,
Mickey Kantor, was a well-connected Hollywood lawyer. Negotiating for
Europe was Sir Leon Brittan, a strident Thatcherite who had left the Iron
Lady's cabinet for the European Commission. Brittan shared Kantor's pro-
market views, but he was under tremendous pressure in Europe to show his
mettle by out-smarting the Americans in the GATT talks.

In early December 1993, Kantor and Brittan conducted tense eleventh-
hour negotiations in Geneva to meet a self-imposed deadline of December

15 for a GATT agreement. Valenti and his Hollywood cohorts were in the Swiss city to follow the talks closely. In fact, they were holed up in the same hotel in a nearby suite. When it appeared obvious that Brittan and his European colleagues would not budge on film and television products, Valenti and his Hollywood bosses began to panic. They urged Mickey Kantor to adopt a scorched-earth strategy. "Blow up the deal," said one Hollywood studio executive. "Have the President go to the American people and explain what happened. Tell him to blame it on the French!"

Valenti's only hope now was President Clinton. A few days earlier, Clinton had attended a $50,000-a-plate fundraiser at the Los Angeles home of billionaire financier Martin Davis. Valenti had prepped all the Hollywood moguls who attended the event, and they each privately lobbied Clinton about the irksome Europeans and their anti-American cultural policies.

On December 15, Mickey Kantor broke away from the Geneva talks to make an urgent telephone call to President Clinton for political instructions. Clinton had been calling European leaders on the telephone to find resolution to the remaining sticking point: audiovisual products. To Kantor's astonishment, Clinton instructed him to back off from movies and TV programs and sign the deal. Europe would get its cultural exemption.

Stunned by news of the White House concession, Valenti furiously lashed out against his adversaries. "In a global treaty supposed to reduce trade barriers, the European Commission erected a great wall to keep out the works of non-European creative men and women," he said. "This negotiation had nothing to do with culture, unless European soap operas and game shows are the equivalent of Molière. This is all about the hard business of money."

Astérix, it seemed, had finally outsmarted Caesar. Still, the GATT accord hardly closed European markets to American movie and television programs. The GATT negotiations may have been a diplomatic setback for the United States, but Hollywood would win in the marketplace. Even in France, with its lavish subsidies for domestic movies, Hollywood would continue to give meaning to the verb *jurassiquer*.

Nearly a decade later, the indefatigable Valenti was still Hollywood's foreign secretary. Valenti was now past 80 years old, but he still had fire in his belly. In early 2002, Valenti delivered a menacing speech before Canadian filmmakers and government officials in Ottawa. "No president, no prime minister, can command great programming to be made nor can any Congress or Parliament order citizens to watch what they do not want to watch," he declared. "That is a truth of the human condition which rhetoric cannot ignore, nor laws distort." →as long as it US

Some affectionately speculated that Valenti would never retire until he turned 100. As *Variety* remarked: "Jack Valenti has outlasted 232 U.S. senators, 13 Supreme Court justices, and seven Presidents. Don't even try to calculate how many studio heads."

Under President George Bush *fils*, the White House had an open-door policy towards Jack Valenti—a privilege he'd already enjoyed under George Bush *père*. It could still be said, with little exaggeration, that Jack Valenti had been one of the most powerful men in Washington for four decades.[13]

Mickey's Good Neighbour Policy

Today the Disney brand evokes a mythical image of America as a place of child-like wonder and innocence. Yet Walt Disney himself was no innocent. In fact, Disney was deeply engaged in the political and commercial battles of his time—especially America's ideological crusade against Communism. What's more, Disney was always willing to lend his name, and Disney brands, to help America's foreign policy objectives throughout the world.

Disney's most famous creation, of course, was Mickey Mouse. Interestingly, Mickey Mouse dates to the earliest days of Disney's career as a young animator in the late 1920s, when an original cartoon rodent called Steamboat Willie morphed into Mickey. By the early 1930s, Mickey was famous in America as the hero of many "triumph-of-the-little-guy" adventures, frequently accompanied by his canine pal Pluto. These were the Depression years, when President Roosevelt was attempting to rebuild the U.S. economy through his America National Recovery Administration. For many Americans, Disney cartoons embodied FDR's campaign to get America back on its feet in the face of adversity. In one of his most famous speeches, FDR told Americans that they had nothing to fear "but fear itself." At the same time, Disney's *Three Little Pigs* hit cinema screens featuring the song, "Who's Afraid of the Big Bad Wolf." The song quickly became a standard in ballrooms across America, and millions of Americans were whistling the tune in the streets. *Three Little Pigs*, which was a huge hit after its release in 1933, seemed to serve as a morale booster for Americans who courageously refused to fear the big, bad Depression.

Walt Disney, ironically, was not a political supporter of President Roosevelt. But in truth, Disney was more patriotic than partisan. When the Depression ended and the Second World War began, Disney put his studio at the disposal of the U.S. government. After Pearl Harbor, Disney began churning out countless propaganda films for the Roosevelt administration. Some were educational documentaries aimed at U.S. soldiers, such as *A Few Quick Facts About Venereal Disease*. Others, however, featured Disney cartoon heroes such as Mickey and Minnie Mouse, and the irascible Donald Duck, who by now was just as famous as Mickey. One of the most memorable animated shorts of the era was *Donald Gets Drafted*, in which Donald Duck triumphs over petty irritations to prove his patriotic duty as a soldier. An anti-Nazi cartoon was *Der Fuehrer's Face*, which features Donald working at a munitions factory in a country called Nutziland. The Oscar-winning film, released in 1943, shows Donald Duck fighting against the torments of totalitarianism and, in the end, saluting the Statue of Liberty and shouting, "I am glad to be a citizen of the United States!"[14]

In *The New Spirit*, a Disney propaganda cartoon shot for the U.S. Treasury Department, Donald Duck is shown as a model of wartime fiscal responsibility. Faced with the annoying duty of paying his taxes, Donald realizes that patriotism and prompt payment go hand in hand. Donald's slogan in the film is "Taxes to Beat the Axis." Some 26 million Americans saw *The New Spirit*, and nearly 40 percent said in a poll that Donald's on-screen fiscal patriotism had inspired them to pay their taxes more promptly. Films like *The New Spirit* gave a tremendous boost to the Disney brand. Newspaper headlines began trumpeting, "Mickey Mouse and Donald Duck Work for Victory" and "Walt Disney Goes to War." *This Week Magazine* observed that Walt Disney was "a propaganda genius for whom the Axis would give a dozen divisions." Indeed, Mickey Mouse was becoming famous throughout the world. In France, he was known as Mickey Souris, in Italy he was Topolino, in Japan he was called Miki Kuchi, and the Spanish knew him affectionately as Miguel Ratoncito. By the early 1940s, it was estimated that roughly 33 percent of the entire planet's population had seen at least one Disney film.

Walt Disney was also keen to promote America's "Good Neighbour Policy" in Latin America. In 1940, the State Department restructured its Inter-American Affairs bureau by instituting a Motion Picture Division. One member was Nelson Rockefeller, the future New York governor and U.S. vice-president. Another was John Hay Whitney, the philanthropist, movie producer, financial backer of Dwight D. Eisenhower, and later President Eisenhower's ambassador to the United Kingdom. After a tour of Latin America, Rockefeller and Whitney—two Eastern establishment aristocrats—came to the conclusion that Hollywood's problem in Latin America wasn't its derogatory portrayal of the local population, but rather its negative portrayal of America. With this in mind, they met with Hollywood executives to encourage them to present "truly American life" to Latin American movie audiences. The result was sometimes ludicrous. After Universal Pictures' Abbott and Costello movie, *In the Navy*, opened in U.S. movie theatres, Rockefeller resolutely opposed its release in Latin America on the grounds that the movie made a mockery of the U.S. Marine Corps. Rockefeller finally secured a compromise from Universal Pictures. [The studio inserted a Spanish prologue at the outset of the film explaining to audiences that the U.S. Navy was not actually as hopelessly incompetent as portrayed in the movie.] ➡ Such cencorshyp

More substantively, the White House's policy objective was to extend and reinforce American influence in Latin America as a bulwark against foreign invasion—especially by the Nazis. Rockefeller, who had long been active in Latin America through the Rockefeller Foundation's public health activities, had shared President Roosevelt's concern about the extent of "Nazi influence and penetration" throughout the region. In the early 1940s, German interests virtually controlled communications infrastructure—notably telephone systems—in Argentina, Uruguay, Ecuador, Paraguay, Chile, and Mexico. There can be little doubt that the State Department wanted, for strategic reasons, to dispossess the Germans of communications systems in Latin America. On a higher moral terrain, however, the Good Neighbour Policy's mission was given the following credo: "To show the truth about the American way." Whitney made this objective explicit in a memo in which he asserted: "The menace of Nazism and its allied doctrines, its techniques and tactics, must be understood from Hudson's Bay to Punta Arenas. Wherever the motion picture can do a basic job of spreading the gospel of the Americas' common stake in this struggle, there that job must be and shall be done."[15]

When looking for a chief cinematic apostle for "the American way." Rockefeller and Whitney immediately thought of Walt Disney. His films, including *Snow White and the Seven Dwarfs*, had been immense box-office hits in the late 1930s, and Mickey Mouse and Donald Duck were charming millions of Americans. Walt Disney immediately accepted their invitation to become the Good Neighbour Policy's unofficial ambassador. Between 1941 and 1943, Disney took his wife, family, and a retinue of staff members on three separate trips throughout Latin America to shoot a series of travelogue and entertainment movies based on their experiences. Some of them were cartoon adventures featuring Mickey Mouse, Donald Duck, Pluto, and Goofy. Many were educational documentaries using Mickey and Donald to teach Latin Americans about basic hygiene issues, such as the dangers of drinking impure water.

Today, Marxist critics of U.S. cultural imperialism have made much of Walt Disney's diplomatic mission to Latin America during the Second World War. Most famously—or infamously as the case may be—is the anti-capitalist treatise, *How to Read Donald Duck*, written by two Marxist polemicists, Ariel Dorfman and Armand Mattelart. Their book argues that Disney characters were industrialized works of fiction whose messages promoted the values of capitalist imperialism and condescendingly treated foreign audiences as children incapable of managing their own affairs. For them, Disney's ultimate capitalist was Uncle Scrooge McDuck, the miser who worships money for itself. Marxists also denounced Disney's use of cultural stereotypes, such as Donald Duck's adventures in *The Three Caballeros*, in which Donald has erotic fantasies about every hot Latin beauty he comes across. More substantively, Marxist critics of the U.S. Good Neighbour Policy argued that Disney films promoted a form of colonial enslavement of Latin America and served to pacify Hispanic populations with "entertainment" distractions that paved the way for further U.S. capitalist control of the "banana republics" in the region. The Marxists conveniently neglected, however, to point out that the imperialist Disney movies were in fact promoting public hygiene in a region where health and sanitation were a serious social issues. It should also be noted that Disney's "Good Neighbour" movies were not entirely American. Disney enlisted the help of surrealist Salvador Dali to generate the graphics for several of the short films.[16]

Still, there can be little doubt that Disney films of the era—such as *El Gaucho Goofy* and *Saludos Amigos*—were propaganda movies intended to promote American values in Latin America. When *Saludos Amigos* premiered in the United States in 1943, the *New York Times* lauded Disney as "the country's No. 1 propagandist" and described Donald Duck as an "ambassador at large, a salesman of the American Way." Another review remarked that *Saludos Amigos* "should do more to cement friendly relations between North and South America than a dozen treaties or a score of diplomatic missions." Walt Disney himself said in a wartime radio broadcast: "While half the world is being forced to shout 'Heil Hitler!' our answer is to say 'Saludos Amigos.'"

After the war, Walt Disney's energies turned towards America's Cold War confrontation with Communism. When the House Un-American Activities Committee arrived in Hollywood in 1947, Disney belonged to a high-profile group of anti-Communist conservatives who had coalesced around the Motion Picture Alliance for the Preservation of American Ideals. Disney, in fact, was the last cooperative witness to appear before HUAC. At the time, Disney still had a bad aftertaste in his mouth from the 1941 strike at his studio. Disney told HUAC that the strike had been concocted by "Commie front organizations." He added, moreover, that the Communist campaign against Disney extended well beyond America's borders: "Throughout the world all of the Commie groups began smear campaigns against me and my pictures." Disney told HUAC he believed Communists should be "smoked out and shown up for what they are."

Throughout the 1950s, Disney's studios played an important Cold War role by producing films that reaffirmed the virtues of the American way of life. These efforts now included the newfangled medium of television, where shows such as *The Mickey Mouse Club* and *Walt Disney's Wonderful World of Color* were immensely popular with kids and families. Disney was, in this respect, a libertarian populist. As Disney historian Steven Watts put it: "Libertarian populism stressed the autonomy of ordinary citizens in the face of overweening authority. The remnants of the older, optimistic, inclusive populism of the Depression era provided an important foundation for this position, but Disney reshaped it to conform to the exigencies of the

Cold War. While offering a sentimental celebration of common American people, working, God-fearing, community-building citizens were inspired by a homogenized vision of the WASP folk whose values he enshrined and prospects he proclaimed." If libertarian populism constituted Disney's domestic policy, so to speak, his foreign policy was pure Pax Americana. Disney espoused the view that "it was America's destiny to export values, institutions, and politics of democracy and capitalism to achieve a peaceful dominion over the rest of the world."[17]

Walt Disney was also influencing U.S. policy towards outer space. Disney's *Man in Space* television series, which consisted of three one-hour segments that first aired in 1955, inspired President Eisenhower to announce a program to build satellites to circle the Earth in geostationary orbit. Some believed Disney was ahead of the U.S. government in space exploration. That became embarrassingly obvious in 1957, when the Soviet Union beat the United States into outer space with its Sputnik satellite launch. As one commentator remarked: "The Russians may have gotten the jump on the United States with their high-flying Sputnik, but they didn't beat Walt Disney."

By the 1960s, Walt Disney was a living icon whose name had become a global brand divorced from his person.

"I'm not 'Walt Disney' anymore," he said. "Disney is a thing, an attitude, an image in the eyes of the public. I've spent my whole career creating that image, and I'm a great believer in what Disney is. But it's not me, the person, anymore."

Now that virtually every Disney character was famous throughout the world, Walt Disney turned his attention to building theme parks as architectural celebrations of the company's pro-American family ideology. But Disney died suddenly in 1966, and consequently did not live to see his company transformed into a multinational corporate conglomerate. It wasn't until the 1980s that Disney emerged as a global media giant under the leadership of Hollywood executive Michael Eisner. He revitalized the company and, in the 1990s, reorganized its operations into five divisions: consumer products, media networks, vacation resorts, studio entertainment, and Internet properties. Disney now controlled not only a Hollywood studio and theme parks resorts, but also the ABC television network, specialty TV channels such as ESPN and Disney Channel, cruise liners, and an international chain of Disney-branded retail stores. But Disney's foreign expansion came at a price. Eisner would quickly realize that, while the all-American, family-oriented Disney Doctrine worked at home in America, as a foreign policy it required delicate finessing.

Family doctrine

Eisner's first international crisis came in 1993 when Disney faced a torrent of protest throughout the Moslem world after the company released its animated movie, *Aladdin*. Many Moslems complained that the movie resorted to pejorative stereotypes of Arabs, alternately riding camels and flying carpets. Others pointed out that, while most characters in *Aladdin* were Americanized to appeal to moviegoers in the West, the movie's villain Jafar was explicitly given Arab-like features. Also, it was noted that Princess Jasmine—called Buddir al Buddor in the original tale—was portrayed as a belly-dancer in the Disney movie. Other Disney movies that came under fire in the Moslem world for similar reasons were *The Return of Jafar, Kazaam, In the Army Now*, and *Rules of Engagement*. But the Disney film that provoked the most concerted Arab backlash was *G.I. Jane*, starring Demi Moore playing a U.S. Navy Seal who goes on a killing rampage against Arabs. After the film's release in 1997, the Arab League issued a strongly worded protest against Disney, calling for "the staunchest collective measures against this company." At the same time, the American-Arab Anti-Discrimination Committee said that many Disney movies were guilty of "undermining our religion and Arab civilization." Leaders of the American-Arab group complained that not only had Disney refused to meet with them since their protests against *Aladdin* four years earlier, but also continued to release movies that "feature a regular flow of negative, degrading Arab images."

Aladdin crisis

While the genie was out of the bottle in the Islamic world, Eisner was facing an even more difficult diplomatic standoff in China following the 1996 release of Martin Scorsese's *Kundun*. The Disney-financed movie, which portrays the Dalai Lama in a favourable light, was bound to provoke the ire of China's communist regime due to political sensitivities about Tibet. China's communist rulers wasted no time issuing a stern warning to Disney: they would put the kibosh on Disney's corporate ambitions in China if the movie were released. Disney, as it happened, was hoping to build a gigantic Disneyland theme park in China. The commercial release of *Kundun* would mean no Sino Disney theme parks. A group of Hollywood movie stars, including Paul Newman, publicly criticized China for playing hardball politics with Disney and "attempting to impose worldwide censorship" on

new US docs

movies about China. Eisner, for his part, didn't flinch. *Kundun* hit worldwide movie screens at Christmas as planned. Eisner meanwhile was making discreet diplomatic overtures to the Chinese regime, including a personal visit to Beijing to meet with propaganda chief, Ding Guagen. The following year, Disney released an animated feature, *Mulan*, which cast ancient Chinese history in an unmistakably positive light. Eisner also had a keen understanding of the inner workings of China's corrupt political system. On his visit, Disney bought the rights to distribute a Chinese film, *A Time to Remember*, produced by the Forbidden City Film Company, which just happened to be controlled by a clique of Chinese apparatchiks with close ties to the ruling Communist Party. The movie was described as a "love story set during the Communist revolution" and a "heavy-handed drama meant to stir Chinese patriotism."

Eisner was a shrewd pragmatist, though it was possible to wonder what Walt Disney would have thought about his doing business with Communists. Still, Eisner's canny dealmaking skills smoothed over ruffled Chinese feathers and kept Disney in China. Now Disney could build its long-planned Disneyland theme park in China—a first in a communist dictatorship.

It's not certain what inspired Walt Disney to build theme parks. Some Disney historians believe Disney was inspired by childhood memories in Kansas City, where he attended the local fair at Fairmont Park. It is also true that Disney, born in 1901, grew up during a period when many American cities boasted bold expositions to flaunt the marvels of modern life. Even before Disney's birth, urban expositions had been temporarily transforming great cities into gigantic theme parks. London vaunted modern industrial technology at its Great Exhibition in 1851, Paris built the Eiffel Tower for its exposition in 1889 and followed up with another Exposition Universelle in 1900. In America, many cities were similarly hosting expositions as tributes to the modern era: Chicago in 1893, Buffalo in 1901, St. Louis in 1904, Seattle in 1909, Philadelphia in 1936, Chicago again in 1933, and of course New York's World's Fair in 1939.

Walt Disney undoubtedly followed the exposition fever sweeping America in the first few decades of the century. While many expositions displayed the wonders of technology and culture, most also featured Ferris wheels and other Coney Island-style attractions. In 1933–34, some 50 million people visited Chicago's Century of Progress Exposition. *Newsweek* magazine described the atmosphere in Chicago as a combination of "the exuberance of an Army-

Navy football crowd with the hysteria of a Day of Judgement throng." It was against this backdrop that, in the late 1930s, Walt Disney began musing seriously about building fantasy parks for his famous cartoon characters.

The Second World War put Disney's plans on hold, but as soon as the war was over Disney was back at the drawing board. In 1948, he wrote a famous memo setting out plans to build a miniature town called "Mickey Mouse Park." But his brother Roy Disney—who controlled the company purse strings—flatly vetoed the idea. Roy Disney thought his brother's theme-park vision was a hair-brained scheme that would bankrupt the company. Roy Disney, needless to say, was wrong. A half century after the first Disneyland opened in the mid-1950s, the global theme-park business is worth roughly $15 billion annually. In 2000, nearly 550 million people visited a theme park. And they had an embarrassment of riches to choose from: some 225 theme parks worldwide—from the Gardens of Babylon to Kubla Khan's Xanadu. The most famous theme parks, of course, are Disney-owned—from Disneyland and Walt Disney World in the United States to EuroDisney and Tokyo Disneyland. By 2010, it is estimated that the global theme-park industry will attract more than 650 million visitors annually and generate roughly $20 billion.

The first Disneyland—which Walt Disney launched by raising money himself—opened in Anaheim, California, on July 17, 1955. Disneyland's inauguration was broadcast live on ABC and hosted by a clutch of Hollywood actors, including Ronald Reagan. The political backdrop of the Cold War was obviously in the air at the opening ceremonies, where Walt Disney led the assembled dignitaries in pledging allegiance to the American flag and singing the national anthem. In his inaugural speech, Disney dedicated the park to "the ideals, the dreams, and the hard facts which have created America." Another speaker was the governor of California, Goodwin Knight, who said Disneyland had been "built by American labour and American capital under the belief that this is a God-fearing and God-loving country." Following these patriotic declarations, Disneyland's baptism was accompanied by the awesome spectacle of U.S. Air Force jet fighters flying overhead while a Marine Corp contingent marched triumphantly down Main Street USA.[18]

Disneyland was an instant success. Soon foreign leaders and other high-ranking figures from the world over were visiting the park, acutely aware of its powerful symbolic connection with the American way. Shortly after

Disneyland opened, U.S. Vice President Richard Nixon took his family to the park. "This is a paradise for children and grown-ups," said Nixon. "My children have been after me for weeks to bring them here." Moroccan king Mohammed V was so thrilled by his first visit to Disneyland in 1957 that he returned for a second time. When former president Harry Truman visited Disneyland, he quipped that he'd taken his wife on all the rides, except Dumbo the Flying Elephant, because of the animal's symbolic link to the Republican Party. Only Soviet leader Nikita Khrushchev was banned from Disneyland. When Khrushchev was on an official visit to the United States in 1960, he specifically requested to see Disneyland—but the State Department turned him down for "security" reasons. Miffed, Khrushchev angrily threatened to build an even bigger theme park in Moscow called "Miracle Land." Soviet citizens, meanwhile, had been reading ludicrous propaganda reports about Disneyland as a symbol of capitalist oppression. According to one report by Russian journalists, Disneyland was holding captive a tribe of American Indians in the park's Frontierland where they were forced to entertain visitors.

Walt Disney's vision for Disneyland's ambitions was openly patriotic. "There's an American theme behind the whole park," he said in 1957. "I believe in emphasizing the story of what made America great and what will keep it great." Most visitors were impressed by Disneyland as a combination of mythological fantasyland and technological marvel. There were some critics, however. Some grumbled about the park's rampant commercialism through corporate sponsors like Pepsi-Cola, Eastman Kodak, Frito, Swift, and Bank of America. In 1958, Julian Halevy wrote a scathing article in *The Nation* comparing Disneyland to the crassness of Las Vegas. Disneyland, he said, was "a collection of midway rides, concessions, hot-dog stands, soft drink counters, peep shows, advertising stunts for big corporations." Science fiction writer Ray Bradbury replied in an outraged letter dismissing Halevy as an intellectual snob and praising Disneyland as "an experience of true delight and wonder."

Flush with success from Disneyland, Walt Disney began scouting east coast locations to build another Disney theme park. Florida was the most obvious location due to the warm climate. Walt Disney eventually settled on the relatively sedate, interior town of Orlando, which was underdeveloped and where land could be purchased cheaply. In November 1965,

Disney announced plans to build Walt Disney World on 27,000 acres of undeveloped land just outside Orlando. Disney was especially attached to the Orlando park because it would feature his "Epcot" project—Experimental Prototype Community of Tomorrow—a real-life model city that embodied the functional and moral values that Disney cherished. Disney died the following year, and therefore never saw Disney World. When the park opened five years later in 1971, like Disneyland it became an instant success and boon to the local economy.

Disneyland's first foreign adventure was Tokyo Disneyland, which opened in 1983 after nearly a decade of negotiations. Disney executives were confident Disneyland would be a huge success in Japan, where children had been watching Mickey Mouse and Donald Duck on television since 1958. Throughout the 1960s, Japan was emerging from its *sengo* period of post-war shame and was starting to embrace modern values—especially American cultural symbols. As one Japanese author put it, Disneyland was "one of the most powerful symbols of the affluent society for which the Japanese were earnestly striving."[19]

Disney decided to let Japanese interests build Tokyo Disneyland under a licensing agreement that would see Disney receive royalties, management fees, plus 10 percent of admissions, 5 percent of food and merchandise sales, and 10 percent of corporate sponsorship revenues. But while Japanese-controlled Oriental Land Company was Tokyo Disneyland's majority shareholder, Disney insisted on total control over the park's design and operations. Tokyo Disneyland made significant compromises to appeal to local Japanese tastes, but the park was a precise replica of the original Disneyland in California. One compromise was Main Street USA, which in Tokyo was called "World Bazaar"—thus erasing any hint of American nationalism that might provoke ambivalent feelings amongst Japanese visitors.

As Disney was hoping, Tokyo Disneyland became immensely popular not only with the Japanese but also with visitors from neighbouring countries such as China and Korea. Tokyo Disneyland became the archetype for a burgeoning theme-park industry throughout Asia, including a Disneyland rival in Japan built by Universal Studios. The Universal Studios theme park, built in Osaka, opened in 2001 with exhibits from Universal movies such as *Jurassic Park* and *Jaws*. A replica of the Universal Studios park in Florida, it was a direct commercial threat to Tokyo Disneyland—and may explain why

Disney countered by opening its Tokyo DisneySea park several months later. In early 2003, when Tokyo Disneyland celebrated its 20th anniversary, self-congratulations were richly deserved. In a Japanese market saturated with "themed" amusement parks—Dutch, German, Swiss, Turkish, Spanish, Russian, even New Zealand—Disneyland was still the real thing. Many other theme parks were going bankrupt due to unattractive concepts and poor planning. Gulliver's Kingdom, for example, featured a 45-metre statue of Jonathan Swift's literary figure at the foot of Mount Fuji. But it was closed down in 2001 when its biggest creditor, a Japanese bank, went bust. Even Universal Studios, owned by media giant Vivendi Universal, was in trouble. Tokyo Disneyland, on the other hand, has been immensely profitable.[29]

China, always circumspect about Western cultural values, has taken a more ambiguous attitude towards the Magic Kingdom. When Michael Eisner was in China in the mid-1990s to defuse diplomatic tensions about the release of *Kundun,* his main concern was China's threat to keep Disneyland theme parks out of the country. In 1999, Eisner was back in Beijing making conciliatory gestures towards the Communist regime. This time, Eisner felt sufficiently confident to announce, though somewhat cautiously, Disney's plans to open a theme park in China—the company's third theme park outside the United States after Tokyo Disneyland and EuroDisney. Eisner, noting the success of McDonald's in China, said he was equally confident that the Magic Kingdom would be just as popular with the Chinese.

"As evidenced by the popularity of McDonald's, we could be getting close to the time for a major Disney attraction in the world's most populous nation," said Eisner. "I am completely confident that the Chinese people love Mickey Mouse no less than Big Macs."

The Chinese were already familiar with theme parks, though very few were commercially successful. In 1990, a theme park called Nine Dragons had opened just outside Beijing, but was plagued with chronic financial pressures. Most theme parks in China were based on legends from China's past, though some exploited purely American themes. In early 2003, a Disneyland-style complex called American Dream Park opened just outside Shanghai. Most attractions at American Dream Park attempt to appeal to aspects of America that Chinese visitors know from Hollywood movies and American television shows. One attraction is an Art Deco exhibit called "Miami Beach."

"This is what most Chinese think of the USA—you know, Miami Vice and all that," said Keith Saunders, president of American Dream Park. But some concessions to local Chinese culture have been made. In the shoot-'em-up Wild West section, for example, Billy the Kid has been replaced with the "Shanghai Kid."

Disney had been seriously contemplating Shanghai as an ideal location for a Disneyland in China. Michael Eisner instead hammered out a deal to build China's first Disneyland near Hong Kong. Financially backed by the local government, Hong Kong Disneyland was announced in 1999 with plans for an official inauguration in 2005. Showing sensitivity to Chinese cultural values, Disney opted to make certain concessions. One was the theme park's slogan. Instead of Disneyland's traditional, "The Happiest Place on Earth." Hong Kong Disneyland's credo is "The Most Harmonious Place on Earth." Accordingly, the 310-acre theme park on Lantau Island was built in strict accordance with the ancient principles of *feng shui*, which ensures harmony between natural elements and buildings.

"Work is progressing on Hong Kong Disneyland," said Eisner in January 2002. "What a site! I think this will be the most spectacular park location we have anywhere in the world. Maybe I'm too enthusiastic, but looking back across the bay to central Hong Kong is awesome."

But Eisner had not forgotten about Shanghai. In early 2003, news leaked that Disney was planning to build another Chinese Disneyland near Shanghai. Hong Kong authorities, who regard Shanghai as an urban rival for economic growth, were infuriated and felt betrayed. The Hong Kong government had put up nearly $3 billion to get their Disneyland built, while Disney had paid only $314 million for a 43 percent stake in the theme park. It appeared that Disney executives had hastily struck a deal in Shanghai as a counter-move against Universal Studios. A few months earlier, Universal had announced with great fanfare its plans to build a gigantic theme park in Shanghai.

Facing the wrath of Hong Kong officials, Eisner hastily organized a ground-breaking ceremony on the site of Hong Kong Disneyland to reassure investors that the project was being fast-tracked. The event, which took place on January 12, 2003, was attended by Eisner and Hong Kong's chief administrator Tung Chee Hwa. The damage-control operation had worked, for now at least. Eisner reassured his Hong Kong partners that, while their

Disneyland would be in business by 2005, Disney's Shanghai theme park wouldn't be opened until 2010.

It was in Europe that Disney first learned the advantages of playing rival cities off one another to land the most advantageous deal. In the mid-1980s, Disney began talks with Britain, France, and Spain about the possibility of building a theme park on the continent. It didn't take long before Britain, an island with a rainy climate, was out of the running. The two preferred cities were Paris and Barcelona. Eisner gave serious consideration to Barcelona, especially given its warm climate. One major disadvantage, however, was Barcelona's relatively isolated location in the southwest corner of Europe. More troubling was a threat from Basque separatists who vowed to bomb Disneyland if Mickey Mouse and Donald Duck came to Spain.

In France, meanwhile, Eisner was examining the possibility of building EuroDisney in Marne-la-Vallée just outside Paris. One potential problem was the Socialist government of François Mitterrand, whose culture minister Jack Lang had already been assailing American cultural imperialism with Mitterrand's tacit, and sometimes explicit, support. But France's young prime minister, Laurent Fabius, seemed more interested in the economic spinoff benefits from EuroDisney, not least of which was 30,000 new jobs. Eisner was surprised when Fabius agreed to lend Disney $700 million at rates well below the market and, what's more, extend the Métro subway line straight out to the EuroDisney site. Even better news came in 1986, when Fabius' Socialist government was defeated. Fabius was replaced by a conservative, pro-business prime minister, Jacques Chirac—the future French president. Eisner made his choice: EuroDisney would be built outside Paris. Millions visited the city every year to see the Eiffel Tower, Notre Dame, and the Louvre. Soon they would come to Paris to visit Disneyland, too.

So confident was Eisner about EuroDisney's prospects that he took a $1 billion public offering on the Paris stock exchange to finance the project. In October 1989, Eisner decided to engage in a spectacle of public grandstanding to publicize EuroDisney's stock market success. In a car driven by Mickey Mouse, Eisner arrived in grand pomp at the Paris Bourse. He marched onto the stock market's outside steps to deliver a speech to an awaiting throng of journalists and press photographers. Just as Eisner began boasting about EuroDisney's brilliant financial outlook, objects began flying through the air in his direction. Volleys of angry shouts also surged from the crowd. A group of anti-Disney agitators, most of them members of the French Communist Party, had shown up to express their outrage at Mickey Mouse's arrival in the Fifth Republic. Mortified, Eisner quickly fled while being pelted with eggs and ketchup. Some voices in the crowd were heard shouting, "Uncle Scrooge Go Home!"

"I rushed through my talk and we all ran off the stage, no longer smiling or confidant," recalled Eisner. "Within hours, images of me and other Disney executives seemingly under siege were flashed around the world. For the first time in my life, I had a sense of what it was like to be a politician during a campaign."[21]

Eisner's problem in France were just beginning. In 1988, the Socialists were back in power and François Mitterrand was still in the Elysée Palace. France's leftist intelligentsia, which traditionally plays a powerful role in shaping public agendas through the French media, was resolutely opposed to American cultural imperialism in general, and to Disneyland in particular. Even before EuroDisney opened in 1992, the project was constantly being scorned and ridiculed in the French media. Labelled a "cultural Chernobyl," EuroDisney was described as a "construction of hardened chewing gum and idiotic folklore taken straight out of comic books written for obese Americans." Snide references to the nutritional consequences of Big Macs and Cokes slipped into denunciations of Disneyland. The French philosopher Alain Finkielkraut, a well-known Parisian media darling, called EuroDisney a "terrifying giant's step towards world homogenization." Even Jack Lang, Mitterrand's culture minister, couldn't resist characterizing EuroDisney as an "enclave of the American leisure industry." Disney attempted some damage control by pointing out that Cinderella was French, Pinocchio was Italian, Snow White was German, and Peter Pan was British. But Parisian intellectuals laughed this off and continued their polemical attacks.

EuroDisney's imminent opening posed a particularly galling threat to Parc Astérix, a French theme park that had opened near Paris in 1989. Now, it seemed, a cartoon invasion led by Mickey Mouse and Donald Duck was coming to French shores to usurp Astérix's place of honour in the local theme-park business. The American cultural Caesar was oppressing the plucky Gaul yet again. But Parc Astérix, like so many theme parks around the world, was not built on the same scale as any Disneyland. Its 28 attractions were based largely on themes related to French history, from ancient times through the Middle Ages and right up to modern France. Not surprisingly, nearly 90 percent of visitors to Parc Astérix were French. Parc Astérix was only one of several French-owned theme parks that operated according to the same parochial attitude. Others were Big Bang Smurf, Zygofolis, and Mirapolis. Like their counterparts in Asia, French theme parks were badly undercapitalized and poorly managed, especially when compared with Disneyland parks. Mirapolis, located near Paris, eventually went bankrupt. Big Bang Smurf, for its part, was forced to live off government subsidies. As for Parc Astérix, it was so poorly designed that it lacked capacity to handle large crowds, and consequently had to shut down on peak days.

Disney had no competitive worries in France. Its main problem, as Michael Eisner would quickly learn, was cultural. Disney made a critical mistake in France by insisting that EuroDisney not only replicate Disneyland precisely, but the company also imposed the Disney "system" on the French theme park. For example, wine was banished from EuroDisney—a gesture that was highly sensitive in the world's biggest wine-producing country. Also, Disney insisted that all EuroDisney employees—or "cast members"—adhere to strict dress codes and hygiene standards. Every employee had to conform to the well-scrubbed, wholesome "Disney look." In other words: no smoking, no chewing gum, no dyed hair, no make-up, no jewelry. This did not go over well with French girls who showed up for work looking like Brigitte Bardot. There were even rumours about EuroDisney managers conducting undercover spying operations on junior employees. French employees, long used to unionized work environments, were particularly resentful towards these "American" procedures. Soon some were calling the Magic Kingdom by another name: "Mouseschwitz."

Almost immediately after EuroDisney opened in 1992, the park was mired in controversy due to these culture clashes. Worse, Europe was going through a severe recession and visitors to the park found the prices outrageously high. Most spent little on rides and food, but contented themselves to walk about and look at EuroDisney's visual marvels. Soon EuroDisney was losing $1 million a day. Michael Eisner was rumoured to be ready to close down the place and pull out.

Eisner quickly realized that Disney had made a big mistake in France. Disney executives had come to Paris with the same arrogant, inflexible attitude that they had imposed on the opening of Tokyo Disneyland. In Tokyo, said Eisner, Disney had insisted on English signs and selling popcorn against the wishes of his Japanese partners who wanted to sell rice cakes. It was that hard-nosed American approach that persuaded Eisner that the same corporate policy had to be applied at EuroDisney. But he was wrong.

"In France, by contrast, the government was deeply interested in having the country's culture and history interwoven through the park," Eisner recalled. "We made a few concessions, but for the most part we were determined to make EuroDisney every bit American as Tokyo Disneyland and our domestic parks—meaning fast food instead of smoky bistros, Coca-Cola and lemonade in preference to wine, and animated movies rather than *film noir*."

Eisner failed to understand one critical difference between EuroDisney and Tokyo Disneyland. In Japan, a post-war colony of the United States, the Japanese were keen to embrace American cultural and commercial symbols to validate their own integration into the modern world. The French, on the other hand, took a culturally superior Old World attitude towards America. France saw in the United States a rival republic with pretensions to universal values. The French, while fascinated by the language of American pop culture, deeply resented American cultural domination. France, moreover, was a highly rigid, unionized society that did not readily embrace American-style capitalism. In a sense, France was too rigid to accept Disney's own rigid standards and codes.

Realizing its mistake, Disney began making cultural concessions at EuroDisney. First, a 45-year-old Frenchman, Philippe Bourgignon, was brought in to run the park. Also, a new roller-coaster ride was based on a recognizably French theme: Jules Verne's *From the Earth to the Moon*. And ticket prices were lowered by 20 percent to attract more visitors from France and other European countries.

Yet these measures were not enough. After two years, EuroDisney was still on the verge of bankruptcy. Then, suddenly, EuroDisney found a dramatic rescuer in a most unlikely figure: 37-year-old Saudi prince Alwaleed bin Talal bin Abdul Aziz. The Saudi prince, while little known in the West at the time, was the nephew of Saudi King Fahd and grandson of Saudi Arabia's founder, King Abdul Aziz. A whimsical billionaire with Western tastes, Prince Alwaleed had attracted attention in 1991 when he shored up Citicorp with a $800 million investment. The Prince, fortuitously, was a Disneyland fan who had taken his family to the theme parks in both California and Florida. He had also recently visited EuroDisney. And when he heard about its financial troubles, he made inquiries via the powerful U.S.-based Carlyle Group, whose principals were a veritable constellation of retired statesmen including George Bush, James Baker, Frank Carlucci, and John Major.

In June 1994, Prince Alwaleed decided to save EuroDisney just as he had propped up Citicorp. He agreed to inject $250 million into EuroDisney as part of a $1.2 billion rescue package to help the company pay down its debt. Prince Alwaleed also gave EuroDisney a low-interest $100 million loan to build a convention centre. The deal probably saved EuroDisney from forced closure. After losing more than $1 billion in 1993, the following year EuroDisney started to earn profits and was on the road to recovery. Attendance also started to increase and was soon reaching 12 million visitors a year—more than either the Louvre, Eiffel Tower, or Notre Dame.

The EuroDisney rescue also put Michael Eisner in bed with a Saudi billionaire. At the same time, Prince Alwaleed was taking sizable investment positions in a number of major American corporations. The Saudi prince owned $2 billion worth of AOL Time Warner stock, and thus controlled a stake in the CNN television network. He also owned about $50 million of Disney stock and a 3 percent stake in Rupert Murdoch's News Corporation, which controlled *The Times* of London, the *New York Post*, Fox Television, Twentieth Century Fox, DirecTV, and HarperCollins publishers. Prince Alwaleed's other corporate holdings included Compaq, Xerox, eBay, Pepsi-Cola, Ford, McDonald's, Gillette, Procter & Gamble, Coca-Cola, and Amazon.com.

Prince Alwaleed insisted that he did not interfere unduly in the affairs of companies in which he held stakes. He confessed, however, that he maintained contact with the executives who ran these companies. "I am always in close touch with them," he said, "but I don't play an active role. If I feel very strongly about something, I convey a message directly to the chairman or chief executive."

That revelation doubtless made Michael Eisner decidedly uncomfortable, especially after Disney's diplomatic crisis vis-à-vis the Arab League. In 1999, Disney was planning to open a new "Millennium Village" at its Disney World park in Florida. Israel had financed a special exhibit featuring a visual tour called "Journey to Jerusalem" in which the Holy City was identified as the capital of Israel. Israel's Foreign Ministry, moreover, had contributed $1.8 million to the $8 million cost of the Israeli pavilion, one of many national exhibits at Millennium Village.

The Arab League immediately threatened to provoke a boycott of Disney products throughout the Moslem world. Eisner knew they were serious. It had recently launched a boycott against Burger King after the fast-food chain had opened an outlet on the West Bank. Burger King had backed down and pulled out of the region. The Arab League had also threatened Sprint and Adidas with similar boycotts. Following up on the Arab League's threats against Disney, in the U.S. the National Association of Arab Americans called on all Moslems to use a boycott against Disney as a "potent weapon" against Israel. It was likely not neglected that Michael Eisner himself was Jewish.

Eisner, meanwhile, received a phone call from one of his major investors: Prince Alwaleed. The Saudi billionaire demanded an explanation for Disney's affront to Moslems. Eisner hastily reassured Prince Alwaleed that, at the Millennium Village exhibit, Jerusalem would not be referred to as Israel's capital. If Prince Alwaleed was satisfied, the Arab League insisted it wished to inspect the Millennium Village site to ensure that both Moslem and Christian claims on the Holy City were not offended by the Israeli pavilion. By now, Eisner found himself enmeshed in another controversy: Jewish groups were accusing him of buckling to boycott pressures from Arab lobby groups.

Eisner fudged his way through this seemingly no-win controversy and eventually placated both sides. He could not know, however, that his Disneyland theme parks were about to find themselves under attack again. One Saudi billionaire had come to Disneyland's rescue. Now another Saudi billionaire was about to threaten Disneyland's existence. His name was Osama bin Laden.

Mickey Mouse and Donald Duck were among the first victims in the aftershock of the Al Qaeda attacks on New York and Washington. Immediately, Disney closed both Disneyland and Disney World. Disneyland, like Wall Street and the Pentagon, was among the most obvious targets of Islamic fundamentalism. What better target, in fact, than the Magic Kingdom, an architectural microcosm of the American Dream.

Paranoia about a possible attack on a Disney theme park proved justified. Within a week of the 9/11 attacks, U.S. police conducted surgical raids in the Detroit area and arrested six Arab men suspected of belonging to a terrorist "sleeper cell" in the United States. The suspected terrorists, some of whom worked at the Detroit airport, were discovered to be members of an Algerian-based militant Moslem group called "Salafi Group for Call and Combat." This group was known to be financially sponsored by Osama bin Laden. During the raids, police discovered forged passports, stolen credit cards, falsified U.S. Social Security cards, and more than 100 audiotapes featuring Islamic leaders exhorting Moslems to kill Jews and Christians. Police also learned that the terrorists were planning to set up a "jihad training camp" in Oregon. Even more alarming, police found surveillance videotapes of Disneyland in California and the MGM Grand Hotel and Casino in Las Vegas. Clearly, an attack on these two symbols of American culture was in the works.

As these terrorists languished in American jails, President Bush prepared for a U.S. invasion of Iraq. And once again, Disney was on the front lines of America's war against a Moslem country. In March 2003, the U.S. Federal Aviation Administration declared that air space over Disneyland and Disney World would become no-fly zones because of the threat of a terrorist attack.

"The Disney parks are a potential target of symbolic value," said FAA spokesperson Kathleen Bergen. A government official from Homeland Security added that "the decision was not made on specific intelligence regarding Disney, but made based on Al Qaeda's dictation that they will carry out attacks on known icons." According to the no-fly zone rule, no pilot was allowed to fly within three miles of a Disney theme park below 3,000 feet. Thus, Disney theme parks were accorded the same military protection as the country's most strategically sensitive sites.

While the U.S. Army occupied Iraq and began the difficult process of reconstruction, the White House turned its attention towards Syria and North Korea—two other despotic regimes that boasted neither a McDonald's nor a Disneyland. While North Korea's communist regime brandished nuclear threats against the American Empire, it was not known when Kim Jong-nam planned his next discreet visit to Tokyo Disneyland. A better solution, of course, would be to build a gigantic Disneyland theme park in Pyongyang. Mickey Mouse, Donald Duck, Pluto, and Goofy may soon be frolicking in the rebuilt precincts of Baghdad, the vaunted cradle of civilization.

From Hollywood to Bollywood

Hollywood's battles in the non-Western world have been infinitely more complex and contentious than its skirmishes with America's industrialized trading partners.

[If Hollywood has frequently clashed with cultural élites in Western countries, the major studios could at least feel confident that their movies were popular with local audiences. Western governments have been forced to strike a balance between protecting domestic commercial interests and allowing freedom of choice in the cultural marketplace. In non-Western nations, local populations do not always clamour for Hollywood products. A local cultural filter gives élites in those nations more autonomy to resist American pressures to provide increased market access to Hollywood movies.]

élites only resist ! culture concessions are holy nice

In Latin America, Hollywood's presence was contentious from the outset. For the first few decades after the invention of cinema, most Latin American countries had no movie industry. This was largely due to the retarded development of electricity in the region. Consequently, the Hollywood studios controlled the motion picture industries in most Latin American countries by the 1920s. Only big countries with large domestic markets—Brazil, Argentina, and Mexico—could afford the luxury of cinematic activity. Argentina, for example, enjoyed a tremendous, albeit short-lived, motion picture boom in the period circa 1915–1920, producing some 100 domestic feature films—many of them *gaucho* (cowboy) and *cangaçeiro* (bandit) films. Historical events—such as the Mexican Revolution in 1910—also served as backdrops for early moviemaking in the region. American movie producers, too, exploited historical turmoil in Latin America to find sensational themes and plots—sometimes to comic effect. The Mutual Film Corporation, for example, actually induced Pancho Villa, Mexico's mythic revolutionary leader, to sign an exclusive contract as a motion picture star performing in what was undoubtedly the first "reality" show ever produced. For a fee of $25,000, Villa agreed to ban all rival film companies from his planned battles. He also committed to fight in daylight to facilitate the technical requirements of Mutual's film crews. What's more, Villa promised to reconstruct battle scenes that had not been captured satisfactorily on the "first take" during the actual conflicts. In 1914, Mutual released *The Life of General Villa*, which consisted entirely of dramatized reconstructions.

By the 1930s, Hollywood's colonial control of the Latin American movie industry was beginning to provoke bitter resentment. The most sensitive issue was Hollywood's allegedly condescending portrayal of Hispanics. There was a feeling throughout Latin America that Hollywood failed to appreciate distinctions among the region's different national cultures and resorted to broad-brush stereotypes. In many Hollywood movies, Latinos were portrayed either as "goodly peasants" or villainous "greasers." Faced with these criticisms, Hollywood made some attempts to appeal to Latin American audiences with movies featuring local themes. The stardom of Carmen Miranda—the "Brazilian Bombshell"—was the result of Hollywood's attempt to cater to local passions.

While America's "Good Neighbour Policy" in Latin America met with resistance, many Hollywood stars were hero-worshipped in the region. In some countries, primary schools used Disney characters such as Mickey Mouse and Donald Duck to teach English. Brazilians were especially fond of Hollywood movies, and it was even believed that Popeye was responsible for a dramatic increase in spinach consumption among Brazilian children. In 1941, journalist Florence Horn wrote in *Harper's Monthly Magazine*: "The movies have done a magnificent job of unconscious propaganda in Brazil. For the movies have made the United States part of the very mental fiber of every Brazilian except those who live in the remotest jungles and isolated river hamlets."

The United States shrewdly played off Latin American nations against one another. In 1936, Mexico and Argentina increased their movie production output after Spain, in the painful throes of a Civil War, cut off its steady supply of films. With a sudden absence of Spanish movies, Mexico and Argentina soon became cinematic rivals to dominate the Spanish-speaking Americas. The United States, by exercising control over celluloid supply, was in a position to determine the winner. Thus, when the Second World War broke out, the United States punished Argentina for its allegedly pro-Nazi neutrality by choking off supply of virgin film stock. Mexico, on the other hand, benefited from a steady supply of U.S. celluloid. This strategic advantage gave a critically important boost to the Mexican movie industry, which would become a major exporter of Spanish-language movies.[22]

In more recent decades, Latin American governments have reacted to Hollywood's grip on domestic movie markets with familiar measures such as taxes and quotas. Just as predictably, Hollywood has reacted with boycotts, though they have not always been effective. When Fidel Castro overthrew Cuba's pro-American government in the late 1950s, a U.S. embargo of communist Cuba exempted Hollywood movies. Washington regarded Hollywood movies as a cultural weapon, not as a consumer good. No matter, Castro promptly seized all Hollywood assets in Cuba and condemned American movies as "obnoxious, childish, and poison for the minds of young people." In 1959, Castro set up a Cuban Institute of Film Art and Industry, which brought all movie production under direct state control. In the 1970s, a new genre of macho adventure Cuban movie emerged—such as *Rio Negro*—in which, not surprisingly, the good guys were always revolutionaries and the villains were invariably counter-revolutionaries.

In Chile, filmmakers in the 1960s rallied around the left-wing Popular Unity coalition that supported socialist leader Salvador Allende. When Allende was elected Chilean president in 1970, the political triumph of socialism triggered a new wave of politically *engagé* films. Hollywood, stunned by the election of Allende, immediately responded with a boycott. No Hollywood movie would be exported to a Marxist regime hostile to the United States. The boycott ended three years later when Allende was overthrown, and assassinated, by American-backed Chilean generals led by Augusto Pinochet. Following the military *coup d'état*, Hollywood quickly recaptured the Chilean movie market, if only because domestic Chilean movies were no longer being produced. Many of Chile's filmmakers had fled into exile, some of them to Cuba where they could work with impunity under the protection of Fidel Castro.

On the whole, however, Hollywood movies have dominated movie screens throughout Latin America for decades. One reason, undeniably, is Latin America's fascination with American culture. Another explanation is economic: Hollywood has benefited from a powerful distribution system while Washington maintained diplomatic pressures to keep local markets open to American movies. A third explanation is political: Latin America's totalitarian regimes have exploited Hollywood escapism to keep the masses passive. As one Hollywood executive put it: "It fit in with the bread-and-circuses idea long followed by dictators as a means of keeping the populace content."

Today, democratic reforms have toppled most dictatorships in Latin America. Liberalization and reform have opened, not closed, market access for Hollywood movies. Murky political arrangements are no longer necessary to ensure a dominant place for Hollywood films on local cinema screens. Cultural reciprocity between the United States and Latin America is being strengthened. This should not be surprising given the significant

Hispanic population in the United States itself and the increasing influence of Latin American pop culture in America. Hollywood is now proactively recruiting Hispanic movie stars, such as Antonio Banderas and Jennifer Lopez, who have played leading roles in major movies, as opposed to making cameo or bad-guy appearances as stereotypical Hispanics. Latin American movies, too, are winning audiences at home and abroad. In 1999, Brazilian director Walter Salles' *Central do Brasil* was nominated for an Oscar for "best foreign film." And in Mexico, the sex comedy *Sexo, Pudor y Lágrimas*, sold 5 million tickets in its domestic market, making it the most successful Mexican film ever. Its box-office record was surpassed by only two Hollywood movies: *Titanic* and *Tarzan*.

Hollywood's relations with the Moslem world have been more difficult. America and Islam are not linked by geographical proximity or cultural affinity. Historically, anti-Western hostility in Moslem countries was aimed at colonial powers, especially Britain and France. The United States actually benefited, to some degree, from Moslem disenchantment with their colonial past. Local Moslem populations often turned towards America—a neutral non-colonial power—as a preferred model for modernity. These attitudes benefited Hollywood movies, though there were some complaints that American films tended to stereotype the Islamic world as a bizarrely exotic place known chiefly for flying carpets, mummies, genies, and opulent harems cluttered with veiled, belly-dancing women.

Arab cinema, while diverse, was dominated for many decades by Egypt, mainly due to its openness to Western influences and relatively large domestic population. Because Egyptian singers were famous throughout the Arab world in the 1930s and 1940s, these same singers appeared in movies to attract their fans into movie theatres. American movies, too, were popular in Arab countries—until, that is, two historical events turned the Islamic world against Hollywood, America, and the West. The first was the creation of Israel. The second was the rise of fanatical Islamic fundamentalism.

Immediately following the birth of Israel in the late 1940s, Arab nations began embargoing American movies. Whatever the official rationale, anti-Hollywood attitudes in Arab countries were based on a widespread perception that Hollywood was controlled by Jews. In some cases, specific Hollywood movies were targeted because they starred actors known for their Zionist sympathies. Egypt, for example, banned all movies starring

Danny Kaye and Mickey Rooney because both stars had contributed money to the cause of Zionism. The United Arab Republic banned movies starring Edward G. Robinson and Elizabeth Taylor because of their "pronounced Israeli sympathies." The 10-nation Arab League compiled a list of Hollywood stars—including Frank Sinatra, Paul Newman, and Joanne Woodward—that it recommended should be blacklisted in all Moslem countries. A second anti-Hollywood backlash came 20 years later, in 1967, when the Arab-Israeli War broke out. Egypt again blacklisted all Hollywood movies, but this time cited "moral" reasons. Officially, the Egyptian government claimed Hollywood movies featured excessive violence and sex and glorified wealth and luxury. But the real reason was political. Arab leaders were not unaware that Hollywood's most powerful moguls—like Lew Wasserman— were Jewish. They also knew that Wasserman and other moguls were influential powerbrokers with close ties to President Johnson's White House.

The United States had a reliable friend in the Shah of Iran, who ruled over the region's main non-Arab country. But even the Shah ended up disappointing Hollywood—not on larger geopolitical issues, but on picayune matters such as the price of movie tickets. Hollywood complained bitterly that movie ticket prices were too low in Iran. For Hollywood, this was particularly galling at a time, in the early 1970s, when Iran and other oil-producing countries in the Middle East were driving up petroleum prices in the Western world through their collusive embargo. In 1975, Jack Valenti initiated negotiations with Iran to have movie ticket prices increased, but the talks failed. The Hollywood majors now had no choice but to resort to their customary tactic: a boycott.

"In these times, it seems to us to be unfair for the U.S. motion picture industry, in effect, to subsidize the Iranian moviegoer," said Valenti.

Valenti could not know that Hollywood's troubles in Iran were about to get much worse. In 1979, Americans were stunned by the overthrow of the Shah and the taking of American hostages by Islamic fundamentalists. The Shah was not the Iranian revolution's only victim. In Washington, President Jimmy Carter lost his 1980 bid for reelection in the wake of America's humiliation in Iran. As Ronald Reagan moved into the White House, he boasted to Americans that he had resolved the hostage crisis in Tehran. But there was little President Reagan could do to reverse Ayatollah Khomeini's outright ban on Hollywood movies. Iran's ruling mullahs declared that no "imperialistic" films would be allowed into the new Islamic republic. Hollywood movies, needless to say, were at the top of the black list. Asian karate and kung fu movies, for less obvious reasons, were similarly deemed to be an affront to Allah. In truth, Iran's fundamentalist theocracy was hostile to all movies. Immediately following the revolution, movie theatres throughout the country were torched. A few years later, few movie theatres remained in Iran. Those that still stood were badly dilapidated. It wasn't until Ayatollah Khomeini's death, in 1989, that Iranian cinema began to re-emerge slowly from a decade of political suffocation.

Elsewhere in the Moslem world, Hollywood became an easy target in the fallout of the Gulf War. In 1993, the Disney movie *Aladdin* triggered angry protests in several Islamic countries because of the movie's alleged racist portrayal of Moslems. In Malaysia, the Muslim Youth Movement called on the government to ban *Aladdin* and its soundtrack. Moslems were particularly offended by a song in movie featuring the following lyrics: *"I come from a land, a faraway place, where the caravan camels roam, where they cut off your ear if they don't like your face—it's barbaric, but, hey, it's home."* As one non-Moslem critic observed about *Aladdin*: "The emancipated genie, with his Goofy hat and other Disney World paraphernalia, is not only an advertisement for Walt Disney Incorporated, he also serves as an unintended symbol of the Mickey Mousing of the world."

Disney met with a similar barrage of complaint only three years later when it released a sequel to *Father of the Bride*, featuring a sleazy, detestable Arab-looking character called Mr. Habib. Arab groups cited other Hollywood movies that allegedly portrayed Moslems as villainous and despicable characters. Movies made by Disney—whose chairman Michael Eisner was Jewish—were frequently singled out. In 2000, Arab-American and Islamic advocacy groups in the United States called for a boycott of the Hollywood movie, *Rules of Engagement*, about the rescue of a U.S. ambassador and his family under siege by an angry mob of Islamic protestors in Yemen. Similar complaints were made about Columbia Pictures' *The American President*, which portrayed Libyans as evil culprits plotting to destroy U.S. weapons systems.

Disney's troubles were not limited to the Islamic world. Hollywood's relationship with China had always been fraught with tension—before and after communism. In pre-communist China, the country's main urban centres were Westernized in virtually every aspect of daily life, including movie-going. The only sensitive issue was religion. At the end of the 1920s, Chinese authorities took the extraordinary step of censoring *Ben Hur* because it was believed the movie glorified "Christian superstition." By the 1930s, however, most Hollywood majors had opened offices in Shanghai, and very few American movies were not released in China. In 1934, nearly 80 percent of all movies screened in China were American, followed by Japanese films with 10 percent. The Chinese movie industry, comparatively retarded in its development, accounted for only 8.5 percent of screen time. Even after the arrival of "talkies" in the 1930s, China continued to produce mainly "silent" movies.

But China's political turmoil turned out to be a no-win situation for Hollywood. The Hollywood moguls were decidedly unenthusiastic about supporting Chang Kai-shek's tax on American movies to finance his crusade against Mao Zedong's communists. But when Mao finally seized power at the end of the 1940s, Hollywood was no longer welcome in China at all. As a state-controlled newspaper in Shanghai put it at the time, Hollywood's sin had been spreading its "imperialist poison" throughout China with lurid stories featuring "sex and legs." Richard Nixon's historic visit to China in the early 1970s did little to open market access for Hollywood. True, some American movies were brought into China to be viewed by Communist ruling élites, but the great mass of China's population remained untouched, and thus unmoved, by Hollywood images.

Jack Valenti visited China in 1979, but his meetings with top officials proved frustrating. China committed to taking some Hollywood movies, but refused to pay top dollar. Valenti's cold reception in China was a humbling experience, especially when compared with his red-carpet treatment in other countries whose leaders were aware of his White House connections. When Valenti went to Beijing, the Communist Party called the shots. And Chinese officials were tough negotiators: they agreed to buy American movies, but they wanted them dirt cheap.

"The kind of price the Chinese want to offer for films," complained Valenti, "does not measure up to what our people believe is the intrinsic marketplace value of those films."

Valenti could complain, but there was little he could do. The Chinese Communist Party's bargaining power was stronger because it controlled access to Chinese audiences. Hollywood could not threaten a boycott—its customary tactic—because Chinese officials felt no pressure from a local population clamouring for the latest Hollywood hits. In any event, China had access to a steady supply of Cantonese-language movies from Hong Kong. Hollywood consequently was forced to live with China's import quota of 10 movies a year, all of which had to be distributed by state-controlled China Film Corporation. Even worse, the few Hollywood movies that China imported often didn't make it onto Chinese movie screens for several years. The first instalment of *Superman*, for example, opened in China in the mid-1980s—eight years after its domestic U.S. release. *Superman* didn't last long in Chinese movie theatres. When Communist authorities realized the movie's slogan was "truth, justice, and the American way," the movie was promptly yanked from all cinemas.

Even more humiliating, Hollywood received no share of box-office receipts. In 1986, Jack Valenti bargained hard for a percentage of box-office receipts. But Chinese authorities flatly refused. It wasn't until the mid-1990s that China finally agreed to distribute American movies on a percentage basis—but took 60 percent of box-office receipts and kicked back only 40 percent to Hollywood. So desperate was Hollywood to gain a foothold in the vast Chinese market that the deal—which would have been considered insulting anywhere else—was lauded as a "major step forward." The same year, *The Fugitive*, starring Harrison Ford, became the first recently released Hollywood movie to open in Chinese cinemas in almost 40 years.

The ink was barely dry on Hollywood's profit-sharing deal with China when controversy over *Kundun* starting making headlines. In 1997, Disney hastily released an animated feature, *Mulan*, an ancient Chinese tale casting China and its history in a positive light. Placated by *Mulan*'s release, China's communist leaders gave Disney the green light to continue doing business in the country. When *Titanic* was released in China the following year, it was not considered offensive to the regime. On the contrary, China's rulers interpreted the movie—which featured a love story across social classes on the doomed ocean liner—as a critique of the deep inequalities engendered by capitalism.

After the phenomenal success of *Titanic*, Beijing agreed to increase its import quota from 10 to 20 movies per year—with the figure rising to 50 films annually over time. But there was a catch. While China agreed to import more Hollywood movies, it reserved the right to ban any American film it found culturally toxic or politically threatening. The deal, which was part of China's attempt to gain entry in the World Trade Organization, was celebrated by the Hollywood majors as a great victory. Jack Valenti, who had once groused about Beijing's intransigence, was now effusive in his praise for his Chinese "friends:" "We are joyful that our friends in China have recognized the worth of American films in their country," he declared.

Unlike mainland China, Hong Kong—a former British territory—was open to Western culture. For Hollywood, however, Hong Kong's embrace of Western-style capitalism didn't necessarily translate into huge box-office receipts. Hong Kong was a prolific producer of its own movies, which were popular throughout Southeast Asia. In fact, Hong Kong movies routinely outperformed Hollywood fare at the box office, not only in Hong Kong itself but throughout the region. Traditionally, the stereotypical Hong Kong film was a martial arts "action" movie, featuring karate and kung fu super-stars such as Bruce Lee and Jackie Chan. In truth, the Hong Kong movie industry had long churned out a rich variety of movies whose stars enjoyed enormous fame throughout Asia. Hong Kong movies form an imaginary world that can be fully understood only from inside its own cultural frame of reference. Hollywood, frustrated in its attempts to break through this cultural barrier, began luring away Hong Kong's brightest cinematic talents, such as director John Woo. His early movies—*The Killer* and *Hard-Boiled*—were major hits in Asia. Interestingly, Woo claimed to have been profoundly influenced by Western directors such as Sam Peckinpah and Stanley Kubrick. His political credentials, too, were laudable in the West. Woo had been outraged by China's repression of the Tiananmen Square and was keen to leave Hong Kong before the former British colony returned to Chinese rule in 1997. Woo arrived in Hollywood in 1993 to make *Hard Target*, starring Jean-Claude Van Damme. But it wasn't until he directed *Mission Impossible 2*, starring Tom Cruise, that Woo became a bankable, top-tier Hollywood director.[23]

When Woo directed *Hard Target* for Universal Pictures, the studio was owned by Japanese industrial giant Matsushita. In the early 1990s, many believed that Japan—following Sony's buyout of Columbia Pictures and Matsushita's purchase of Universal—would soon control Hollywood from

Tokyo. It wouldn't quite turn out that way. Sony's initial experience with Columbia was a disaster. And Matsushita, for its part, ended up selling Universal.[24] It could nonetheless be argued that, if Japan failed to conquer Hollywood, neither had Hollywood conquered Japan. Despite its fascination for American popular culture, Japan has remained essentially an Asian culture.

Japan's relationship with Hollywood has been ambivalent. When the Great Kanto Earthquake destroyed much of Tokyo in 1923, most of the nascent Japanese movie industry was decimated in the rubble. This tragedy created a cinematic vacuum that encouraged the importation of Hollywood movies that would inspire a generation of young Japanese filmmakers. In the 1930s, however, the Emperor's government took a hands-on approach towards the domestic movie industry as part of its policy of "national imperialism" that inspired Japan's belligerent invasion of China. During this period, many Japanese films were censored, and some filmmakers with Marxist inclinations were executed. Movie distribution was strictly controlled by a cartel of two Japanese companies: Toho and Shochiku. All Hollywood movie imports had to pass through the Toho-Shochiku cartel. Hollywood's frustration with this situation became irrelevant when the Second World War broke out. Japan, allied to Nazi Germany, shut the door completely on American movies. Pearl Harbor—which later would inspire many Hollywood movies—rendered the boycott meaningless, as America and Japan were now at war.

After the war, when a humiliated Japan fell under American control, the Japanese entered a period of forced emulation of American institutions, values, and habits. Constrained by Washington to adopt U.S.-style political institutions, Japan also adopted Hollywood's model of a vertically integrated movie studio combining production, distribution and theatrical exhibition. This industrial model was highly efficient and produced many superlative Japanese movies. Akira Kurosawa, arguably Japan's greatest movie director, emerged in Japanese cinema during this period. In 1950, Kurosawa made *Rashomon*—about the mysterious death of a samurai—which won the Oscar for "best foreign film." Kurosawa's debt to American cinema was more evident in his *Seven Samurai*, which inspired the Hollywood movie, *The Magnificent Seven*. For Hollywood, however, imitation was a form of flattery that paid no dividends. Japan's movie industry, a closed self-feeding circuit focused on domestic output, could casually spurn Hollywood imports with little anxiety about American commercial or diplomatic retaliation. By the 1960s, Hollywood boasted no more than 20 percent of the Japanese movie market.

When Sony bought Columbia Pictures from Coca-Cola in the late 1980s, many feared a new form of "yellow menace" had arrived in America. The American media sounded alarm bells again when Japanese interests bought New York's Rockefeller Center. After Matsushita purchased Universal Studios, two Hollywood studios were Japanese-controlled. *Time* and *Newsweek* magazines featured cover stories warning that Japan was buying the "soul" of America. The Hollywood studios, always quick to seize the mood of American audiences, began producing movies in which Asian characters were the villains. One Hollywood movie in particular, *Rising Sun*, exploited deep-seated fears in America about the Japanese threat. The movie, starring Sean Connery and Wesley Snipes, was a story about attempts by a Japanese conglomerate, Nakamoto, to take control of a major U.S. computer giant, MicroCon. *Rising Sun* was a compelling tale. A decade later, however, Japan was a spent economic force while America, despite its declinist detractors, was once again in ascendancy. In the late 1990s, Hollywood felt sufficiently self-confident to produce a blockbuster called *Pearl Harbor* with no hard feelings.

In smaller Asian countries that don't benefit from Japan's large population, Hollywood has overwhelmingly dominated domestic movie screens. In Thailand, for example, American movies traditionally have taken up more than 85 percent of screen time. But in other Asian countries, especially those with large populations and strong religious-based identities—notably Indonesia and Malaysia—Hollywood's presence has been more controversial. Indonesia's President Sukarno visited Hollywood in 1956 with the unexpected message that American movies were "revolutionary." Hollywood films, said Sukarno, showed ordinary people owning refrigerators and automobiles, which incited envy and emulation—not jealousy and bitterness.

"That is why I salute you," Sukarno declared to Hollywood executives.

Only a few years later, however, Sukarno denounced liberalism and vowed to bring Indonesia back to the values of a strictly national ideology. Soon massive boycotts of "evil" American movies were organized, especially by Indonesia's Communist Party. When anti-American riots spread to the streets, Hollywood stopped exporting its movies to Indonesia, though private screenings for the country's élites were discreetly arranged in luxurious hotel ballrooms. It would take years of hard-nosed trade negotiations to pry open Indonesia's doors to American movies. Indonesia finally relented in a trade-off: it would import Hollywood movies if the United States remained open to Indonesian tile exports. In late 2000, *The Year of Living Dangerously*—the Hollywood film about Suharto's overthrow of Sukarno in the 1960s—was finally screened in Indonesia more than 17 years after its original release.[25]

Another Asian trouble spot for Hollywood was South Korea, whose government prohibited American movie distributors from establishing offices on its territory. As in Japan, the Hollywood majors were forced to hand over their product to local distributors. In 1987, the Korean government finally relented by allowing the Hollywood studios to set up local offices. The following year, the movie *Fatal Attraction*—starring Michael Douglas and Glenn Close—became the first American film to be distributed directly in South Korea by a Hollywood studio. But anti-American sentiment was so high that *Fatal Attraction*'s release provoked violent riots in which movie theatres were vandalized. Protestors also intimidated moviegoers buying tickets for the film. Slogans such as "Drive Out Yankee Movies" were sprayed-painted on movie screens. Some protestors let snakes loose inside movie theatres where *Fatal Attraction* was showing. Some 30 movie theatres in Seoul were shut down amid the protests.

India provides the best example of an Asian country whose ethnic and religious identities have culturally insulated its population from the powerful impact of Hollywood's images. Within India itself, cultural references have been largely ethno-centric, which often has created ethnic animosity among Hindis, Moslems, Sikhs, Tamils, and other groups. Attitudes towards the West, in like manner, have been shaped by religion and social class. While India's liberal élites have tended to be receptive towards the West, other castes among India's majority Hindu and minority Moslem populations have manifested more ambiguous attitudes towards Western influences. Generally speaking, these ethnic realities have constructed a cultural rampart against foreign influences that has greatly benefited India's domestic movie industry.

India's movie industry easily rivals Hollywood in size, output, and economic success. First of all, the Indian movie industry benefits from the economies of scale provided by a domestic population of roughly 1 billion people—more than three times the size of America's population. More than 500 films are produced in India every year, and every week some 100 million Indians buy a ticket to see a domestically produced movie in the country's 12,000 movie theatres. India's biggest movie production center is Bombay, whose local film industry is known popularly as "Bollywood." With an annual output of some 250 films, Bollywood's star system is so culturally powerful that local screen idols are almost always more famous than leading Hollywood actors. If Hollywood has a global rival beyond America's borders, it is unquestionably Bollywood.

Sylvester Stallone learned this first-hand in 1998 when attending a Dubai film festival in the United Arab Emirates. Throngs of movie fans virtually ignored Stallone as they ecstatically mobbed Indian film star Amitabh Bachchan. In America, Bachchan is virtually unknown beyond the Indian immigrant community. Most Americans would not even know how to pronounce his name, let alone recognize him in the street. But thanks to the popularity of Bollywood movies, the handsome Indian actor—known as "The Big B"—is a superstar in India and throughout much of the world, including the Middle East. He is especially famous in Britain, which boasts a large Indian population. When Britain's BBC television network took a poll to discover the world's most famous movie stars, Amitabh Bachchan came first—ahead of Laurence Olivier and Marilyn Monroe.

Hollywood's cultural status and economic performance in India has never been solid. During British colonial rule, it is true, India's movie screens were overwhelmingly dominated by American movies. In the late 1920s, only 15 percent of screen time was devoted to domestic Indian films. But the roots of anti-Hollywood hostility were already germinating, especially among India's Hindu population. In India's legislature, Hindu politicians called upon the government to counter Hollywood's "evil stream of misrepresentation." Unlike in France and Britain, opposition to Hollywood in India was not based on cultural snobbery or commercial rivalry, but on deeply rooted moral and religious values. In India—despite its multi-ethnic, multi-linguistic, and multi-religious composition—local populations preferred domestic movies to American movies because they resonated with familiar cultural, moral, and religious values.

Following India's independence in the late 1940s, local films began to supplant Hollywood imports. Among classics of the era were Satyajit Ray's

Apu Trilogy, which followed a single family through life while touching on the themes of death and exile. Another Indian film of the era, *Aan,* was a low-budget movie that nonetheless outgrossed all Hollywood imports combined. By the 1950s Hollywood was taking a minuscule 3 percent of India's national box-office receipts. The success of Indian films in their own domestic market was all the more remarkable given that Hollywood controlled the best first-run movie theatres in the country's major cities.

Eric Johnston, head of the MPAA, regarded India as Hollywood's most serious foreign challenge. Johnston understood the forces behind India's resistance to Hollywood product. "The problem isn't so much one of attendance," he said, "as one of native preference for local product."

In the 1960s, the Hollywood majors called on Washington for assistance in their fruitless efforts to penetrate India's movie market. Hollywood complained, in particular, about India's import duty on film reels brought into the country. The Indian government relented slightly on these taxes, but only in exchange for guaranteed exposure for Indian movies in America. The deal worked in spirit, but not in practice. In 1971 the Indian government took action by setting up a state-owned agency as the monopoly clearing house for all movies imported into the country. India's State Trading Corporation thus could show preference to movie distributors that bought and popularized Indian movies in their own home markets. Hollywood was outraged by this state-owned import cartel—even though, ironically, the Hollywood majors had been prosecuted in the United States for their own cartel-like behaviour. As a gesture of protest, Hollywood adopted its time-honoured tactic of boycotting the Indian market. But India had the luxury of benign indifference to a paucity of Hollywood movies. A measure of the Indian government's nonchalance was the four years that passed before it decided to negotiate with Hollywood to end the boycott. According to the terms of the bilateral agreement, India restricted Hollywood to 100 films per year—a fraction of India's annual domestic output.

The precise source of Hollywood's frustration in India was deeply entrenched in Indian society—in a word, xenophobia. Indian hostility to the outside world boiled to the surface in the 1990s with the rise of the Hindu nationalist Bharatiya Janata Party and its "India first" policy. The Hindu nationalists successfully tapped into a deep-seated, religiously based xenophobia that found expression in a rejection of American-style imperialism in the form of global brands such as Coca-Cola, McDonald's, and Disney. Economic progress was one thing, cultural pollution something else. Hence the party's slogan: "Microchips yes, potato chips no." In India, Bollywood benefited from Hindu nationalism. At the same time, Bollywood movies enjoyed access to a huge export market in countries with large Indian populations. In Britain, for example, Bollywood movies rivalled Hollywood at the box-office in 2000 with three movies in the top ten.

Despite commercial success, or perhaps because of it, Bollywood has undergone profound, and sometimes troubling, changes in recent years. In the past, Bollywood movies tended to deal, albeit in a melodramatic manner, with serious social issues. In recent years, however, Bollywood has followed Hollywood's example of churning out more escapist fare. One reason for this shift has been economic. Like the Hollywood studios, Bollywood producers have been adopting risk-reduction strategies by producing movies with guaranteed mass appeal. Another reason is more disturbing: criminal infiltration of India's movie industry. In the 1990s, gangsters gravitated towards Bollywood to escape the uncertainties of traditional mafia-like activities such as racketeering and smuggling. Controlling export rights to Bollywood's massive film libraries was an attractive opportunity that, once seized, proved immensely lucrative. The result, however, was rampant crime and corruption in every aspect of the Indian movie business, including the casting of actors and actresses.

In the late 1990s, Indian movie fans were shocked to learn that Sanjay Dutt, one of Bollywood's biggest stars, had been arrested and jailed on charges related to a series of bomb explosions that had killed more than 300 people. A year later, Rakesh Roshan, a top Bollywood director, survived a shooting after a quarrel over money. In early 2001, Bollywood was struck again by scandal when movie producer Bharat Shah—called "Mr. Moneybags"—was arrested by Bombay's organized crime squad for making movies with funds provided by Chota Shakeel, one of India's most vicious gangsters.

There has been some positive news for Bollywood. In early 2002, a Bollywood film, *Lagaan*, was nominated for an Oscar—the first time in 14 years that a movie from India was in the running for an Academy Award. The previous Oscar nomination for an Indian film was for *Salaam Bombay* in

1988. In Britain, *Lagaan* and another Bollywood film, *Kabhi Khushi Kabhi Gham*, were among the top ten box-office hits in 2000. In May 2002, a Bollywood film, *Devdas*, became the first mainstream Hindi movie to be screened at the Cannes Film Festival. These successes have sparked Hollywood interest in the fast-growing market for Indian movies. Some hope Bollywood's association with Hollywood will help eradicate its infestation by organized crime by imposing legal business practices on the industry's operations.[26]

During the summer of 2002, Bollywood movies were starting to resurface in post-Taliban Afghanistan. Posters of Bollywood stars could be seen in the shops of Kabul and Kandahar, and Bombay-produced action movies like *Burning Heat* were broadcast on Afghan television. Bollywood movies had been popular in Afghanistan long before Osama bin Laden's fundamentalists took power, but were banned by the Taliban, which ordered the destruction of all movie theatres. Today, most Afghans watch Bollywood movies on television, usually via satellite TV services aimed at the Indian market.

Despite its success, Bollywood can never hope to rival the global influence of Hollywood. The appeal of Bollywood movies, while powerful in many parts of the world, will remain restricted to countries with Indian diaspora populations. The universal appeal of Hollywood movies will continue to reinforce America's status as the planet's most powerful cultural model.

Hollywood Imperialism Today

A century after the first American movie moguls emerged from the nickelodeons of New York, Hollywood is the most powerful cultural force on the planet. And its historical alliance with Washington is stronger than ever.

Following the terrorist attacks on the World Trade Center and Pentagon, a group of Hollywood studio executives held secret meetings with top White House officials to discuss how American movies and Hollywood-produced television shows could combat global terrorism. Attending the meeting was Bryce Zabel, chairman of the Academy of Television Arts and Sciences, who said later that the meeting produced a consensus that America needed to do more to promote its strengths internationally.

"We have not done a good job communicating to people about who we are when so many people in the world think ill of us, and many wish us harm," Zabel said. "It's possible the entertainment industry could help the government formulate its message to the rest of the world about who Americans are, and what they believe."

A year later, the Hollywood blockbuster *The Sum of All Fears* opened in American cinemas. The movie, based on the Tom Clancy novel about nuclear terrorism, could have been billed as a Hollywood-Pentagon co-production. During the film's shooting, the Pentagon provided an arsenal of authentic military hardware—B-2 bombers, F-16 fighter jets, Marine Corps and U.S. Army helicopters, plus the nuclear-powered John Stennis aircraft carrier with its crew of 5,000 soldiers. What's more, top military and CIA officials worked with Paramount Pictures as consultants on the film.

The Sum of All Fears provoked complaints that the Pentagon was using American taxpayers' money to parade its military hardware in Hollywood movies. Others argued that the Pentagon was manipulating Hollywood to project a positive image of the U.S. military establishment. But Philip Strub, the Pentagon's special assistant for entertainment media, put it differently: "We want an opportunity to communicate directly to the American public through that powerful medium."

The Pentagon undoubtedly approved Hollywood's provocation of North Korea with the James Bond movie, *Die Another Day*. Even though North Korea's communist dictator Kim Jong-il was an avowed Hollywood movie buff, he was outraged by the Bond film released in late 2002. In the movie, agent 007 is captured and tortured in North Korea, where one of Bond's sexual conquests occurs in a Buddhist temple. In protest, North Korea's official news agency issued a statement: "The U.S. should stop at once this dirty and cursed burlesque," adding that *Die Another Day* was a "deliberate and premeditated act of mocking and insulting the Korean nation." Obviously sensitive to George W. Bush's presidential rhetoric, the North Korean protest added that the United States was "an empire of evil" that "spreads abnormality, degeneration, violence and fin-de-siècle corrupt sex culture." It was uncertain whether Kim Jong-il's dislike for the latest James Bond flick was related to North Korea's nuclear arms provocation against America at precisely the same moment. But the North Korean despot obviously had forgotten one key fact about James Bond: He is a British agent of Her Majesty's government, not the United States.

Hollywood's soft power can sometimes produce unintended consequences. In the spring of 2003, as U.S. bombs rained down on Baghdad, Saddam Hussein frantically distributed copies of the Hollywood movie *Black Hawk Down* to boost morale among his besieged commanders. In the movie, U.S. soldiers suffer a humiliating defeat in Somalia when two Black Hawk helicopters are shot down by local paramilitaries. *Black Hawk Down* was inspired by the real-life U.S. intervention in Somalia after President Bill Clinton responded to a United Nations pleas for humanitarian aid in the war-torn country. Saddam Hussein evidently believed that, by screening *Black Hawk Down* to his troops as U.S. soldiers encircled Baghdad, the Iraqi resistance could take inspiration from the precedent in Somalia. But not even a Hollywood movie could save the Iraqi despot from the awesome force of U.S. hard power.

America's invasion of Iraq undoubtedly will inspire several heroic movies, thus continuing a longstanding relationship between Hollywood and the Pentagon. In fact, Hollywood and the Pentagon have been working together since the earliest days of cinema a century before—as far back as the 1915 classic, *Birth of a Nation*, on which director D.W. Griffith used West Point engineers as technical advisors. A century later, the world's six biggest media conglomerates have at their core a Hollywood movie studio: AOL Time Warner, Disney, Viacom, News Corp., Universal Studios, and Sony. Yet while Hollywood is located in the United States, it is no longer an exclusively American industry. Of the six Hollywood giants, only three are controlled by American companies: Warner Bros., Disney, and Paramount. Shifting ownership structures may explain, in part, why Hollywood has adopted a different, more cooperative, approach towards "foreign" countries—especially in the West. Hollywood no longer regards foreign markets as a dumping ground for its products. In Europe, Hollywood now invests in movies through partnerships with local producers. Hollywood's lesson over the past several decades has been that it must treat foreign countries like an opportunity to be seized, not as a stubborn obstacle to be overcome.

There are, to be sure, pragmatic reasons for Hollywood's new international strategy. It would be naïve to claim Hollywood is not chiefly driven by economic imperatives. But beyond bottom-line considerations, Hollywood conveys an enduring commitment to a core set of values and beliefs: individualism, capitalism, liberalism, and democracy.

Where these values are shared, Hollywood's presence has been strong. Where these values are rejected, Hollywood has been zealously resisted.

→ doesn't talk about why core set of values + beliefs are shared → just talks about cultural protectionism + elite influence

two

Television

Lotusland as Global Empire

TELEVISION, AS any casual viewer of CNN knows, has become an indispensable instrument of global soft power.

The same images—bloody revolutions, Olympic sporting events, political assassinations, rock mega-concerts, Academy Awards ceremonies, royal marriages, funerals of princesses, smart-bomb military campaigns—can be watched simultaneously, in real time, by nearly every person on the planet. Satellites made this technologically feasible toward the end of the 20th century. Today, broadband video on the World Wide Web has extended, and intensified, the electronic nervous system of post-modern civilization.

But if global television is a technological reality, it is not always embraced with enthusiasm. Television can be a powerful force of free expression, creativity, and liberation. But it is also resented as a homogenous agent of oppressive mono-culture. In some cultures, television has produced unintended consequences. In Fiji, female plumpness was traditionally a sign of beauty. "You've gained weight" was a flattering compliment to a Fijian. But after teenaged Fijian girls began watching American television soap operas, constant exposure to images of attractive, blonde, rich—and thin—female characters introduced new canons of beauty on the tropical island. Following American television's invasion of Fiji, local health officials began observing troubling levels of bulimia and low self-esteem among young women.[1]

While television's role as a global purveyor of taste and fashion should not be underestimated, its most controversial role in international affairs has been political. Media mogul Rupert Murdoch famously declared that satellite television represents an "unambiguous threat to totalitarian regimes everywhere." He was right. There is nothing more exasperating to ruthless tyrants and their oppressive regimes than foreign television signals beamed directly into the homes of their suffering populations. When dissident Lech Walesa—Poland's future head-of-state—was asked what had triggered communism's collapse in Eastern Europe, his response was succinct: "Television." When the Berlin Wall was being smashed apart in 1989, East German youths taking sledgehammers to the detested Soviet rampart brandished "MTV" logos. In the Islamic world, satellite TV dishes that pick up MTV signals have been banned by theocratic regimes. In Africa, autocratic rulers revile CNN because its news reports show images of repression inflicted on their local populations. In Asian countries with free-market economies, political leaders—Singapore's Goh Chock Tong, Malaysia's Mohamad Mahatir—howled against the "poisonous" influence of Western television.

Television sometimes serves as an unofficial ambassador of goodwill. During the Soviet occupation of Afghanistan in the 1980s, an English woman in Kabul suddenly found herself being aggressed by an angry crowd that mistakenly believed she was Russian. Fearing for her life, the woman began frantically screaming: "British! British!" But this desperate declaration of her nationality failed to appease the mob's wrath. Then, instinctively, the woman changed her approach. "BBC! BBC! BBC!" she cried. Suddenly, the hostile crowd stopped, fell silent, and moved back. Many years later, television continued to play a role in Afghanistan's tormented political life. After the Soviets had been evicted by an even more brutal Islamic regime, the Taliban's first priority was to send their fundamentalist thugs throughout the country on a violent search-and-destroy mission. Their targets: TV sets and videocassette machines. And yet, ironically, Osama bin Laden was not averse to using videocassettes to shake his fist at the West.

In retrospect, it's surprising television took so long to impose itself as a global medium. For decades, television was stubbornly contained in strictly national spaces, and usually operated under the tight control of states. It took nearly a half-century for television to fulfill its global destiny.

Cold War TV: The American Way of Life

Television exploded as a mass medium at the outset of the Cold War. Not long after Winston Churchill made his famous "Iron Curtain" speech on a Missouri college campus in 1946, millions of American families were moving to newly built suburbs and buying television sets as symbols of post-war prosperity.

The tube, of course, was not new. TV had been invented many years before. The word "television" was first coined circa 1900 at the Universal Exhibition in Paris, where technological marvels were on proud display at the dawn of a brave new century. In the following years, several TV prototypes were developed by rival inventors in Russia, Germany, France, Britain, and America. By the 1920s, major American corporations such as General Electric, Westinghouse, and AT&T were financially backing competing efforts to manufacture TV sets. These same companies launched Radio Corporation of America—a forerunner of NBC—to make programs that would feed their mass-produced TV sets. In Britain, John Logie Baird invented another TV prototype, which in the 1930s competed against a television apparatus invented by Marconi-EMI.

Television's most highly publicized debut occurred in April 1939, when RCA chairman David Sarnoff—anxious to be first in the field with a mass-produced model—demonstrated a TV set at the World's Fair in New York City. President Franklin Roosevelt was on hand for Sarnoff's historic television broadcast. FDR even made a brief speech at the unveiling of the new video contraption.

Sarnoff, still burdened by his radio bias, failed to grasp the full potential of the new medium when he declared: "Now we add radio sight to sound."

Optimism about Sarnoff's newfangled invention evaporated five months later when Nazi Germany invaded Poland in September 1939. In America, commercial television was put on indefinite hold two years later following Japan's bombing of Pearl Harbor.

Sarnoff, meanwhile, began to see television's potential to transform American society. During the Second World War, he predicted that television, along with automobiles, would drive the growth of a new suburban lifestyle in the United States. His timing was propitious. In the late 1940s, post-war prosperity triggered a burst of optimism, and TV sets took off as mass-produced consumer goods. America's new culture of consumption was elevated to the status of patriotic ideology: the American way of life. Against this backdrop, television served a double function. First ownership of a TV set was a sign of material achievement, and early television shows reflected the values that made Americans desire to consume more. As James Burke, former president of Johnson & Johnson, recalled: "I sincerely believe that television saved us after the Second World War. Without television, we'd have gone back into the Depression."[2] Second, America's patriotic materialism also served an ideological function at a time when the United States faced a new global adversary in Soviet Communism. America was a prosperous and confident nation that saw itself as the leader of the free world. In contrast, the dull, grey, authoritarian Soviet Union was an impoverished, barren police state. The Kremlin, which was channelling a huge portion of the Soviet Union's domestic productivity towards military spending, nonetheless constituted a dangerous threat to the United States and its allies. The Cold War thus gave television a timely function as an ideological weapon to promote American values. Throughout the 1950s, millions of Americans watched reassuring television shows—like *Ozzie and Harriet* and *Leave It to Beaver*—that comforted the white-picket-fence ideals of Pleasantville, U.S.A.

Inside the television industry, however, the picture was not so reassuring. While McCarthyism purged Hollywood of alleged communist infiltration, a red scare similarly was sweeping through the corridors of the major U.S. television networks. In 1950, a right-wing lobby group published a document titled *Red Channels: The Report on the Communist Influence in Radio and Television*. Its publication led to the so-called "Red Channel purges" in which of dozens of television industry figures were blacklisted. One of them was actress Jean Muir, who was dropped from the General Foods-sponsored television comedy, *The Aldrich Family*. Broadway actor Philip Loeb was, in like manner, removed from the popular CBS situation comedy *The Goldbergs*. Loeb was a tragic victim of the House Un-American Activities Committee. When Hollywood director Elia Kazan and movie star Lee J. Cobb, appearing before HUAC, identified Loeb as a former member of the American Communist Party, General Foods ordered CBS to fire him. The show's producers refused, so in 1951 General Foods cancelled the show. The following season, *The Goldbergs* moved to NBC—but Loeb was replaced in the starring role. Depressed, Loeb committed suicide in a New York hotel room in 1955.

In most cases, the U.S. networks—like Hollywood—were eager to prove their unflinching anti-Communist credentials. The networks, in fact, attempted to turn the red scare to their advantage, arguing that television was a strategic weapon that could be deployed to combat Communism. CBS president Frank Stanton argued that strong TV networks were necessary as a civilian mobilization system against the Communist threat. Appearing before Congress, he declared: "To curtail or destroy the networks' unique quality of instantaneous national interconnection would be a colossal step backwards." The networks thus conferred upon themselves the highest moral purpose: to bind America together in the anti-Communist cause.

Others believed the new medium—and especially American television—had an even higher purpose. Television could be harnessed not merely as an instrument of anti-Communist mobilization, but also as an electronic panacea for the entire planet's ills.

David Sarnoff, the ubiquitous RCA chairman, was so enthusiastic about television's global prospects that, in 1952, he confidently predicted that TV would be an international medium within five years. It didn't matter that, at home in America, network television was shamelessly commercial. For Sarnoff and others, television's global mission would be a utopian project. In 1954, comedian Bob Hope declared that global television networks would, within ten years, bring "mutual understanding between the world's peoples." The equation was simple: Global television equalled global peace.

Pervasive anxiety about the Soviets getting a technological head start in global television was, of course, not unrelated to these high-minded declarations. The U.S. government had already launched its Voice of America radio service as an electronic weapon against the Soviets. Voice of America supporters soon began lobbying in favour of a concerted U.S. offensive to secure an American lead in the spread of global television. The idea had little trouble finding support in Congress. U.S. Senator Alexander Wiley, for example, asserted that television "would spread the truth concerning the epic battle of the forces of the free world against Communist dictatorship." The media, too, liked the idea. In 1955, *Variety* reported that global television would "give the lie to Commies," adding that "it's Communism versus the

American way." On the same theme, NBC president Pat Weaver declared: "It's through television that we can expect to answer the charge of the Communists that ours is an empty society without interest in the better things of life."

Weaver, who headed NBC throughout the 1950s, articulated his own plan for global television. He understood that TV sets, as consumer goods, were a luxury that could not be afforded by the vast majority of the planet's population. In the 1950s, television was limited to rich industrialized countries where, thanks to relatively high disposable incomes, middle-class and wealthy people could afford to buy TV sets. Even in the United States, it took several years for television to become a mass medium. In 1947, there were only 60,000 TV sets in the United States, most of them in New York City. Many Americans watched television in public places, such as taverns and bars. In Europe, television penetration was even lower. In 1959, while North America boasted 287 TV sets for every 1,000 persons, the European figure was 48 television sets per thousand.[4]

Facing this economic barrier, Weaver proposed what he believed was a more feasible solution: the United States would construct an international network of transmitters and install some 10,000 TV sets in public places throughout the world in a high-tech campaign aimed at exposing foreign populations to American values. If implemented, said Weaver, an American-owned global television network would "leave the Russians gasping for breath and out of the running."

Weaver's global television system was never built. However noble in principle, early optimism about television's global reach, and moral mission, was naïve and unworkable. For one thing, national governments, keen to assert jurisdiction over virtually every aspect of their local broadcasting spheres, were natural adversaries of a global television system that escaped their control. Governments had technology on their side. Before the advent of broadcast satellites in the 1970s, television was transmitted via off-air frequencies that could not be picked up by antennas beyond a certain radius. Consequently, TV signals tended to be limited to local, regional, or national spheres. Most governments saw television as a political instrument that could be used to promote social cohesion and reinforce citizenship loyalties. In Europe, governments not only regulated broadcasting, but also owned and operated their own television networks, produced programs, and acted as state censors. In Britain, the venerable BBC—founded as a radio broadcaster in the 1920s—expanded into television in the late 1940s as a state-controlled monopoly. The BBC model was exported to other British Commonwealth countries, notably Canada and Australia. In continental Europe, virtually every government imposed state control over its national broadcasting landscape, often manipulating television for partisan purposes. In France, Charles de Gaulle's attitude towards state-owned broadcasting was, in effect: "La télévision, c'est moi." This state-centric attitude was pervasive throughout Europe during the 1950s and 1960s. Even in free-market America, the federal government controlled the airwaves through the Federal Communications Commission, which Franklin Roosevelt had set up during the Depression.

If building a global television system was unworkable, selling television programs internationally, country by country, was not only commercially possible, but highly lucrative. In many countries, nascent television networks, desperate for programs to fill their schedules, turned eagerly to foreign suppliers. Given America's advantageous economies of scale thanks to its huge domestic market, the United States quickly became a global exporter of television programs. Most foreign networks were only too happy to buy American shows such as *I Love Lucy* and *San Francisco Beat*.

In most countries, however, television networks remained under strict state control and abided by an arsenal of regulations. American television executives quickly realized that, to maximize foreign sales, they would have to export the entire American model of television—namely, commercial advertising-supported. Their chosen agent to achieve this objective was the powerful clutch of major U.S. advertising agencies—notably J. Walter Thompson and McCann Erickson—as well as corporations selling global brands like Colgate, Kodak, Johnson & Johnson, Goodyear, Max Factor, Procter & Gamble, and Bristol-Myers. As Donald Coyle, a senior executive at ABC International, put it: "It is highly desirable from the standpoint of the economies of these countries that television be brought in, so it can fulfill its natural function as a giant pump fueling the machine of consumer demand, stepping up the flow of goods and services to keep living standards high and the economy expanding."

Thus inspired by a global mission, the U.S. advertising industry organized itself internationally, mainly through lobbies such as the International Advertising Association. Television was now advertising's privileged conduit. American television became, in effect, an electronic extension of the Marshall Plan. But American-style television was not always an easy sell. At the first World Congress on Commercial Television, held in London in 1957, the tacit agenda was to promote commercial television as an alternative to state-owned broadcasting. Some progress had already been made on this front, especially in Britain where the commercial ITV stations were now competing for audiences against state-controlled BBC. In many European countries, however, hostility toward private television remained adamant. The London conference's sponsor, Johnson & Johnson, consequently was obliged to accept the more limited objective of promoting commercial advertising on Europe's state-controlled television networks.[5]

In the United States, meanwhile, the domestic television industry frequently was the subject of controversy and criticism. In 1961, when President Kennedy appointed Newton Minow as head of the Federal Communications Commission, the new FCC chairman shocked and angered many industry executives with his famous declaration that television was a "vast wasteland." Minow's comments garnered support from establishment sources, including legendary broadcaster Edward R. Murrow. President Kennedy had just appointed Murrow as head of the United States Information Agency (USIA), which was the State Department's bureaucratic arm responsible for promoting America's image abroad. Kennedy had vowed to restore America's deteriorating image overseas and, once he was installed in the White House, the USIA became the administration's chosen instrument to achieve that goal. Murrow, a former CBS broadcaster, was one of JFK's most high-profile appointments. Kennedy made sure, moreover, that Murrow was kept in the loop, especially at meetings of the National Security Council. Murrow made no secret of his view that American television was not fulfilling its role as an ambassador for American cultural diplomacy. In a widely anticipated speech to the National Association of Broadcasters in 1962, Murrow cautioned the U.S. networks to be mindful that television programs were a "strategic commodity" in the global combat against Communism.

Television's geopolitical role—whether as an altruistic promoter of world understanding or a marketing instrument for the American way of life—depended as much on common technical standards as on shared moral values. This technological imperative came sharply into focus during the 1960s, as viewers throughout the world began abandoning their black-and-white TV sets and replacing them with sets offering crisp colour images.

The geopolitical stakes of colour-TV were high. And, predictably, the race to establish a global colour TV standard got caught in the Cold War cross-fire of superpower rivalry between the United States and Soviet Union.

TV Standards and International Politics

From the earliest days of television, the United States understood the strategic importance of imposing American technical standards internationally. By establishing its standard on TV reception, the U.S. would effectively become a powerful gatekeeper, commercially and culturally, as television extended its reach into foreign countries.

When black-and-white television first emerged in the late 1940s, the United States adopted the "NTSC" standard—for National Television Systems Committee. Originally developed by RCA, the NTSC standard was automatically adopted in neighbouring Canada, whose broadcasting system was, de facto, an extension of the American system. Japan, which had become an American puppet state after the Second World War, also adopted NTSC. One key advantage of imposing a single technical standard was improved mass-production efficiencies for electronics manufacturers—General Electric, Zenith, Philco—that produced TV sets.

Europe, in keeping with its traditional reflexes, would prove much less compliant towards the United States—especially when colour TV emerged in the 1960s. France, in particular, was resolutely opposed to adopting an American colour TV standard. This was not surprising given that, in the 1960s, France's social and political climate was tacitly, if not explicitly, anti-American. Charles de Gaulle had installed himself in the Elysée Palace as a republican monarch. Few Western leaders personified anti-Americanism more than General de Gaulle. His politics of French grandeur emphasized, above all, the principle of *indépendance nationale*.

French anxieties about America's industrial threat were expressed in particularly urgent terms by the influential journalist Jean-Jacques Servan-Schrieber. In his bestselling 1967 book, *Le Défi américain*, Servan-Schrieber called for a common European strategy to counter American industrial hegemony. If Europe failed to meet the "American challenge," he warned,

Europe would become a mere colony of the United States. Servan-Schrieber could marshall convincing evidence to support his claim that America was Europe's most threatening technological adversary. In the early 1960s, the U.S. government had prohibited IBM's subsidiary in France from selling computers to the French government to support France's development of nuclear weapons.

The emergence of colour TV provided De Gaulle with a timely pretext to assert France's high-tech superiority by sponsoring French industrial champions in the electronics sector. De Gaulle was launching other high-profile industrial projects—including the Franco-British construction of the supersonic Concorde jet—to establish France's prestige and independence vis-à-vis the United States. Colour TV standards were accorded similar status in France's vainglorious industrial strategy. De Gaulle was determined that France would not buckle to American pressures to adopt the NTSC standard and, as he put it, be "tied like a dog to a leash."

In a Gaullist snub to America, France defiantly adopted its own colour TV standard, called SECAM—for "*séquence à mémoire*." Adopting SECAM was not only a defensive tactic. France also planned to promote its colour TV standard internationally as a rival to NTSC. The French government, taking a state-centric approach that found its origins in the longstanding French tradition of industrial mercantilism, bought a 25 percent stake in the firm Compagnie Française de Télévision, which owned the SECAM patent. De Gaulle declared to the nation that SECAM was a "*grande technique française*" that would conquer the planet. Ironically, in the 1960s many French households still didn't own a black-and-white television set, let alone a colour TV set.

Despite De Gaulle's bold declarations, France's strategy was based chiefly on discrediting the U.S. standard as technologically inferior. The French dismissed NTSC as "horse-and-buggy vintage," adding that NTSC stood for "Never Twice the Same Colour." In Europe, the French also cleverly promoted SECAM as a "European" colour TV standard that would reduce the continent's technological dependence on the United States. In the American press, SECAM soon became known as an acronym for "Supreme Effort Contra A-Merica."

But France's attempt to lead a European technological coalition against America soon encountered predictable obstacles. France attempted to rally Germany to the SECAM cause, but the German government had its own electronics sector to protect and promote. Germany therefore developed its own standard, called PAL—for "Phase Alternation Line." Most technical experts agreed that Germany's PAL was an improvement on France's SECAM. The French nonetheless were outraged that Germany had shattered "European" solidarity by developing a rival colour-TV standard. Feeling betrayed, De Gaulle turned towards Britain for support. At first, the British government endorsed SECAM. But a heroic Franco-British technological accord soon became victim of nasty backroom Euro-politics. When De Gaulle vetoed Britain's entry into the European Common Market, Britain abruptly pulled out of the proposed SECAM consortium.

France was now isolated with its lofty SECAM gambit. So De Gaulle changed tactics. This time, he turned to a more reliable ally: the Soviet Union. It was not the first time De Gaulle had played the Soviet card to send a defiant message to "*les Anglo-Saxons.*" The Soviets, for their part, were gratefully receptive to France's colour TV industrial project. SECAM gave the Kremlin a technological pretext to spurn the American and German standards.

With the Soviets in the picture, the colour-TV wars were now getting dangerous. The United States could not afford to be indifferent to a Franco-Soviet *rapprochement* in the high-tech sector. Fearing widespread adoption of SECAM among Soviet allies, the United States adopted a policy of technological containment. Leading the U.S. campaign, RCA launched a blitzkrieg campaign to promote NTSC internationally, including in the Soviet Union. RCA's efforts were frustrated, ironically, by the U.S. Commerce Department, which opposed the export to the Soviet Union of sophisticated colour TV technology that, it was feared, could potentially be used for military purposes. But the White House overruled the Commerce Department. President Johnson's secretary of state, Dean Rusk, hastily wired embassies in Moscow, London, Paris, and Vienna to inform them that the U.S. was ready to export the NTSC colour TV technology to the Soviet Union.

But it was too late to court the Soviets. In 1965, Moscow officially embraced SECAM by signing an accord with France. The Franco-Soviet colour-TV accord, while today erased from the annals of international diplomacy, was given the grandiose treatment of a monumentally significant event between the two countries. The bilateral deal entailed a straightforward trade-off. Thanks to the Kremlin's cooperation, France would gain a captive export market for its colour-TV standard in the Soviet Union and throughout Soviet-controlled Eastern Europe. The Soviets, for their part, would share the credit for "inventing" SECAM. Thus, a double agenda was simultaneously served: France's national industrial grandeur was given a badly needed boost, while the Soviets were able to create the impression that they were on the leading edge in the high-tech sector. In March 1965, France's Gaullist minister of Information, Alain Peyrefitte, proudly declared that the Franco-Soviet accord marked a "glorious day for the human race."[6]

The United States, irked by the Franco-Soviet accord, quickly made common cause with Germany to sandbag SECAM in Western Europe. As part of a U.S. counter-strategy, NTSC and Germany's PAL standard were merged to create a single colour-TV technology called QUAM—for "Quadrature Amplitude Modulation." The U.S.–German manoeuvre succeeded in thwarting France's industrial aims in Europe. Henceforth, France would have to settle for export markets in Russia, Soviet Bloc countries, and the Third World.

Undeterred, the French government pursued high-level diplomatic efforts to sell SECAM technology to other friendly countries, including Iraq, Egypt, Iran, and Lebanon. To make their sales pitch more persuasive, the French strategy frequently linked the sale of French Mirage fighter jets to the adoption of SECAM. In 1974, French prime minister Jacques Chirac—who later would become France's head of state—visited Iraq to preside officially over the signing of industrial and military contracts worth some $3 billion, including the construction of a petro-chemical plant and military hospital. During that meeting, Chirac warmly embraced a rising Iraqi political figure called Saddam Hussein. Iraq had earlier decided to adopt the PAL standard, but the prospect of French-made armaments made the Iraqis reconsider. Suddenly, they were persuaded by the superior technological virtues of the SECAM standard. Iraq reversal was a diplomatic "gift" to France. Chirac's tour of the Middle East was not over. In Iran, he convinced the Shah to adopt SECAM despite the Iranian government's official preference for PAL. Once again, politics prevailed over other considerations. The Shah's reversal could be explained by his personal friendship with French President Valéry Giscard d'Estaing. Giscard d'Estaing, in fact, had personally intervened in the matter, insisting to the Shah that Iran's adoption of SECAM would be received in France as a sign of the "special relationship" between the two countries.

Despite these diplomatic successes, France's grand industrial plans for SECAM failed against the NTSC standard. SECAM, was, in effect, a non-tariff barrier aimed at protecting France's domestic television industry and securing an export market for French industrial champions. The strategy worked only partially. In the final analysis, the existence of three rival colour-TV standards—NTSC, SECAM, PAL—produced unnecessary confusion in the international television market.

In the 1980s, the advent of "high definition" television—or HDTV—set the stage for yet another Byzantine saga of geopolitical rivalry. In 1986, Japan developed an HDTV technology called MUSE, which was compatible with the NTSC colour TV standard. The Europeans, led again by France, vigorously opposed MUSE. Major European manufacturers, notably French-controlled Thomson and Dutch-owned Philips, had ambitious HDTV plans of their own. European industrial champions knew that the commercial adoption of an HDTV standard would have billion-dollar ramifications for the manufacture of high-definition TV sets. At the same time, French President François Mitterrand called on Europe to develop a high-tech strategy to counter U.S. President Reagan's so-called "Star Wars" military project. A European HDTV standard would be at the center of that strategy.

France cobbled together a European HDTV consortium sponsored by the European Commission, which announced a billion-dollar subsidy package for a new HDTV program called "EUREKA." In the United States, meanwhile, regulators decided to take a hands-off approach towards HDTV. This was partially dictated by unavoidable realities: There were no longer any major U.S. manufacturers of TV sets. The United States had retreated from that sector. For this reason alone, HDTV offered little strategic advantage to the U.S. consumer electronics industry. Still, U.S. regulators shrewdly understood that the massive size of the American domestic market would be sufficient to give America tremendous clout in the selection of an HDTV standard. Any media mogul with global ambitions in the television industry would feel compelled to adopt standards compatible with U.S. market demands. It was for this reason that, in Europe, broadcasters such as Rupert Murdoch's BSkyB satellite service refused, despite billions in subsidies, to accept a European Commission-imposed HDTV standard.

Murdoch was proved right. In 1993, the European Commission abandoned its EUREKA project altogether. Market forces, not political fiats, would determine which HDTV standard would be adopted in Europe. Billions in EC subsidies had been squandered on HDTV to promote European industrial champions. Now European manufacturers joined a wider HDTV consortium—called the "Grand Alliance"—whose standard would be commercially adopted in the United States. It would take several more years, however, before HDTV would resurface as a consumer electronics product.

By 2000, the HDTV saga had produced precious little after two decades of industrial lobbying, political jockeying, and massive government subsidies. The only lesson learned was that, for a technical standard to succeed globally, it must be adopted in America. → point

— anecdot that tries to show US is the only real testing ground for electronics

Hollywood and Global Prime Time

Since the birth of television in the late 1940s, Hollywood's relationship with the small screen has been ambiguous.

At first, Hollywood moguls were terrified that television would put them out of business. These fears were not entirely unfounded. Box-office receipts started to decline in the 1950s, forcing Hollywood to respond with new-fangled gimmicks such as "3-D glasses." Hollywood quickly realized, however, that television also presented opportunities. Television was an ideal showcase for movies following their initial box-office run. More importantly, Hollywood studios could diversify into making television programs.

As early as 1954, Disney began producing TV shows for ABC, and Columbia Pictures set up its own television production arm, Screen Gems. By the end of the decade, the major U.S. networks were turning to Hollywood as key program suppliers. By the 1960s, Hollywood-produced television programs were becoming popular in foreign markets, too. In 1961, Raymond Burr, the star of the TV courtroom drama *Perry Mason*, conducted a worldwide publicity tour that included countries such as Britain, Australia, France, Germany, and Sweden. The following year, a young actor called Clint Eastwood, who was starring in a CBS series called *Rawhide*, embarked on a publicity tour of Japan. Screen Gems produced *Rin Tin Tin*, a series starring a German shepherd dog, and was sold in more than 40 countries. It was even joked that, to promote foreign sales of the show, the dog could "bark in 17 different languages."

American television programs were so successful in foreign markets, in fact, that U.S. producers began pushing for the creation of a Hollywood-style cartel to act as a unified "State Department" to negotiate sales with foreign governments. Thus, the Television Program Export Association was born in 1960. Its first president was John McCarthy, who had been vice-president of Hollywood's Motion Picture Association of America before working in the U.S. State Department as director of the Office of Economic Affairs.

Like the Hollywood studios, the American television industry benefited from U.S. government financial assistance through programs such as the USIA's Informational Media Guaranty, which protected television exports from currency devaluations and blockages. The U.S. government guaranteed convertibility by ensuring payment to TV producers in dollars at favourable rates. But there was a quid pro quo: American television shows, before they could be exported, had to portray the United States "in a favourable light." The State Department also covered travel expenses for foreign television producers to visit the United States and see first-hand how American television shows were produced.

State Department-sponsored exchanges with neighbouring Canada were not necessary, of course, since English-speaking Canadians already watched American television programs directly on U.S. networks. Excluding Canada's French-speaking minority, the Canadian broadcasting landscape had been Americanized from the beginning of television in the late 1940s. The state-owned CBC network was created in 1952, but even it aired many American programs. Only severe ownership restrictions prevented the Canadian television industry from becoming completely American-controlled. The Canadian government—pressured by nationalistic élites—adopted regulations aimed at limiting the cultural impact of American television. Canadian nationalism was surging in the 1960s, and many intellectuals and politicians looked upon American cultural influence with suspicion and disdain. In 1967, the year of Canada's centennial anniversary, the country's culture minister, Judy LaMarsh, remarked: "I just don't think it's good enough to sit around all evening and let the culture of another country pour into your ears and eyes." In reality, however, there was little distinction between the American and Canadian audiovisual spheres. Canadians watched American television as if the programs were their own. Many Canadian actors—such as Lorne Greene in *Bonanza* and

William Shatner in *Star Trek*—gained global fame working in the U.S. television industry.

Australia, though much farther from the United States than Canada, was similarly awash in American TV shows throughout the 1950s and 1960s. But, as in Canada, popular taste for American shows did not always sit well with Australian élites. Local television unions, too, felt threatened by the massive presence of American shows on the tube. The Actors' Equity lobbied the government to impose quotas and other measures to stem the tide of American programs. In 1958, American domination of Australian television was sufficiently contentious to become an issue in the country's national elections. The Labour Party vowed to impose a strict quota on U.S. television imports. But Australian voters were not moved by Labour's electoral promise. The Liberal Party triumphantly returned to power. The quota issue persisted, however, as Australian-made programs increasingly vacated prime-time slots to make way for American imports. In Sydney, the *Sunday Telegraph* offered an explanation: "Few people watched the homebrew shows when they had the alternative of watching the world's best." *Variety* made a similar observation from its not unbiased vantage point of California: "The average Aussie viewer prefers imported fare with No. 1 preference to the American brand."

[margin note: Foreigner prefers US]

In the 1960s, the emergence of private Australian TV stations brought competition to the market, which increased inflows of American programs. As in Canada, the economics of television production was the underlying reason for American domination of Aussie TV screens: Australian broadcasters could buy a U.S. show for a tiny fraction of the cost to produce a similar homemade program. This didn't prevent Australian television stations from attempting to establish a cartel vis-à-vis U.S. program suppliers to hold down the price of American television shows. But the Aussie cartel fell apart when an upstart media baron called Rupert Murdoch made a foray into local television in Adelaide and began bulk-buying American programs. At the time, Murdoch's Australian television operations were allied to the international division of the U.S. network, ABC.

[margin note: But really what marketplace becomes most effective]

In Britain, the situation was decidedly more complicated. Like viewers in Canada and Australia, average Britons enjoyed watching imported American shows like *I Love Lucy, Dragnet,* and *What's My Line?* The British government, however, was concerned that acquisitions of American television shows were adversely affecting Britain's balance of payments. This was precisely the same issue that, in the late 1940s, had triggered the British government's efforts to limit imports of Hollywood movies. In the mid-1950s, a Labour MP rose in the House of Commons to express his astonishment that the publicly owned BBC, aping the commercial strategies of its private rivals, had fallen into the habit of airing "many rubbishy American films which are a complete waste of money." Harold Macmillan, the Chancellor of the Exchequer—and future Prime Minister—was forced to admit, somewhat embarrassed, that the BBC and ITV were indeed spending $4 million a year on the acquisition of American television programs. At the time, $4 million was a not inconsiderable sum. Another Labour MP remarked wryly that $4 million was "rather a large sum of money for the sake of getting *Hopalong Cassidy*." In London, the *Daily Express* grumbled about Britain's private ITV stations: "Do they imagine that commercial TV was brought into being here in order to turn our children into little Americans?"[7]

American television enjoyed some political support in Britain. Sir Robert Fraser, head of the Independent Television Authority regulatory body, warned against "anti-American" demagoguery. "And remember this," he said to his critics, "Americans have acquired such a mastery of TV film techniques that we can apply no better stimulus to our producers than to let them see how it is done."

Fraser had put his finger on the real issue. As in Canada and Australia, anti-American attitudes in the British media found their origin in the mix of interests of cultural élites and trade unions. The Association of Cinematograph, Television, and Allied Technicians had successfully lobbied for an 86 percent British-content quota to counter the "ever increasing amount of American material" on the BBC and ITV stations. By the late 1950s, however, there were renewed complaints that many "British" programs were either U.S. co-productions or shows that, while they starred British actors, were written and directed by Americans. British unions, moreover, were exasperated that U.S. television networks showed little interest in buying British programs for their domestic American market.

By the early 1960s, more than a dozen British unions had formed an ad hoc lobby called the Radio and Television Safeguards Committee, which in 1961 issued a report castigating a "deplorable tendency towards Americanization." The group also called for "safeguards against the domination of the

[margin handwritten note: oppositions from élites + trade unions]

British airwaves and British screens by a foreign ethos." Targeting Britain's private ITV stations, the unions observed: "They have done much to advertise the American, rather than the British, way of life." A year later, the British government's Pilkington Committee on Broadcasting submitted its final report, which echoed the anti-American sentiment of the U.K. trade unions. While the Pilkington Report praised the non-commercial BBC, the privately owned ITV stations were criticized as "vapid" and "cheaply sensational"— epithets that, as everyone knew at the time, were code words for "American." British–American commercial tensions over television programs had become so sensitive that Washington decided to act. State Department officials met with John McCarthy, the head of the U.S. Television Program Export Association, before he held emergency negotiations in London to defuse the looming crisis. In the end, British production unions—through the imposition of the 14 percent ceiling on foreign imports—largely succeeded in resisting the dreaded Americanization of U.K. television.

In 1967, Jack Valenti became president of the powerful Hollywood lobby. One of his first diplomatic targets was the British television quota. GATT negotiations aimed at liberalizing international trade were entering their final stages, and Valenti saw an opportunity to pressure the British to relax their stringent quota blocking U.S. television imports. But the British production unions had tremendous clout with Harold Wilson's Labour government. In the end, Valenti's campaign failed: the 14 percent import ceiling was maintained. Similar quotas were adopted in Canada and Australia, but proved either unworkable or unenforceable. In Britain, however, the effectiveness of the 86 percent minimum quota on U.K. programs was due to the enormous clout of British trade unions. The U.S. State Department adamantly opposed the U.K. quotas, but diplomatic pressures failed to dissuade Harold Wilson's Labour government—the same Harold Wilson who, as trade minister two decades earlier, had fought Hollywood and lost. Faced with British intransigence, McCarthy's TPEA changed tactics. The U.S. television lobby began demanding higher fees for popular U.S. television series, which in the 1960s included *Batman*, *Mod Squad*, and *The Fugitive*. British television would continue to be dominated by the public-private duopoly of highly unionized BBC and ITV stations, which acted as an effective cartel. The liberalization of British television would have to await Thatcherism in the 1980s.

Jack Valenti was more successful at twisting arms in the familiar precincts of Washington. In the late 1960s, the so-called "Big Three" television networks—CBS, NBC, and ABC—were capturing more than 90 percent of the American viewing audience. As a quasi-cartel, the Big Three exercised tremendous gatekeeper power over any non-affiliated television producers seeking to get their shows on the air. The Hollywood studios resented the Big Three's market power. But Valenti shrewdly saw an opportunity, via federal regulations, to strengthen Hollywood's role as a major supplier of network TV programs. Valenti argued before the Federal Communications Commission that the Big Three were exploiting their market power by self-dealing programs produced by their own production arms. Valenti called on the FCC to open up network TV schedules to unaffiliated producers—namely, to the Hollywood studios.

U.S. regulators agreed. In 1970, the FCC forced the networks—through "Financial and Syndication" rules—to air programs supplied by non-affiliated producers. What's more, the FCC imposed rules that prohibited the Big Three from monopolizing foreign sales of the programs they aired in the domestic U.S. market. The FCC restricted the networks to selling foreign rights only to programs they produced themselves. Valenti had hit the jackpot. The combined effect of these FCC rulings opened up two hugely lucrative markets to the Hollywood studios: U.S. network television at home, and foreign television rights abroad. Valenti's triumph marked the consummation of Hollywood's long love affair with the television industry.

By the mid-1970s, there were only five countries on the planet that did not broadcast any American television shows: China, North Korea, North Vietnam, Albania, and Mongolia. All were communist. The most receptive markets to American television, not surprisingly, were Anglo-American: Canada, Britain, Australia, and New Zealand. Television audiences in these countries were as familiar as Americans with *M*A*S*H*, *All in the Family*, and *The Mary Tyler Moore Show*. There were complaints, of course, that the U.S. networks were not reciprocally open to imports from their Anglo-American cultural allies. Even hugely popular British shows—such as *Monty Python's Flying Circus* and *Fawlty Towers*—were snubbed by the U.S. networks. These shows, along with *Masterpiece Theatre*, were broadcast on America's publicly financed network, PBS.

While it was true that the U.S. networks were effectively closed to foreign imports, they were nonetheless receptive to Americanizing concepts that worked in other countries. *All in the Family*, for example, was inspired by Britain's BBC series *Till Death Us Do Part*. Also, the popular U.S. series *Sanford and Son* was based on the hit British series, *Steptoe and Son*. Another British sitcom, *Man About the House*, was transformed into *Three's Company* on U.S. network television. This form of cultural cross-pollination continued, in the United States and elsewhere, throughout the 1980s and 1990s. Television series in many countries took inspiration from British and Australian shows, especially in the "soap opera" genre. The long-running Australian soap *The Restless Years* produced numerous offspring in several languages. Another Australian soap, *Sons and Daughters*, was readapted in Germany as *Verbotene Liebe* and in Sweden as *Skilda Varlder*. The German series *Lindenstrasse* was based on the British soap, *Coronation Street*, which first aired in Britain in 1960. Another German soap, *Gute Zeiten, Schlechte Zeiten*, was inspired by the Australian series, *Good Times, Bad Times*. In Spain and Portugal, the most popular prime-time television dramas were frequently imported from former colonies, Mexico and Brazil.[8]

The Latin American market presented a unique challenge for the U.S. television industry. Latin America was generally open to American-style commercial television due to widespread rejection, or marginalization, of state-owned broadcasting. The United States had played an instrumental role—especially through organizations like the Inter-American Association of Broadcasting—in establishing commercial television as the predominant model throughout the region. At the same time, however, television audiences manifested a strong appetite for "Latin" television programming, which strengthened the Latin American television industry.

Critics of American cultural imperialism might be surprised to discover that Latin America—though frequently regarded as a victim of American domination—is itself an imperial power in television. The region's two most populous countries—Brazil and Mexico—have each produced broadcasting powerhouses that today are global in scope, ambition, and influence. In Brazil, Globo—founded by Roberto Marinho, director of the Rio de Janeiro newspaper, *O Globo*—is a media giant capable of toppling and installing political leaders. In 1964, Globo played an instrumental role in the downfall of reformist—and anti-American—President Joao Goulart and the installation of a military dictatorship. Globo enjoyed the military regime's favour because its escapist "entertainment" programs were regarded as a powerful opiate for the masses. Also, Globo's role in binding together a regionally diverse country served the dictatorship's goal of imposing modernization and centralization.

Globo's influence eventually became threatening. In 1980, Brazil's military government moved to break up its monopoly and divide its licences among new rivals. This provoked Marinho to use his TV network to support a civilian candidate, José Sarney Costa, in Brazil's presidential elections of 1985. With Globo's backing, Sarney won. It was once said that Brazilian society is buttressed by four pillars: the Church, the Army, the Communist Party, and Globo—and, it was invariably added, "the greatest of all is Globo."[9]

By far the most popular form of television distraction throughout Latin America is the *tele-novela*. A hybrid genre combining the narrative techniques of American soap operas and mini-series, *tele-novelas* are indigenous to Latin American culture. While inspired by American television forms, *tele-novelas* convey traditional "Latin" values. And they attract huge audiences. One Brazilian *tele-novela*, *A Próxima Vitima*, once boasted a 100 percent share of the nation's television audience—or about 40 million viewers. A classic Brazilian *tele-novela* was Globo's *The Right to be Born*—sponsored by Colgate-Palmolive—about the relationship of a poor wet nurse and a wealthy family. When the series finished its run in 1964, some 25,000 Brazilians gathered in a Rio stadium to honour the show's stars in a mass ceremony of public adulation.[10]

Mexican *tele-novelas* are not only popular throughout Latin America, but dubbed versions have won audiences in unlikely places, including the Moslem world. Today, Mexico boasts the most powerful broadcasting industry in the Spanish-speaking world. Mexican television is dominated by the private Televisa network. Globo cannot rival Televisa as a dominant regional player in Latin America due to a simple linguistic reality: Brazilians speak Portuguese, while most of Latin America is Spanish-speaking. Some Globo *tele-novelas*, such as *O Bem Amado*, have been successful in Latin America in dubbed versions. But Globo has turned to other international markets for its *tele-novelas*—especially Portugal and its colonies in Africa. In the Spanish-speaking television market, Mexico is a cultural imperialist.

Despite the power of Brazil's Globo and Mexico's Televisa, the presence of U.S. media companies in Latin America cannot be overlooked. As early as the 1950s, the U.S. networks were making direct investments in Latin America television. In the 1960s, Time-Life invested in Globo, though it was obliged later to divest its stake due to Brazil's ownership restrictions. ABC was the most active U.S. network in Latin America, partnering with a Mexican program producer headed by Miguel Alemán Velasco, son of a former Mexican president. Global advertising agencies, such as J. Walter Thompson, also moved into the region and brought with them the American soap-opera model of advertising-commissioned shows. In Brazil, U.S.–style sponsoring was pervasive on television, with shows such as *Cine Max Factor*. There was, it is true, some negative cultural reaction to American-style television. In Brazil, the government passed a decree in 1963 banning prime-time television shows that showed "police events of any nature, the Far West, or sex." Globo, for its part, began strengthening its ties to the United States through programming deals with Time Warner and Disney. Globo also sold a minority stake in its cable TV business to Microsoft. Televisa, meanwhile, expanded into cable TV with Cablevisión, which offered a variety of American channels including a local version of Home Box Office.

But it's not a cultural one-way street. Today, there are three major Hispanic television networks—Univision, Telemundo, and Azteca America—operating in the United States, whose Spanish-speaking population is expected to reach more than 40 million by 2010. Univision, the biggest of the three, features TV shows—including *tele-novelas*—that draw more viewers than the major U.S. networks. With some 25 stations throughout the United States, Univision carries the programs of the Mexican network, Televisa. Univision is controlled by Venezuelan media tycoon, Gustavo Cisneros, a personal friend and fishing companion of former U.S. President George Bush. Cisneros, who was educated in the United States, was reportedly behind the short-lived coup against populist Venezuelan leader, Hugo Chavez. The second network, Telemundo, was originally owned by a consortium including Sony and AT&T, but NBC later bought it for $2 billion. Azteca America—a joint venture with Mexico's TV Azteca—was launched to compete with Univision and Telemundo[If America dominated the world's television screens, at home its TV screens were open to foreign influences.] → no really proven

→ another important point

By the 1980s, American television shows such as *Dallas* and *Dynasty* blanketed the planet. Critics of American cultural imperialism complained of "wall-to-wall *Dallas*." But claims about the noxious influence of American television were contestable. For one thing, there was little evidence that international audiences interpreted shows like *Dallas* in the same way. Also, as numerous examples of cultural cross-pollination demonstrated, direct importation of TV programs was supplemented by the adaptation of foreign television shows to local cultural realities. Even game shows, such as *Wheel of Fortune*, were transformed into local versions in dozens of countries—including in culturally hyper-sensitive France. As the influence of Hispanic television in the U.S. demonstrated, cultural influence via television was diverse, complex, and multi-layered. American television nonetheless was a powerful global export commodity, and would find even readier access to foreign markets thanks to new technologies such as satellite TV, privatization of state television networks, and deregulation of national broadcasting landscapes in the 1980s.

The main beneficiary of these trends was Hollywood, which increasingly could count on revenues from foreign markets. In the domestic U.S. market, the Hollywood majors won a stunning regulatory victory in Washington in the early 1990s. After two decades, the Federal Communications Commission deregulated ownership restrictions that had prevented movie studios and TV networks from merging. Suddenly, Hollywood studios were free to buy their own TV networks. And that's precisely what they did. Disney bought ABC, Paramount took control of CBS, Twentieth Century Fox owned Fox TV, and Time Warner controlled The WB network. By the mid-1990s, only NBC—owned by industrial giant General Electric—was without a Hollywood parent. With the completion of these mega-mergers, Jack Valenti's power was considerably reinforced. He spoke not just for the Hollywood studios; the interests of U.S. network television, too, were now part of Valenti's "State Department" approach to Hollywood's international strategy.

One of Valenti's first battles on the television front was against his *bête noire*, the European Commission. The EC had drafted a "Television Without Frontiers" directive that included a 60-percent minimum quota on European films and television programs. This pro-European quota had been inspired by France, where television producers benefited from massive state subsidies. France's objective was to secure European markets for

French television programs with a minimum degree of competition from Hollywood. Captured by France's agenda, the EC took the position that television programs were "cultural" and hence should be exempted from the terms of the GATT multilateral trade agreement. Washington, on the other hand, argued that movies and TV programs were "services"—and therefore should be captured by GATT.

Valenti assailed Europe's "Television Without Frontiers" policy as anathema to the American principle of free choice. Employing characteristically grandiloquent language, Valenti argued that the quota would do more harm to Hollywood than it would help European cinema: "Is a thousand, two thousand years of an individual nation's culture going to collapse because of the exhibition of American TV programs?" he asked. "The quota is there, it hangs with Damoclean ferocity over the future. And it will, in time, as its velocity increases, bite, wound and bleed the American television industry."

As usual, Valenti boasted support in high places in Washington. "The President of the United States, the secretary of state, the secretary of commerce, and the U.S. trade representative have all been supportive," he declared. "They have made it clear to the chancelleries of Europe that the imposition of this quota is an intolerable thing for the United States."

Within the EC, Valenti found a reliable ally in Britain, which resolutely opposed "Television Without Frontiers." Beyond cultural affinities, Britain had commercial reasons to support the American position. Unlike other European countries, Britain exported television programs to the United States. The public PBS network, in particular, acquired most of its *Masterpiece Theatre* drama programs—such as *Brideshead Revisited* and *Sons and Lovers*—from the United Kingdom. The British government could not be indifferent to the implied threat of an American boycott of British television shows. Britain's support was not sufficient, however, to soften the EC's resolve. In late 1993, the EC declared victory when its "cultural exception" was maintained in the GATT accord.

But if Jack Valenti lost the battle, he would win the war. At best, "Television Without Frontiers" was a temporary victory. In subsequent years, the EC policy was diluted and European television markets became, even more than previously, open to American imports. Parisian intellectuals would continue grumbling about the baffling popularity of *Columbo* and *Wheel of Fortune* among French television viewers.

Information Wars: Television News

"I learn more from CNN than I do from the CIA," George Bush *père* once remarked. That's quite a statement from the President of the United States—even more so given that Bush Sr., in a previous career, had been director of the Central Intelligence Agency.

Much has been written about the geopolitical influence of Cable News Network. Some praise CNN as a fearless crusader for freedom of information and liberal democracy. Others berate CNN as an agent of the U.S. State Department. Most world leaders, whatever they say in private about CNN, are eager to appear on the network, especially if they wish to send a message to Washington. In the mid-1990s, Boutros Boutros-Ghali, secretary-general of the United Nations, described CNN as the "sixteenth member" of the UN's fifteen-member Security Council.

The thought of Ted Turner sitting on the UN Security Council would alarm many, especially among those who know the unpredictable maverick. The flamboyant founder of CNN nonetheless has many admirers who would applaud his active role in world affairs. Turner, the champion of many altruistic causes—including global peace and world hunger—is an eccentric genius with a gambler's canny instinct for brilliant timing. He was the first American broadcaster to grasp the potential of satellites to send television signals to distant places. He also understood that U.S. television, dominated by the Big Three networks since the late 1940s, would increasingly become fragmented with the arrival of dozens of niche channels on cable TV. As Turner put it when addressing an audience of advertising executives in the late 1970s, there was no reason why television should be controlled by "three nincompoops in New York"—a dismissive reference to NBC, ABC, and CBS.

"Where you have idiots watching idiot shows, I guess you can sell them idiot products," Turner told the American Association of Advertising Agencies. "Not with us."[11]

Turner got his start in business after inheriting his father's billboard company, Turner Communications, which diversified into television in 1970 when it bought a money-losing Atlanta TV station, WGTC. By the end of the 1970s, the station—egocentrically rebaptized WTBS for "Turner Broadcasting System"—had expanded beyond its local market. It was now a national "superstation" whose signal—offering a package of old movies and syndicated TV series—was beamed via satellite to cable systems throughout the United States. Emboldened by WTBS's success, Turner struck upon an even bigger idea: A round-the-clock, all-news network that would be beamed via satellite to the entire planet.

When CNN debuted in June 1980—in the middle of America's foreign policy débâcle in Iran—the network was immediately dismissed as amateurish and few believed it would survive. The cold numbers certainly looked bad: CNN counted only 1.7 million subscribers in the United States and was losing $2 million a month. Critics scoffed that CNN stood for "Chicken Noodle Network." But CNN persevered, and quickly expanded globally, starting in Europe in the mid-1980s. By the end of the decade, a succession of cataclysmic world events—the fall of the Berlin Wall, the collapse of the Soviet Union, the San Francisco earthquake, Tiananmen Square—made CNN an indispensable source of live, breaking news around the globe. CNN's big break, however, came in 1991 with the Gulf War. That global conflict indelibly put CNN on the map as the planet's most powerful information conduit. → in the West

"I don't think there is any question that we are the world's number one provider of television news," asserted Turner. "More than any other TV and radio news entity, CNN has a global reach and a global mission."

CNN's global influence, to be sure, attracted persistent criticism. During the first Gulf War, CNN was castigated for airing pre-censored raw video footage obtained directly from the Pentagon's Military Joint Information Bureau. Yet, at the same time, CNN took heat for broadcasting uninterrupted speeches by Iraqi dictator Saddam Hussein. Responding to the network's detractors, CNN president Tom Johnson stated: "Our goal at CNN is neither to assist, nor to inhibit the diplomats of any country as they seek a solution for this or any other crisis. It is our goal to provide fair and balanced reporting of all news and all views that are relevant to the events of the day." Turner, for his part, was characteristically cockier when confronted with questions about journalistic ethics: "What is news? You know what news is? News is what we at CNN interpret it as."

Turner's assertion, however smug, accurately described how news-gathering services had operated since the birth of international news agencies in the mid-19th century. They had always filtered the "news" through their own particular political and cultural biases—to say nothing of the economic interests of their home countries. Whatever their national origin, news agencies served a double function. First, the journalistic function of reporting news for their commercial clients: newspapers. Second, the strategic function of gathering information to be used by the imperial powers with which they were aligned.]

news Bias

The first international news agency was French. In 1835, when the liberal-minded King Louis-Philippe ruled France, Charles-Louis Havas founded the news agency Agence Havas. By the 1850s, during Napoleon III's Second Empire Havas faced competition from two rival European agencies. In Germany, the Continental Telegraphen Compagnie—known as the Wolff Agency—had been created in 1849. In London, Reuter Telegram Company—or Reuters—had followed two years later in 1851. Thus, by the mid-19th century Europe's three major powers—France, Germany, and Britain—each had its own news agency transmitting financial data and news via telegraph and cable.

For more than a decade, the three agencies competed aggressively. But in the late 1860s they settled on an arrangement that suited their mutual interests. Henceforth, each agency would concentrate its news-gathering resources in its respective sphere of political and cultural influence. Thus, Reuters would focus on the British Empire and the Far East; Havas would cover the French Empire and Latin countries such as Italy and Spain; and Wolff gained exclusive rights to operate in Germany, Austria, Russia, and Scandinavia. This cartel arrangement was formalized with the signing of the Agency Alliance Treaty. In effect, these three European agencies carved up the world according to the geopolitical interests of their political masters. While the agencies were nominally independent, in reality they served the trade, diplomatic, and political interests of their imperial sponsors. As journalistic vehicles for cultural diplomacy, the correspondents for Havas, Reuters, and Wolff were generally regarded as quasi-diplomats who served the interest of their home countries. In political circles, these linkages were taken for granted. Bismarck, for example, bitterly resented the influence of Havas. During the First World War, the head of Reuters, Sir Roderick Jones, also served as Director of Propaganda in the British Department of Information.[12]

As the United States emerged as a world power circa 1900, America felt the need to have its own international news agency. Associated Press, it is true, had been founded in 1848 by six New York newspapers, but it was little more than a junior member of the European news cartel. In 1906, press baron William Randolph Hearst founded the International News Service, and the following year publisher E.W. Scripps created the United Press Association to compete with AP. It wasn't until after the First World War, however, that AP and UPA expanded their operations internationally. One of AP's first geopolitical incursions into the territory of the big European news agencies was its entry into Latin America, a region that been strategically important to U.S. foreign policy since the "Monroe Doctrine."

Not surprisingly, the fortunes of news agencies rose and declined with those of the imperial powers they served. When London and Paris stood imperiously at the center of world affairs, Reuters and Havas were major forces in international news-gathering. But their influence waned as the British and French empires declined in the 20th century. The outcome of the two world wars produced particularly devastating effects on the prestige of news agencies. Berlin-based Wolff saw its prestige irreparably suffer with Germany's defeats in 1918 and 1945. Havas, too, had become an unfortunate victim of fascism. In 1940, France's pro-Nazi Vichy regime took control of Havas to use the agency for propaganda purposes. After the war, the stigma associated with the Havas name was such that Agence France-Presse (AFP) emerged from its ashes. But AFP also fell under quasi-state control. During the Fourth Republic in the 1950s, a young French minister of the Interior, François Mitterrand, was personally appointed the head of AFP. Three decades later, Mitterrand—installed in the Elysée Palace—was still providing state funding for AFP. Neither did Mitterrand neglect to appoint his political friends to senior executive positions within the French news agency. AFP, like Reuters, continued to regard itself as a major international news agency, though in truth its glory had faded with the collapse of France's imperial ambitions. AFP nonetheless continued to devote most of its coverage to France's former colonial sphere of influence. Reuters, for its part, transformed itself into a financial information service. As geopolitical forces, however, both had been eclipsed by the rise of American rivals.

The world's most famous post-imperial media system was the British Broadcasting Corporation. Created in 1922, the BBC quickly became a cherished radio voice that informed Britons of events in their far-flung Empire. The BBC's "Empire Service" began in 1932 with a short-wave radio service, thus extending its technological reach into the colonies. That year, King George V became the first British monarch to address the entire Empire in a BBC radio broadcast. The king's radio address was written, fittingly, by imperialist author Rudyard Kipling, famous for his poem, "White Man's Burden." Shortly before the Second World War, the BBC Empire Service—a forerunner of BBC World Service—began radio broadcasts throughout Europe in several languages—French, German, Italian, Portuguese, and Spanish. By the end of the Second World War, the BBC was broadcasting in some 50 languages. There was some irony in the BBC's imperial pretensions: its Empire Service was expanding at precisely the moment the British Empire was in rapid decline. Even after the British Empire had effectively collapsed, the BBC continued to promote an elitist corporate culture associated with Britain's imperialist past. It has even been suggested that, paradoxically, the BBC was partly responsible for Britain's decline as an imperial power. Since the BBC recruited the brightest and best from Oxbridge, British élites were no longer attracted to the civil service—in particular, the Foreign and Colonial Services.

In the United States, with its free-market ethos, most media, including news organizations, were privately owned. But the U.S. government found a rationale for state financing when ideological wars were being fought. The State Department created Voice of America a few months after the Japanese attack on Pearl Harbor in 1941. Following the war, Voice of America—whose motto was "telling America's story abroad"—became the State Department's official Cold War broadcasting weapon, producing programs in some 50 different languages. In the 1950s the U.S. government created Radio Liberty to target the Soviet Union, which had its own propaganda news agency, TASS. Radio Free Europe, for its part, aimed its broadcasts at Soviet Bloc countries in Eastern Europe. Based in Munich, both Radio Liberty and Radio Free Europe were covertly funded by the CIA. If their financing was secret, their mission was unambiguous: the destabilization, dismantling, and destruction of Soviet-style communism. A measure of their effectiveness was the considerable effort by the Soviets and other Eastern Bloc countries to jam signals spilling over their borders from U.S.-backed "Liberty" broadcasters.

In the early 1980s, President Reagan announced a soft-power offensive called Project Democracy. Fittingly, President Reagan unveiled Project

Democracy in a speech delivered in the British Parliament at the invitation of his conservative ally Margaret Thatcher. The U.S. initiative, part of America's "war of ideas" offensive, was aimed at fighting Soviet propaganda by spreading American values in favour of democracy and capitalism. In Latin America, a region targeted by Project Democracy, the Reagan administration created an Hispanic broadcasting service, Radio Martì. In 1985, Radio Martì began transmitting radio programs into Cuba from the Florida Keys. Five years later, TV Martì added television programs to its anti-communist offensive. The combined efforts of Radio/TV Martì were a source of constant irritation to Fidel Castro, whose government worked tirelessly to jam their signals. In 1997, Radio/TV Martì's headquarters were relocated from Washington to the Miami offices of the State Department's United States Information Agency, a move that further incensed Castro since the USIA's broadcasting outfit was closely linked to the anti-Castro Cuban-American National Foundation. The USIA had previously launched a television service with more global aspirations: Worldnet, which spread American values internationally by making program packages available to TV stations and cable TV channels. To avoid stigma of straight propaganda, Worldnet sometimes mixed its own programs with mainstream news shows, such as PBS's *NewsHour with Jim Lehrer*.

Throughout the Third World, autocratic regimes hostile to democracy and capitalism intensely resented the global domination of Western newsgathering operations. Many of these regimes found an institutional ally in UNESCO, which in the 1970s had become an ideological vehicle for protests against the so-called "Free Flow Doctrine" advocated by the United States. As a counter-measure against Western domination of information flows, UNESCO attempted to establish news agencies in Third World countries, such as Pan-African News Agency and the Non-Aligned News Agencies Pool. But these organizations lacked resources and could do little more than edit reports from Western sources. Throughout the 1970s, UNESCO—under the leadership of Senegal-born Amadou-Mahtar M'Bow—grew increasingly anti-Western.

UNESCO's anti-Western crusade culminated in 1980 with the publication of its MacBride Report—officially titled *Many Voices, One World*—which denounced Western control of global information flows. Heavily involved in the report's drafting was a top Soviet official, Sergei Losev, who

Marxist enemy

UNESCO

at the time was director of TASS. The MacBride Report marked a euphoric moment for Third World regimes and Marxist intellectuals who had long been vehemently critical of American cultural imperialism. Now their doctrinaire anti-American rhetoric had an official UNESCO-sanctioned manifesto. It even gave birth to yet another anti-Western buzzword: "news imperialism."

By the mid-1980s, UNESCO had successfully spread its anti-American mantra throughout the West. These efforts were aided by the proselytizing efforts of a left-leaning, jet-setting priesthood of government bureaucrats, university academics, and ideologically like-minded journalists who socially mingled and professionally networked at UNESCO-financed conferences that invariably concluded with "manifestos" vilifying American cultural imperialism. By historical serendipity, UNESCO's agenda found a convenient ally in the pervasive ideology of political correctness. In this newly radicalized intellectual climate of the 1980s, the imperialist culprit was no longer America alone. The sins of the entire course of Western civilization were now on trial. The West—from Plato to NATO—stood accused as a racist, sexist, imperialist monoculture created and propagated by Dead White Males. In truth, UNESCO's New World Information and Communications Order concealed an anti-liberal political agenda that was hardly surprising. Many of the Third World countries that found a voice within UNESCO were ruled by totalitarian states with little interest in democracy or free expression.

In Washington, the White House was running out of patience with UNESCO. The Reagan administration regarded the UN agency as a bloated bureaucracy that, despite its professed educational mission, had degenerated into a hotbed of leftist agitation and anti-American diatribe. Even more galling, the United States was UNESCO's main financial contributor. White House officials were incensed that Amadou-Mahtar M'Bow was taking American money to finance UNESCO's incessant campaign of denigration against the United States and the West. In 1984, the United States pulled the plug on UNESCO. Margaret Thatcher, showing solidarity with President Reagan, likewise pulled Britain out of UNESCO the following year.

M'Bow, faced with a huge funding shortfall following the U.S. and U.K. withdrawals, took the extraordinary—and somewhat comical—step of suing the United States to enforce its financial contributions. The gesture, dismissed by Washington as "legal nonsense," went nowhere. But M'Bow persisted in his attacks against the United States, claiming the Reagan administration was exploiting UNESCO to play hardball with the United Nations.

"Some people have sought to make the failings of the UN system responsible for the most flagrant flaws in international relations," said M'Bow.

M'Bow failed to see the writing on the wall. For one thing, his own leadership at UNESCO was troubled by persistent rumours about his personal conduct. M'Bow was a notorious autocrat who—during his long UNESCO tenure in the 1970s and 1980s—never let his hostility towards capitalist America to interfere with his personal taste for a lavish lifestyle. Like most autocrats, he immensely enjoyed the perquisites of power and stubbornly refused to leave office. After thirteen years, his second term was due to expire in 1986, but he suddenly announced that he would seek an "unprecedented" third term as UNESCO's director-general. But the Anglo-American alliance would have none of it. After a series of tense backroom manoeuvres, M'Bow's bid to stay at the helm of the UNESCO boondoggle failed. A compromise candidate, Spaniard Federico Mayor Zaragoza, was elected to the post. The Soviet Union's collapse a few years later delivered another blow to the UNESCO clique. The UN cultural agency realized that its Marxist-inspired crusade against America was irredeemably out of fashion. UNESCO officially disavowed its doctrinaire campaign against American "cultural imperialism."

With the end of the Cold War, the U.S. government felt less compelled to deploy enormous financial resources to operate international broadcasting facilities to fight communism. Some countries were still considered nuisance targets—notably Cuba and North Korea—but Voice of America and other State Department broadcasters were no longer seen as critical soft-power instruments of U.S. foreign policy. At the same time, coincidentally, CNN was rapidly becoming America's window on the world. CNN thrived on international military conflicts. Indeed, the network's unofficial motto was: "Oh, what a lovely war!" Margaret Thatcher had provided CNN with its first war in the Falkland Islands. President Reagan, too, provided CNN with military interventions in Latin America, plus a dramatic bombing of Libya. Then came the first Gulf War in 1991. When American bombs rained down on Baghdad under cover of dark, the entire planet— including leaders in the Arab world—simultaneously watched the Pentagon's videogame-like images transmitted by CNN.

By the mid-1990s, few were scoffing at the "Chicken Noodle Network," which was now beamed globally via satellite to some 150 countries. CNN counted more than 3,000 employees worldwide—1,000 of them working in 42 foreign bureaus. CNN was frequently criticized, it is true, for presenting a jingoistic American perspective of global affairs. International viewers, it was said, learned more about America than they did about their own countries or other foreign nations. Ted Turner, who envisioned CNN as a truly global network, was not insensitive to this criticism. To remedy this perception, Turner made cosmetic changes to CNN newscasts. The word "foreign" was banned from all CNN news reports. Turner also took structural measures, such as the creation of a dedicated global network, CNN International, which was available, via a network of 23 satellites, to roughly 160 million households worldwide.

Ironically, just when Ted Turner seemed to have conquered the planet, CNN found itself in a deep crisis. The main threat was competition from rival news networks with similarly global aspirations. BBC World already existed, but was now joined by Rupert Murdoch's Sky News. In Latin America, CBS had launched TeleNoticias. As a defensive strategey, CNN launched CNN en Español. In Europe, state-owned broadcasters had jointly created Euronews to sandbag CNN's growing presence on European TV screens. As *The Economist* put it: "After CNN won the Gulf War, European public-service broadcasters decided to combat American imperialism." At home in the United States, NBC and Microsoft teamed up in 1996 to launch a rival news network, MSNBC. Rupert Murdoch would soon follow with Fox News. CNN, once a pioneer in the all-news television business, now had many imitators—and competitors.[13]

In 1996, Turner made a decision that he would live to regret: he sold his entire broadcasting empire to media conglomerate Time Warner. Swallowed whole by one the world's biggest media giants, CNN was now merely one small division inside a corporate colossus with a huge stable of global brands that included Bugs Bunny, *Time* and *People* magazines, pop star Madonna, Home Box Office, and Warner Bros. Four years later, Time Warner itself would be taken over by America Online in the biggest media merger ever, creating AOL Time Warner. While these deals made Turner a billionaire, CNN was no longer under his control. Some began to question the future of the all-news network that Turner had built. By 2001, CNN appeared to be suffering from the effects of "imperial overstretch." Its influence had been declining since its glory days during the Gulf War, yet CNN was still maintaining expensive bureaus all over the world. Worse, CNN was becoming banal—a hotel television channel good for baseball scores and weather reports. In August 2001, *The Economist* published a damning article on CNN that asked: "Short of a war, what can revive the fortunes of CNN?"[14]

Osama bin Laden answered that question only a few weeks later. Al Qaeda's attacks on the United States thrust CNN back into the international spotlight as its images of the collapsing World Trade Center were beamed, live, to the entire planet. Within hours, CNN's star foreign correspondent, Christiane Amanpour, had flown to Afghanistan to cover the impending war. Amanpour conducted an exclusive interview with Pakistan's president, Gen. Pervez Musharraf, and later interviewed U.S. Defense Secretary Donald Rumsfeld. Iranian-born Amanpour was an interesting case study herself. Despite her journalistic celebrity, she embodied the direct linkages between American television and U.S. foreign policy: Her husband was James Rubin, who had been a top adviser to Secretary of State Madeleine Albright and, later, spokesman for the State Department. Those who argued that CNN was a broadcasting extension of the State Department could point, at least anecdotally, to the Rubin-Amanpour couple.

When the United States invaded Iraq in March 2003, millions of television viewers throughout the world again tuned into CNN to follow the conflict. This time, however, CNN had strong all-news rivals. At home in America, Fox News was attracting more viewers than CNN thanks to its populist and patriotic coverage of the war. In the Arab world, viewers could now turn to Al-Jazeera, a formerly unknown news network whose name was rapidly becoming familiar throughout America. Based in the tiny Persian Gulf emirate of Qatar, Al-Jazeera had been launched in 22 Arab countries in 1996 via satellite. In the Arab world, Al-Jazeera instantly became successful—and notorious—because it eschewed the established model of state-controlled Middle East broadcasters, which traditionally were sheepishly reverential to political and religious authorities. With Al-Jazeera, the Islamic world had its own CNN.

The birth of Al-Jazeera was the result of a bizarre saga that unfolded inside Qatar's royal palace. In 1995 the Emir of Qatar took a fateful holiday in Europe. His son, crown prince Sheik Hamad bin Khalifa al-Thani, seized on his father's absence to oust the Emir in a palace coup. Installed as Qatar's usurper Emir, the young reform-minded Sheik Hamad promptly set a new tone that was resolutely defiant of established customs. He shocked the region's other Moslem regimes, especially Saudi Arabia, by imposing sweeping top-down reforms, including the abolition of the Information Ministry, an end to censorship of newspapers and broadcasting, political rights for women, and municipal elections. The main thrust of Sheik Hamad's revolution, however, was the launch of Al-Jazeera. At that very moment, Britain's BBC was planning to make a foray into the Middle East by launching an Arabic news service on a Saudi-backed satellite system called Orbit. The Saudi-BBC venture suddenly fell apart, however. The Saudis—sensitive about criticism of Saudi Arabia's ruling family—refused to grant the BBC complete editorial independence. When the BBC refused to accept this condition, its contract with Orbit was cancelled. Sheik Hamad, freshly installed in Qatar's royal palace, couldn't believe his luck. He quickly hired the BBC journalists and technicians who had just lost their jobs in Saudi Arabia. It was this rump of BBC-trained journalists who played a key role in launching, with a $150 million start-up investment from Sheik Hamad, the Arab world's first Western-style television news channel.

Shortly after its debut in 1996, Al-Jazeera was reaching some 35 million Arabs who received the all-news network via satellite dishes. The dishes were soon sprouting like mushrooms throughout the Arab world—from sordid Cairo slums to opulent Dubai palaces. Even in the United States, some 150,000 Arab-speakers—and undoubtedly the U.S. government too—paid a monthly fee to the Dish Network to receive Al-Jazeera as part of a multi-channel "Arab package."

For his impudence, Sheik Hamad was ostracized within the Arab world. Some claimed the maverick Emir, despite his liberal appearances, had launched Al-Jazeera as a "nuisance factor" to gain small-state leverage vis-à-vis larger neighbours, notably Saudi Arabia. Others claimed Qatar was exploiting Al-Jazeera as a propaganda weapon in a territorial dispute with its Persian Gulf neighbour, Bahrain. Whatever Sheik Hamad's motives, Al-Jazeera's arrival was regarded throughout the Islamic world as a provocation—especially in countries like Iraq where satellite dishes were banned altogether. Many Iraqis furtively watched Al-Jazeera programs on smuggled videocassettes sold at local bazaars.

Al-Jazeera's main sin was its obvious emulation of CNN's aggressive reporting, fast-paced editing, and thirst for scoops. Al-Jazeera's Western format and tone shocked many sensibilities in the Islamic world, whose television networks traditionally had been servile, sycophantic, and self-censoring. Al-Jazeera, on the other hand, did not shrink from controversy. Its current affairs programs boasted titles such as *Akthar min Ra'i* (*More Than One Opinion*). A popular debate show, *Al-Ittijah al-Muaakis* (*The Opposite Direction*) was modelled on CNN's *Crossfire*, featuring free-for-all debates on contentious issues. But in the Middle East, a free exchange of ideas provoked the wrath of regimes unaccustomed to open debate and public criticism. Jordan, one of the most pro-Western regimes in the region, shut down Al-Jazeera's bureau in Amman after a commentator, while condemning Jordan's peace treaty with Israel, declared Jordan was populated by "a bunch of Bedouins living in an arid desert." Kuwait likewise shut down Al-Jazeera's local bureau after an Islamic militant, participating in a phone-in show, stated that Kuwait's ruler, Sheik Jaber al-Jaber al-Sabah, should be deposed for extending the vote in Kuwait to women. In May 2002, Qatar's neighbour, Bahrain, banned Al-Jazeera on the ludicrous pretext that its news reports on the Middle East crisis were "Zionist." If anything, Al-Jazeera, despite its American-style gloss, was known for its pro-Islamic bias.[15]

If Al-Jazeera has embraced a political view, it is pan-Arabism—a shrewd posture given the network's commercial aims in the Arab-speaking world. Also, the network's support of a pan-Arab sphere conveniently flatters the regional insecurities of a small territory such as Qatar. Al-Jazeera has become, in some respects, a broadcasting extension of Qatar's foreign policy aspirations. Al-Jazeera has given the Qatari government a degree of regional influence far beyond its military and economic strength. It is believed, for example, that Iran's president, Mohammad Khatami, used Qatari diplomatic channels to send a message to the United States asking the White House to relax pressures on Iran in a run-up period to Iranian elections.

The Saudis have been particularly irritated by Qatar's broadcasting ambitions, because Saudi Arabia has long considered itself to be the region's most powerful pan-Arab presence in satellite television. Before Al-Jazeera appeared, the Saudis controlled a number of pan-Arab satellite channels. Middle East Broadcasting Center (MBC), though London-based, is owned by a group of Saudi investors including members of Saudi Arabia's royal family. MBC was launched by the Saudis in late 1991, in the fallout of the Gulf War, as part of Saudi Arabia's strategy to extend its influence in the Islamic world. While MBC's stated mission was to "correct the false image of Islam throughout the world," [the station has tended to feature shows such as an Arabic version of *Who Wants to Be a Millionaire*— proof that Moslems are not adverse to American-style escapism.] MBC also airs five news broadcasts that, unlike Al-Jazeera, rigorously conform to the standard Arab style of journalistic servility. The Saudi royal family also controls two private pay-TV channels. One is ART, controlled by Shaikh Saleh Kamel, who is also a part-owner of Arab Media Corporation. The other is Orbit, which unlike ART offers English-language channels mixed with Arab-language versions of Western programs.

Besides MBC, Al-Jazeera's main competitor in the region has been Syrian-controlled Arab News Network. While Al-Jazeera has attempted to adopt Western-style journalistic practices, including objectivity, ANN's biases are more obviously pro-Moslem and anti-Israeli. Some have accused ANN of inciting hatred throughout the Middle East with a constant barrage of images of Israeli soldiers brutalizing Palestinians.[16] Behind the scenes, ANN has been plagued by a family saga at the summit of the Syrian state not unlike the uncanny plot twists that led to the creation of Al-Jazeera.

ANN was founded in 1997 by Soumar al-Assad, nephew of the late Syrian president, Hafez al-Assad. The young broadcaster's father, Rifaat al-Assad, had once been one of the most powerful and feared men in Syria. Rifaat proved just as ruthless as his brother, Hafez, who regularly purged the top ranks of Syria's army to maintain loyalty. In the early 1980s, Rifaat—who also enjoyed the support of the Syrian army—crushed an insurrection in which an estimated 18,000 people had been killed. Rifaat committed a tactical blunder in 1983, however, when he led a coup attempt to overthrow his brother, who had been recovering in hospital after suffering a heart attack. When the coup failed, Rifaat was forced into exile in France and Spain, where his humiliation was undoubtedly attenuated by an extravagant lifestyle in opulent homes. With a personal fortune estimated at $4 billion, Rifaat's many indulgences included a round-the-clock escort of 30 bodyguards. In France, where Rifaat was said to have financed the electoral campaigns of prominent politicians, the French government provided him with official protection. In his gilded exile, the flamboyant brother of Syria's long-serving president also became a media mogul. One of Rifaat's many lucrative business ventures was his son Soumar's satellite news channel, Arab News Network, which operated from London.

In the 1990s, Rifaat was finally allowed to live in Syria, and for several years it was believed he would succeed his brother. This impression was confirmed in 1998, when French President Jacques Chirac accorded Rifaat a grandiose welcome at the Elysée Palace. President Chirac was clearly sending a signal that Rifaat al-Assad had been designated as the next president of Syria. On June 10, 2000, it seemed Rifaat's rendezvous with destiny had finally arrived. President Assad, the cunning dictator known as the "Lion of Damascus," dropped dead of a heart attack while speaking on the telephone with Lebanon's president, Emile Lahoud. His 30-year rule, marked by pan-Arab ideology, pro-Soviet diplomacy, hostility towards American imperialism, and aggressive anti-Zionism, was now over. The future of Syria was suddenly in doubt, and many were nervous about implications for stability in the Middle East.

Seizing the moment, Rifaat al-Assad promptly declared himself to be the late president's rightful heir. "I will keep on the oath and there will be a new 'correctionist movement' with a new trend covering all political, social and political levels," he declared. "Freedom will prevail in Syria as well as democracy. The average citizen will take his due role in building the homeland and in choosing his representatives in Syria."

Syria's political elite had other plans. Succession instead fell to the late president's 34-year-old son, Bashar al-Assad. An oculist by training—hence his "Dr. Bashar" appellation—Syria's new 34-year-old president had relatively little experience in politics. In fact, President Assad's intended successor originally had been his eldest son, Basil, but he died in an automobile accident in 1994. When Bashar al-Assad was selected as Syria's president, his uncle Rifaat was infuriated. He was further outraged when the Syrian government banished and banned him from his brother's funeral and, what's more, warned him that if he returned to Syria he would be arrested. Another insult came from his old friend Jacques Chirac, who flew to Syria to attend the late Syrian president's funeral—a diplomatic sign widely interpreted to signify France's support for Bashar al-Assad's succession.

Incensed, Rifaat al-Assad issued a terse statement: "What is happening in Syria is a real farce and an unconstitutional piece of theatre which is a violation of the law and the constitution."

At Arab News Network, meanwhile, Soumar al-Assad was faced with a dilemma. His first loyalty was to his father, who was also a financial backer of ANN. Thus, combination of filial duty and business realities undoubtedly influenced his public declaration. "I know my father and he is not somebody who wants power," he told the British newspapers. "If he is sure that security has returned to Syria and that power is in the hands of the people he will rest quietly at home."

Soumar described his uncle's state funeral as "completely inhuman" and lashed out at the Syrian establishment who had put his cousin Bashar in power. "They are trying to profit from the crying of the people to create some kind of political gain," he said. "Now they are trying to make the people of Syria pay the price of creating an inexperienced leader purely because he's the son of his father. They are doing this by jumping over the will of the people. This is very dangerous for the stability of Syria and the stability of the Middle East. The people of Syria are mostly in favour of Rifaat, not because he has beautiful eyes but because he has fought all his life for what they want."

In London, where ANN was licensed to broadcast its signal, the network's coverage of the al-Assad family power struggle was closely monitored by British broadcasting regulators for impartiality—a principle not normally applied to television news in the Arab world. But the most damaging blow to Rifaat al-Assad's political aspirations came from ANN's rival, Al-Jazeera. Its reporters had discovered a stunning breach of loyalty in Rifaat's own family. His other son, Mudar al-Assad, appeared on Al-Jazeera to declare: "We are all with Bashar. He is the legitimate successor for the late president. There is no time for us for sorrow. What is of concern to us is continuity and stability under the leadership of Dr. Bashar who was chosen by President al-Assad and all the Syrian people." At the end of his statement, Mudar al-Assad added these devastating words: "Our father is Hafez al-Assad and there is no father but him in the whole world." Following this stunning act of media patricide, Rifaat al-Assad remained in frustrated exile while his implausible nephew Bashar ruled Syria.

At Al-Jazeera, meanwhile, the network's brash style and independent positions continued to affront authoritarian regimes in Arab countries unfamiliar with the principles of editorial autonomy. Throughout the Middle East, Al-Jazeera was referred to as the "Arab CNN." In Saudi Arabia, it was dubbed "the suspicious network," and a Saudi government spokesman called the network "poisonous." In Algeria, when Al-Jazeera began broadcasting reports investigating torture and murder in the country's bloody civil war, the Algerian government reacted by cutting electrical power to ensure the population could not watch television. The Arab States Broadcasting Union refused to admit Al-Jazeera as a member unless it agreed to obey a "code of honour of the Arab media." Despite these pressures, Al-Jazeera persisted—and attracted millions of viewers. Even powerful leaders in the Arab world watched Al-Jazeera, albeit grudgingly, to stay abreast of world events from an Arab perspective. During one live phone-in show, Libyan dictator Muammar al-Qaddafi called in to contribute his views on Arab nationalism.[17]

Al-Jazeera's president, Mohammed Jassem al-Ali, insisted that, despite widespread criticism in the Arab world, the network was determined to break from the traditional reflex of Arab satellite broadcasters who serve governments, not viewers. "It's time to have channels that satisfy viewers and their mentality and to respect them, which is what Al-Jazeera is doing," he said.

One influential Arab who was a great admirer of Al-Jazeera was Osama bin Laden. Al-Jazeera's relationship with bin Laden pre-dated Al Qaeda's attacks of September 11, 2001. Two years earlier, the *New York Times* had made the following observation in a report on Al-Jazeera, then virtually unknown in the West: "Sometimes, viewer interest has been piqued by scoops like the lengthy interview the channel broadcast three weeks ago with Osama bin Laden, the Islamic militant who has been indicted as the alleged mastermind of the bombings of American embassies in East Africa last year that killed 224 people, including 12 Americans. The interview gave Arab audiences their first opportunity to hear Mr. bin Laden speak uncensored, and in their own language. Ironically, for an enterprise often accused of acting as a mouthpiece for American ideas, Al-Jazeera's management faced pressure not to broadcast the interview from American diplomats who expressed fears that Mr. bin Laden's calls for new attacks could heighten risks for Americans in the Middle East."[18]

After the 9-11 terrorist attacks, bin Laden once again turned to Al-Jazeera—this time to speak to both the Arab world and the West. In fact, Al-Jazeera stole CNN's thunder. The Taliban regime expelled all foreign journalists from Afghanistan. The only television network allowed in Afghanistan was Al-Jazeera, which was accorded exclusives on all statements by Osama bin Laden. Consequently, throughout the fall of 2001 the world watched Al-Jazeera's footage of the world's most infamous terrorist defying the might of America. Even American political leaders—Secretary of State Colin Powell, Defense Secretary Donald Rumsfeld, National Security Adviser Condoleezza Rice—appeared on Al-Jazeera to communicate their positions to the Arab world. Charlotte Beers, appointed by President Bush as undersecretary of state for public diplomacy, said: "If I have to buy time on Al-Jazeera, I would certainly consider it." At the same time, ironically, Al-Jazeera was accusing the United States of bombing its bureau in Kabul.

By Christmas 2001, the White House came up with an alternative strategy: The U.S. would launch a state-sponsored Arabic-language television network to rival the influence of Al-Jazeera. The U.S. plan, part of a Broadcasting Board of Governors project called "Initiative 911," envisaged investing $750 million in the television network. Senator Joseph Biden, the driving force behind Initiative 911 in Congress, sold President Bush on the idea of a U.S.-backed TV network to fight a "war of words" with broadcasts in 26 languages to some 40 Moslem countries. The network was the third pillar in a three-pronged strategy that included Voice of America and the newly created Radio Free Afghanistan, modelled on Radio Free Europe.

Senator Biden said the satellite TV project was even more urgently needed than Voice of America during the Cold War. "If, for example, we had satellite TV in 1949, 1950 and 1955," he said, "I doubt whether anybody would have wondered whether we should have used it to broadcast into Hungary or Poland or Czechoslovakia. The twist here that's a little different than during the Cold War is that we want to target young men between the ages of 15 and 30, the recruiting grounds for terrorist and radical organizations. And the kind of program we were talking about is what would make a 21 year old living in Sri Lanka turn on the television to watch that particular station? It may be their version of MTV. We will go out in the same way we decide what makes somebody want to buy a Ford product in Indonesia. We're going to go to the various folks who do their version of focus groups in Madison Avenue. ... You want to sell a product!"

American frustration with Al-Jazeera did little to improve its reputation in the Arab world. In early 2002, authorities in Bahrain barred Al-Jazeera from covering local elections because, they said, the network was guilty of

"Zionist infiltration in the Gulf region." The real dispute between Qatar and Bahrain, in fact, was territorial: Both were making claims on the Hawar Islands due to their popularity as a tourist destination. Saudi Arabia, meanwhile, continued its policy of harassment of the Qatar-based network. The Saudis were intensely irritated by Al-Jazeera's airing of Osama bin Laden tapes, because bin Laden was a Saudi citizen who railed ceaselessly against the Saudi government for its close relationship with the United States. The Qatari daily newspaper, *al-Raya*, openly accused Saudi Arabia of waging a "hidden war" against Al-Jazeera by banning Saudi companies from buying commercial advertising on the network. In the fall of 2002, Saudi Arabia took further steps by recalling its ambassador in Qatar. And in February 2003, the Saudi government barred Al-Jazeera from covering the annual pilgrimage—or *hajj*—to Mecca.

Shortly before the U.S. invasion of Iraq, Qatar was unequivocally in the American camp. In fact, the U.S. Army's command centre set up in the Qatari capital of Doha. It was there, in Al-Jazeera's own backyard, where hundreds of foreign journalists attended official Pentagon briefings on the progress of the war. Ironically, U.S. generals seized on these rituals to express irritation at Al-Jazeera's war coverage. Millions of viewers throughout the Arab world were watching Al-Jazeera as an alternative to CNN. This time, however, Al-Jazeera had an Arab rival in Abu Dhabi TV, operated from the United Arab Emirates. Even CNN and U.S. television networks used images supplied by Al-Jazeera and Abu Dhabi TV, which enjoyed preferential access in Iraq during the war.

It was believed that some regimes, fearing that Saddam Hussein's defeat would presage their own downfall, blamed Al-Jazeera for fomenting popular discontent in the Arab world. There were even rumours that the Saudis had been plotting to overthrow the Emir of Qatar. No wonder Saudi Arabia's royal family was incensed when news leaked that the Saudi ambassador to the United States, Prince Bandar bin Sultan Abdul Aziz, had bought a financial stake in Al-Jazeera. Prince Bandar, a nephew of Saudi crown prince Abdullah bin Abdul Aziz, justified his investment by saying Al-Jazeera was desperate for cash. One of the reasons Al-Jazeera needed a cash injection, however, was the Saudi-led boycott against commercial advertising on the network.

Hostility towards transnational all-news networks—whether CNN or Al-Jazeera—confirm Rupert Murdoch's assertion that satellite TV represents an "unambiguous threat to totalitarian regimes everywhere." In reality, however, Murdoch has been obliged to put pragmatism before principle. It was a lesson he would learn when attempting to gain access to the biggest market on the planet: China.

Closed Circuits and Channels of Resistance

In 1993, Rupert Murdoch bought a majority stake in Star TV from Hong Kong billionaire Li Kashing with plans to transform the satellite TV system into a pan-Asian version of his BSkyB service in Britain. Star TV's satellite footprint covered all of Asia and the Middle East—reaching a potential audience of some 3 billion people. The satellite service was already broadcasting popular American programs such as *Dynasty* throughout southern China. But Murdoch had bigger plans. He believed Star TV could dominate the Asian television market because it had something local Asian broadcasters lacked: programming.

"They have nothing," Murdoch remarked after a visit to Vietnam. "If you left them a cassette, the next day it would be broadcast on national television."

Above all, Star TV had popular sports. And sports programs were, along with movies, the main drivers of the television industry.

But Murdoch still had a problem. Millions of Asians were watching Star TV, but few were actually paying for it. To make Star TV a legally authorized subscription channel, Murdoch needed the approval of Asian governments—especially China's Communist regime. That wouldn't be easy, however, due to Beijing's traditional distrust of Western culture. True, China's state-controlled television reflected a bizarre mixture of official propaganda and fascination with Western pop culture. The regime-controlled Chinese Central Television (CCTV), for example, featured a predictable cycle of censored newscasts and Revolutionary Operas, yet every afternoon CCTV showed *Popeye* and other familiar cartoons dubbed into Mandarin. But one thing was certain: Chinese television was state-controlled. This meant that any Western broadcaster seeking entry into the Chinese market had to deal with the Communist regime.

Murdoch was encouraged to discover that Chinese leader Deng Xiaoping enjoyed watching sports on Star TV. He was discouraged, however, to learn that Chinese rulers had remembered his highly publicized comment about satellite TV's potential to destabilize totalitarian regimes. Beijing had responded to Murdoch's remark, in fact, by banning satellite dishes in China.

Murdoch quickly understood that the only way to win approval for Star TV was currying favour with Chinese leaders, even if it meant shamelessly exploiting his media outlets to ingratiate himself with Deng Xiaoping. In his attempts to placate Beijing, Murdoch pulled out all the stops. In 1994, Basic Books—a publishing division of Murdoch-owned HarperCollins— released a flattering biography of Deng Xiaoping written by the Chinese ruler's own daughter, Deng Rong. More controversially, Murdoch ordered HarperCollins to jettison its planned publication of *East and West* by former Hong Kong governor Chris Patten, due to the book's possible affront to Chinese rulers. Murdoch also removed BBC World from Star TV's channel lineup to appease Chinese concerns about political messages in Western news reports beamed into China. Murdoch even publicly criticized Star TV for repeatedly airing film footage of the Tiananmen Square massacre. What's more, Murdoch invested millions to launch an online version of China's official propaganda sheet, *The People's Daily*. He also financed a Chinese-language channel on Star TV in partnership with Hong Kong businessmen known to have close links with the Chinese military establishment.

In 1999, *Time* magazine asked Murdoch, a longtime anti-Communist, if his pandering to China was perhaps hypocritical. His answer was evasive. "I don't think there are many communists left in China," he said. "There's a one-party state, and there's a communist economy, which they are desperately trying to get out of and change. The real story is an economic story, tied to the democratic story."[19]

It seemed Murdoch's obsession with China was affecting his personal life, too. In 1999, he divorced his wife of 32 years, Anna, to marry a 31-year-old Chinese beauty called Wendi Deng, an executive at Star TV. In 2001, 70-year-old Murdoch and his young Asian bride produced a child—Murdoch's fifth—when Wendi Deng gave birth to a baby girl, Grace. This was not the first time Murdoch had made extraordinary personal gestures that appeared to be calculated, at least in part, to advance his business interests. In the 1980s, Murdoch—an Australian—had taken out American citizenship in order to extend his media empire into the United States. Murdoch pleased the Chinese regime even further by publicly dismissing the Dalai Lama as "a very political old monk shuffling around in Gucci shoes."

Murdoch's indefatigable courtship of communist China finally paid off. In December 2001, he announced an historic agreement with Beijing permitting Star TV to provide service to some 100 million Chinese living in the country's affluent Guangdong province surrounding Hong Kong. In a reciprocal twist to the deal, Murdoch agreed to use Fox TV to broadcast the Chinese government channel, CCTV, in the United States. Murdoch's new wife, Wendi, played a key role in the negotiations with Chinese officials. Wendi Deng-Murdoch was also overseeing the creation of a Murdoch-controlled global satellite TV empire, called Sky Global Networks, incorporating satellite television properties in Asia, Europe, and Latin America.

In March 2002, Murdoch formally announced that he would soon be broadcasting his new Mandarin-language channel, Xingkong Weishi, in China. The channel promised to feature quiz shows, dance programs, situation comedies, and a nightly talk show. The launch of Xingkong Weishi, along with another channel called Phoenix, made Murdoch a major media player not only in China, but also throughout Asia.

Xu Guangchun, China's minister of State Administration of Radio, Film and Television, gave Murdoch an enthusiastic endorsement: "It is hoped that your channel will bring quality television entertainment to the Chinese viewers. We look forward to expanding our collaboration in other areas," Murdoch, for his part, declared: "I expect the new channel to be the first in a series of many successful projects we can achieve here."

In truth, Murdoch was not the only global media mogul making inroads into the Chinese market. Beijing, in fact, was signing deals with other American media giants. AOL Time Warner struck a deal allowing the U.S. media colossus to begin legally broadcasting its satellite service, China Entertainment TV, in the Guangdong province. In return, AOL Time Warner agreed to offer state-controlled CCTV channel on its U.S. cable television systems. The Chinese channel featured mainly news broadcasts, cooking shows, and Mandarin-language classes.[20]

When Murdoch's interest turned to India, he was determined to learn from earlier mistakes and pander to local audiences. Star TV originally had beamed into India a package of mostly foreign channels, including MTV, CNN, BBC, and Prime Sports. Star TV had failed to understand that

Indians generally prefer local cultural products. To increase its audience, Star TV added a local Hindi channel called Zee TV to its lineup. The new formula worked. Soon Zee TV dominated Indian television with a 50 percent audience share. Also, an Indianized version of MTV, called Channel 5, was added to Star TV's offering.

India's main challenge in the television sphere was not an invasion of foreign cultural messages, but deep internal cultural divisions within the vast, popular, and ethnically complex country. While India has a large Moslem population, its dominant majority is Hindu. Hindu nationalism is a powerful force in Indian politics, and violent clashes between Hindus and Moslems are tragically frequent—to say nothing of Sikh and Tamil violence. Despite these deep divisions along religious and linguistic lines, the Indian government established a state-owned broadcasting system, Doordarshan, that largely served India's majority Hindi culture. Early Indian television programs were inspired mainly by Indian cinema, conveying themes rich in Hindu tradition. It wasn't until the 1980s that Indian television began developing TV series with "entertainment" appeal. An early example was *Hum Log*, which debuted in 1984. Throughout 156 episodes, *Hum Log* followed the travails of a lower-middle-class family faced with issues such as corruption and superstition. The series was sponsored by food giant, Nestle, which used the show to sell its Maggi Noodles product in India.

By the 1990s, Indian television was undergoing a revolution. The success of Zee TV put pressures on state-owned Doordarshan to "dumb down" its programming in a newly liberalized television market. Doordarshan began reserving slots for Disney and MTV shows. Indians also acquired a taste for localized versions of U.S. television formats, including game shows such as *Wheel of Fortune*. Similarly, *High Life* was an Indianized version of *Lifestyles of the Rich and Famous*. And *The Zee Horror Show* featured vampires and zombies against local backdrops. American soaps, such as *The Bold and the Beautiful* and *Baywatch*, were dubbed into Hindi. Several well-known American channels—Home Box Office, ESPN, NBC, CNN, and MTV—had leased transponders on direct-broadcast satellites with "footprints" covering the whole of Asia. In India, the influence of American soft power had the merit of providing the country's youth with a global frame of reference that could mitigate ancient animosity among Hindus, Moslems, Sikhs, Tamils, and other minorities.

In the Islamic world, television has long been regarded with deep suspicion as an instrument of subversion. And yet, as the example of Saudi Arabia's King Saud demonstrates, reactions towards television in the Arab world are fraught with contradictions. It is said that King Saud first experienced the marvels of a new medium called television during a stay in a Boston hospital. The king, who succeeded his father King Abdul Aziz in 1953, evidently became so addicted to watching American TV shows in his private hospital room that, upon his return to Saudi Arabia, he decreed that his desert kingdom must have its own television service.

The story may be apocryphal. There can be no doubt, however, that the introduction of modern technologies in Saudi Arabia have generally required the force of a royal edict. As a rule, religious leaders in Saudi Arabia have strenuously opposed new technologies, such as telegraph and wireless radio systems inherited from the Turks following the First World War. Radio was finally accepted in Saudi Arabia in the 1950s because Egyptian radio services—notably Voice of the Arabs—were launching virulent over-the-air attacks on the Saudi monarchy. Like radio, television came late to Saudi Arabia. Hostility towards the new medium was inspired more by Islamic orthodoxy than by hostility towards American cultural imperialism. Saudi religious leaders—or *ulema*—claimed television, like cinema, was a form of idolatry and therefore violated the Koran. But once again, the Saudi royal family had more pressing secular concerns, not least of which was national unity, state control, censorship of information, and countering the relentless broadcasting assaults from Egypt. In 1963, the Saudi royal family decided it was time to build a national television system.

The Saudis automatically turned to the United States to get the job done. Saudi dependency on American expertise stretched back to the 1930s, when King Abdul Aziz granted a concession to Standard Oil and formed the joint petroleum exploitation firm, Arabian American Oil Company. The Saudis also depended on the United States for military protection. In 1945, King Abdul Aziz and President Franklin Roosevelt signed an "oil-for-security" agreement that brought Saudi Arabia under the American security blanket. From the early 1950s onwards, the U.S. maintained a permanent military presence in Saudi Arabia that included a U.S. Army corps of engineers who constructed Saudi defence installations. It was these same American military engineers who, in the early 1960s, built the first Saudi television system under the supervision of the U.S. State Department. Hardware was supplied by RCA, and Saudi broadcasting personnel were trained by staff from the U.S. television network NBC. The Arabian-American Oil Company also played an important role in Saudi broadcasting. Aramco, as the company was known, operated its own broadcast facilities in Saudi Arabia, and in 1957 began airing television shows—in English and Arabic—for its American and Saudi employees. It was Aramco's broadcasts, in fact, that first created an appetite for American-style television programs in Saudi Arabia.

Predictably, the advent of television in a religiously orthodox country like Saudi Arabia soon triggered controversy. In 1964, King Saud—a spendthrift monarch who plundered the Saudi treasury—was forced to abdicate in favour of his more moderate brother, Crown Prince Faisal. Opposition to television, meanwhile, had been intensifying amongst Saudi Arabia's fundamentalist leaders who regarded the medium as a non-stop bombardment of "graven images." One orthodox zealot who violently opposed television was a lesser-known member of the Saudi royal family, Khalid bin Musad, who was one of the king's nephews. In mid-1965, Khalid led a violent march on Riyadh's local TV station in an attempt to destroy its transmission tower. The incident erupted in violence, and Khalid was shot and killed by a policeman. When Khalid's family insisted to King Faisal that he punish the policeman, the Saudi monarch refused. King Faisal could not know it, but his clemency would prove tragically fateful. In 1975, Khalid's younger brother assassinated King Faisal during a royal ceremony in Riyadh. After murdering the king—his own uncle—the assassin shouted: "Now my brother is avenged!"[21]

Throughout the Islamic world, television produced equally passionate and paradoxical reactions. In most Moslem countries, television fell under strict state censorship. But state control worked only when broadcasting remained national in scope. With the advent of satellite TV, signals could easily be beamed down on any territory from virtually any foreign source. Even state-controlled, pan-Arab broadcasting cartels—such as ARABSAT and the Arab States Broadcasting Union—could do little to control information flows via satellite TV. Satellite dishes were banned in many Islamic countries—including Saudi Arabia—but in most cases authorities were forced to turn a blind eye to chronic violation. Even in Iran, ruled by ultra-

orthodox ayatollahs, an official interdiction of satellite TV was not sufficient to deter thousands of satellite dishes from mushrooming on buildings
throughout Tehran's populist north end, which in Iran became known as
"suburb of the West." Other technologies, such as videocassettes, could be
smuggled into Moslem countries and used to propagate "dangerous"
images and audio messages. Ayatollah Khomeini himself, when in exile in
Paris, had tapes of his subversive speeches smuggled into Iran to destabilize
the Shah's regime. Khomeini clearly had not been averse to exploiting, for
tactical political purposes, the same Western technologies that later, when
ruling over his neo-medieval theocracy, he fiercely denounced.

In many Moslem countries, including Iran, there had long been
simmering resentment towards Hollywood's stereotypical portrayal of the
Islamic world with crude images of mummies, flying carpets, sheiks,
harems, and turban-headed terrorists. As early as 1926, Felix the Cat was
featured fighting an Arab sheik. In subsequent generations, millions of children throughout the West grew up watching cartoon characters—Bugs
Bunny, Woody Woodpecker, Porky Pig, Popeye, Richie Rich, Heckle and
Jeckle, and Scooby-Doo—expressing comically anti-Arab sentiments.
Critics of Arab stereotyping claimed that, during the OPEC oil embargo of
the early 1970s when Arab countries were blamed in the West for provoking
a global economic crisis, American movies and TV shows renewed their
denigration of Arabs. American shows such as *Dynasty* featured Arab characters who were untrustworthy and lascivious. Comedian Bob Hope joked
on one of his television variety shows: "Now that the Arabs own Beverly
Hills there'll be caravans down Rodeo Drive." In another show, *Hail to the
Chief*, a U.S. army general combating Libyan terrorists, remarks: "Give me
a unit of Green Berets and I'll level falafel land in a half hour."[22]

Iran's Islamic Republic, realizing that transnational audiovisual flows
were impossible to stop, eventually opted to encourage imports from
cultures other than America. Of all places, the ayatollahs turned to Japan—
a country whose culture and religion was just as remote to Islam—for alternatives to American culture. To this day, one of the most popular imported
TV dramas ever shown in Iran is the Japanese series, *Oshin*. The story of a
Japanese girl who is sold into bondage but struggles against her abject
poverty, *Oshin* had been a hit in Japan in the early 1980s. The show
premiered in Iran in 1987, and immediately transfixed Iranian television

audiences. *Oshin* was so popular, in fact, that the streets of Tehran evacuated every Monday night during its broadcast. It has been suggested that *Oshin* owed its success in Iran to the compatibility of the heroine's personal morality—including female submissiveness—with the tenets of Islam. Some Iranian fans took their devotion to *Oshin* to the point of offending the country's religious rulers. One Iranian woman provoked the anger of Ayatollah Khomeini, then a dying old man, by declaring that she identified more with Oshin than with Fatima, daughter of the Prophet.

Within the Arab world itself, the most powerful cultural imperialist is Egypt, whose pan-Arab ambitions stretch back to Gamal Nasser in the 1950s and 1960s. Egypt's first television service was launched in 1959 thanks to technical assistance provided by U.S.-based RCA. After Egypt's military defeat in 1967, however, the country's state-controlled broadcasting system turned towards the Soviet Union. But in 1973, President Anwar Sadat expelled Soviet advisors, and Egyptian television reconnected with America and the West. Following Egypt's peace treaty with Israel in 1979, the country found itself diplomatically isolated from its Arab neighbours. One result was Egypt's expulsion from the ARABSAT satellite broadcasting system. Egypt, no longer regarded as a cultural leader in the Arab world, gravitated more and more towards the West, diplomatically and culturally.

It was at precisely this time that the American series, *Dallas*, made its debut in Egypt—and immediately was a huge success. *Dallas* was soon followed by other American imports, such as *Falcon Crest* and *Love Boat*. Many of Egypt's urban youth population were not indifferent to the images of wealth and luxury projected by *Dallas* and *Dynasty.* But the popularity of American television was potentially explosive. While Egypt's secular, Western-oriented bourgeoisie adopted American habits—money, leisure, sex, fashion—the lower classes generally remained loyal to Islamic traditions and thus were potential agents of fundamentalist zealotry against America. Egyptians who were not seduced by *Dallas* and *Dynasty* seized on these American TV shows as proof of a corrupt America. In the early 1990s, the soap opera *The Bold and the Beautiful* was so successful in Egypt that the show provoked violent anti-American protests, including the attempted assassination of the country's minister of Information, Safwat al Cherif.

The Egyptian government faced a serious domestic problem regarding *The Bold and the Beautiful.* If the show remained on the air, further Islamic violence was certain. But Egyptian officials did not want to appear to be caving in to Islamic extremists. So the government decided to wean Egyptians gradually from their *The Bold and the Beautiful* addiction. The show was first aired only on Sundays, then it was pulled from television schedules altogether. Its replacement, interestingly, was the same Japanese series that had been popular in Iran: *Oshin*. At first, Egyptian viewers believed *Oshin* was moral punishment for over-indulgence in American soaps and sitcoms. But *Oshin* quickly became popular, as Egyptians—like Iranians—identified with the show's underlying values emphasizing the virtues of marriage and sexual timidity. The impact of *Oshin* in Egypt was enormous. After the show's success on television, Egyptians were fascinated by anything Japanese, which they called *yabani*. Sales of imported Japanese consumer products—fridges, dishwashers, stereos—soared in Egyptian cities. Also, Egyptian television commercials for Japanese products made explicit mention that they were made in Japan. Egyptians were so enthralled by Japanese culture that they hungrily watched any television programs about Japan—shows about Japanese gardens and cooking, even live news reports about Christmas festivities in Tokyo. Anything from Japan was deemed newsworthy. When Egyptian President Hosni Mubarek made an official state visit to Japan in March 1995, observers believed the trip was not unrelated to *Oshin*'s popularity in his own country.

The success of *Oshin* in the Islamic world should not be overstated. Japanese television shows may have provided useful alternatives to American cultural influences, but other geopolitical dynamics were simultaneously at work. Traditionally, France had been the biggest foreign power spreading its cultural influence in the Arab world, especially the Maghreb. France's sphere of cultural influence extended even further to include sub-Saharan countries—Benin, Congo, Mali, and Senegal. Television was delayed in many sub-Saharan countries because it arrived during a turbulent period of decolonization. France, the main colonial power in the region, was originally reluctant to provide technical assistance to support the broadcasting interests of its rebellious colonies. By the early 1960s, however, France saw a strategic advantage in using francophone Africa to promote French technologies and national industrial giants such as Thomson. France was particularly jealous of potential British influence in Africa. Thus, in the early 1970s, France moved hastily to build a national television system in Togo to prevent the country's audiovisual absorption into the British Commonwealth. French President Georges Pompidou even visited Lomé, in July 1973, to inaugurate Togo's new television system. In Zaire, France competed fiercely with U.S.-based RCA to build television facilities in Kinshasa. Zaire ended up using RCA technology, but relied on French technical personnel and television programs. In the Central African Republic, the self-styled emperor Jean-Bédel Bokassa snubbed France in favour of using Israeli expertise to build a national television infrastructure.

Television in Africa served a "bread and circuses" function. In some cases, African dictators built television systems so their populations could watch World Cup soccer matches. In virtually all sub-Saharan countries, television was tightly controlled by states, but the emergence of satellite transmission produced two undesired consequences. One was privately owned broadcasters. The other was the invasion of signals from sources such as CNN, which frequently broadcast news reports that were deeply resented by African dictators. In the early 1990s, Mobutu Sese Seko, Zaire's flamboyant dictator, expressed his annoyance with satellite television. "It's possible today, by pushing a button, to pick up virtually every Western television signal. And our political opponents are using these technologies to stir up confusion—and they are doing it from Paris, Brussels, and Washington."[23]

Considered equally menacing was the francophone satellite channel, TV5, available throughout post-colonial Africa, the Maghreb, and in the Middle East. TV5, a consortium of French-language broadcasters, was created in 1984 as a French-led project to counter the Anglo-American influences of CNN and BBC World Service. Besides France's three main television networks (TF1, France 2, FR3), other consortium members were Belgium's RTBF, Canada's Radio-Canada, and Switzerland's SSR. During its startup phase, France continually expressed frustration with TV5, mainly because its own broadcasters were unable to exercise control despite paying most of TV5's budget. At one point France wanted to shut down TV5, but changed its policy when TV5's influence in Africa promised strategic geopolitical advantages as an extension of France's cultural ambitions in its former colonies.

TV5 has sometimes provoked bitter controversies in Africa—especially in the Maghreb—where its news and current affairs programs have probed into domestic political issues. In 1990, TV5 broadcast a literary talk show on which French author, Gilles Perrault, was discussing his new book, *Notre Ami le Roi*. The book was a vitriolic diatribe against the Moroccan king,

Hassan II, accusing the monarch of corruption and torture and calling into question France's traditional friendship with Morocco. Hassan II—though Westernized in his education, personal habits, and close personal friendship with many French political leaders—was an authoritarian figure in his own country. He moreover claimed to exercise "divine right" powers due to his putative lineage back to the Prophet. During Hassan II's reign, any hint of *lèse majesté* was considered a serious crime in Morocco. Hassan II had already been outraged by the publication in France of *Notre Ami le Roi*. But TV5's broadcast of the Gilles Perrault interview infuriated the Moroccan monarch. The affair quickly degenerated into embarrassing diplomatic incident. Hassan II was convinced, rightly or wrongly, that the French government—under socialist president François Mitterrand—had tacitly agreed to the TV5 broadcast to subtly mark its growing distance from the Moroccan king. It was remarked, for example, that Mitterrand's wife, Danielle, had publicly taken issue with the Moroccan regime for imprisoning dissidents. While Hassan II could do little about the copies *of Notre Ami le Roi* being smuggled into Morocco, he banned transmission of TV5, via local relay stations, throughout his kingdom. TV5 was replaced with the signal of Saudi-controlled MBC.

Despite these incidents, by the mid-1990s the Arab television landscape was becoming increasingly penetrated by foreign programming from the United States, France, and other Western countries. In 1994, the satellite service Orbit—launched by Saudi Prince Khaled bin Abdel Rahman Al Saud—featured a package of 16 channels, including CNN International, Fun Channel, Hollywood Channel, Discovery Channel, America Plus, Music Now, and a news channel with reports from ABC, CBS, and NBC.[24] Though Saudi-controlled, the Orbit satellite service was—like Al-Jazeera—highly influenced by Western taste and formats. Orbit, a subscription satellite service that launched in 1996, boasted a *Larry King Live* talk-show imitation, called *Aala al-Hawa*, on the Al-Thania channel. In 1997, Orbit and Disney negotiated a deal to broadcast a Disney channel tailored for Arabic viewers. Disney's squeaky clean image in America, it seemed, suited the puritanical mores of Islamic culture. Other channels available on Orbit included Discovery, Paramount, MTV, VH1, Nickelodeon, and Bloomberg. Orbit also offered a package of channels from Rupert Murdoch's Star TV, including CNBC, Sky News, Fox Kids Network, Star Movies, and Star Sports.

Meanwhile, another Saudi prince, Alwaleed bin Talal bin Abdul Aziz, was building an impressive network of business co-ventures with Western media giants, including Rupert Murdoch's News Corp. and Disney. Ranked by *Forbes* magazine, in 2000, as the sixth richest person in the world, Alwaleed was the grandson of Saudi Arabia's founder and nephew of the late King Fahd. His own father, Prince Talal, had been a champion—like the young Emir of Qatar many years later—of constitutional reform and representative government. A leading figure in the so-called "Free Princes" movement in the 1950s and 1960s, Prince Talal had been stripped of his Saudi passport in 1962 as punishment for his reformist views. The young Prince Alwaleed grew up in a liberal family setting, which was reinforced by his Lebanese mother, Mona al-Solh, the daughter of Lebanon's first prime minister, Riad al-Solh. Alwaleed, moreover, received an American university education at Syracuse University in upstate New York, and began his career in international finance at Citicorp. After amassing a personal fortune, Alwaleed began investing heavily in global media properties, including Netscape, News Corp., and Motorola, and Bill Gates' Teledesic satellite project.

In rare interviews, Alwaleed liked to compare himself to other billionaire investors such as Warren Buffett and George Soros. "I'm a billionaire and I'm international—a Buffett, Soros type," he said in 1998. "I'll leverage my assets as best I can. I have alliances with everybody and I don't have enemies."

This was hardly the view of a Moslem with a deep-seated suspicion of Western cultural imperialism. On the contrary, Alwaleed became internationally famous in the Western media as a Saudi billionaire with enough cash to make, or break, global corporate empires. It was Alwaleed whose rescue financing saved the EuroDisney theme park outside Paris.

Thanks to Alwaleed, Saudi Arabia—the Islamic kingdom that produced Osama bin Laden—owned a piece of Mickey Mouse and Donald Duck.

Globalization or "Glocalization"?

It's tempting to conclude that television failed to live up to its early promise as a global medium promoting greater world understanding. But as we have seen, this vision was largely based on a naïve post-war utopia that, in truth, was partially inspired by America's Cold War campaign against the Soviet Union. It may have been a noble cause, but television remained stubbornly national—and state-owned—for several decades. And yet, thanks to satellite technologies, television finally succeeded in liberating itself from its state-controlled shackles of heavily politicized regulation.

Today, television is finally global—and yet, at the same time, it is profoundly local. Both trends—globalization and localization—can harness television's potential as a window on the world. We may all be citizens of Rome, but we lead lives deeply rooted in a particular local experience. Television can, and does, reflect both these realities.

But what about the persistent critics of American cultural imperialism who argue that global television is merely an American mirror reflected onto the planet's diverse cultural realities? Their fallacy has been in measuring American global domination by quantities—or "flows"—of U.S. television programs exported around the world. They believe, falsely, that merely because America exports massive amounts of television programs, the automatic result is cultural homogenization. The observable reality, however, is manifestly different.

The term cultural imperialism, as it pertains to television, fails on a number of levels.

First, it portrays America as an external threat to regional cultures, as if America represents a "false" culture and other national cultures are somehow authentic or "real" cultures. But as we have seen in many examples—India, Latin America, and the Middle East—regional cultural spheres have their own internal dynamics that can present issues and tensions that have little, or nothing, to do with Americanization. In fact, the influence of American culture is sometimes a welcomed antidote to local cultural suffocation.

Second, international flows of television programs do not—despite UNESCO's persistent claims—demonstrate a pattern of centre-periphery domination by the United States. Television has been the subject of considerable cross-cultural hybridization and regional exchanges that, in many instances, do not even involve American programs. Soaps from Mexico, Brazil, and Japan are frequently more popular in many countries than shows from the United States. If there is American cultural imperialism via television, it is not a unique phenomenon. Brazil and Mexico exercise similar influence vis-à-vis their regional cultural spaces and mother countries in Europe. Egypt has extended its cultural dominance in the Arab world. France is an imperial cultural power in parts of Europe and the Maghreb. And Hong Kong culturally dominates the Chinese-speaking sphere. If television is an imperial medium, there are many imperial powers exploiting its symbolic resources. America is the most powerful, but not the only, television empire.

Third, the cultural imperialism theory assumes that television audiences are passive receptors of foreign television messages. But as numerous studies have demonstrated, television viewers actually tend to be active negotiators of meaning when they watch foreign television programs. Whether *Dallas*, *Baywatch*, or *The Bold and the Beautiful*, these shows are interpreted differently depending on the national cultural context in which they are received. In like manner, the Japanese series *Oshin* is decoded differently according to national cultural experiences. So-called "wall-to-wall *Dallas*" is denounced as American cultural imperialism, whereas the phenomenal success of *Oshin* in Iran, Egypt, and elsewhere is never cited as evidence of Japanese cultural domination. In truth, there can be no cultural domination without the complicity of those who receive and interpret the message. To be sure, American commercial domination in the global television market is indisputable. But that is precisely the trap into which cultural imperialism proponents have fallen: They mistakenly equate commercial success with cultural domination. Yet there is no solid evidence about allegedly negative effects of American television exports. In fact, empirical research tends to affirm that local cultures "negotiate" the sense and meaning of American television programs through cultural filters. What's more, while American television formats have been adopted in many foreign countries, audiences generally prefer to watch local programs that reflect specific cultural realities. There is, as noted, a global empire of American television, though it serves as an overarching frame of reference whose conveyed values are not a mono-culture juggernaut, but rather penetrate local cultural values in a complex process of transmission and reception of meaning.

Finally, there is no country in the world more penetrated by foreign television signals than the United States itself. True, most Americans prefer to watch prime-time programs on U.S. network television, though even that well-established habit is in decline. Many Americans today are watching specialized TV channels, including signals from virtually every part of the world. One of them is a TV channel owned by China's ruling Communist Party. Today, America may be a massive exporter of television programs, but it is also a huge importer of television signals. The experience of Hispanic television in the United States is particularly instructive.

In Western countries, it is true, the importation of American television programs, has sometimes challenged the interests of local cultural élites and threatened commercial arrangements between governments and unions. High-minded evocations about "cultural sovereignty"—notably in Canada and France—have generally been transparent attempts to protect local cultural industries against competition from foreign imports. In non-Western countries, American television channels—notably CNN and MTV—have been resented because they threaten to destabilize despotic regimes or provoke undesirable lifestyle attitudes among youth populations. Surely the values of protectionism and authoritarianism cannot be permitted to constitute a justification for restrictions against the global circulation of television programs. Whatever their origin.

In recent years, the American television industry has fundamentally changed its export strategy. Today, Hollywood studios and U.S. television producers prefer local co-productions to dumping massive amounts of domestic programming on foreign markets. Disney, Warner Bros., Universal, and Fox would rather invest in local production projects to tailor programming for culturally distinct markets. True, they have made a virtue of necessity. With more than half of Hollywood's revenues coming from foreign markets, showing sensitivity to foreign markets is eminently sensible from a strictly bottom-line point of view. Instead of treating Europe as an incremental spillover market for its movies and TV shows, Hollywood is now investing in European projects through partnerships with local producers. Time Warner, for example, invested in satellite TV in Scandinavia and in pay TV in Germany. Disney, for its part, formed joint ventures to produce children's programs in France, Germany, Italy, and Spain. News Corp, controlled by Twentieth Century Fox owner Rupert Murdoch, operated Britain's BSkyB satellite TV service, and Warner Bros. studio announced a joint movie deal with France's pay TV outlet, Canal Plus.[25] In all-news television CNN today is a global news network, not a domestic U.S. network. At the same time, CNN has shown sensitivity to regional cultures.

In 1997, CNN International was regionalized into six divisions: CNN International Europe/Middle East/Africa; CNN International Asia Pacific; CNN International South Asia; CNN International Latin America; CNN International USA; and CNN International North America.

In some countries, it cannot be doubted, fundamental cultural values have erected strong cultural barriers against American television. This is particularly the case in countries—such as India and Iran—where nationalism is based on deeply entrenched religious identities. But even in these countries, as we have seen, satellite TV has brought the signals of MTV, CNN, and HBO—and these channels have been embraced by the local youth and urban populations.

In the final analysis, not even the interdictions of ayatollahs can prevent people from installing satellite dishes on their balconies and pointing them toward the sky. As Rupert Murdoch correctly asserted, satellite television represents an unambiguous threat to totalitarian regimes everywhere—including, sooner or later, Communist China.

three
Music
Pop Goes the World

ON VALENTINE'S DAY in 2002, MTV sent a message to the world's youth: "Be Heard."

The global video channel invited the planet's MTV generation to join a live discussion with General Colin Powell, hero of the Gulf War and now President Bush's foreign secretary. In a publicity blitzkrieg, MTV declared: "Young people from the U.S. to Russia, Europe to the Middle East, get the chance to ask Secretary of State Colin Powell questions about the war on terrorism and issues that affect them directly."

The same day, U.S. Army and allied troops were routing out Osama bin Laden's terrorists in Afghanistan, whose detested Taliban regime had banned television and all forms of popular music. At MTV's New York studios, finishing touches were being put on the live broadcast billed as "A Global Discussion with Colin Powell." Questions to the Secretary of State could be submitted by telephone or via email on MTV.com.

It may have seemed presumptuous for an American music TV channel to assimilate the entire planet's youth into a discussion about U.S. foreign policy. But MTV could well afford that pretension. MTV and its sister channel, VH1, boasted a global reach of nearly 1 billion viewers in 140 countries.

MTV's Valentine's Day appeal to the world's youth was a diplomatic success. Powell took questions from teenagers from South America, Europe, Asia, and Africa. Some probed into issues beyond the U.S. war on Islamic terrorism. A young Italian woman asked the Secretary of State for his opinion on the Pope's ban on condoms in the AIDS era.

"I certainly respect the judgement of the Holy Father and the Catholic Church," replied Powell. He insisted, however, that he personally advocated the use of condoms by the world's young people. "I not only support their use," added Powell, "I encourage their use among people who are sexually active and need to protect themselves."

Many more questions—from London, Moscow, Cairo, New Delhi, Sao Paulo, Italy, Norway—flooded in during the hour-long broadcast. Powell impressed MTV's global audience with his knowledge of pop music. As a Jamaican immigrant to the United States, he said he still had a soft spot for calypso music—in particular Bob Marley. He also confessed being a fan of the Swedish pop band, ABBA, famous for 1970s hits such as "Dancing Queen."

Powell's appearance on MTV was more than a global goodwill gesture from the U.S. State Department. There were strategic reasons for Powell's appeal to the world's youth. His MTV performance was part of a concerted strategy to get the Bush administration's message to the planet's young people, especially in the non-Western world, where popular music was systematically being exploited as an instrument for anti-American propaganda. At that very moment, the Egyptian-based television channel, Nile TV, was broadcasting so-called *intifada* music videos featuring Arab singers chanting belligerent anti-American slogans.

Pop music Challenge

The Bush administration took this Islamic pop music assault as a serious threat. In early 2002, the White House's Broadcasting Board of Governors—which oversees Voice of America and U.S. "Liberty" radios—sponsored a pop music countercampaign to bring American values to the Middle East. Working through Los Angeles businessman Norman Pattiz—whose company Westwood One is the biggest U.S. distributor of commercial radio programming—the White House launched an Arabic radio station called Radio Sawa. Pattiz, a Democratic fundraiser who had been close to President Clinton, sat on the U.S. Broadcasting Board of Governors along with former Secretary of State Madeleine Albright. As the White House's radio crusader in the Middle East, Pattiz conducted focus groups in Cairo to determine which kinds of American pop songs would win over Moslem youths. It was decided that young Arabs would prefer the soft pop sounds of Britney Spears and Cher, not the hard-edged hip-hop anger of rappers like Puff Daddy.

"Will the religious extremists like it?" asked Pattiz rhetorically. "Probably not. But you've got to go after the hearts and minds you can get. After all, it was MTV that brought down the Berlin Wall."

The White House also enlisted the support of MTV in its campaign to win the hearts and minds of Moslem youths. MTV was already airing a show, *Mashaweer*, mixing Arabic songs with Euro-pop and Latin American music. MTV also planned to launch a 24-hour video channel in Arabic. For Washington, MTV was a powerful soft-power weapon that could be deployed strategically against Mad Mullahs and dangerous tyrants who opposed Western values.

The MTV generation may have coalesced around pop music. But MTV is much more. The pop-video channel is a pulsing electronic extension of the American Empire.

theme

Music's Imperial March

Humankind, it can confidently be asserted, was making music many millennia before the emergence of empires, kingdoms, nations, and the *Billboard* charts.

The ancient Greeks believed music could produce a profound emotional effect on human behaviour, including the stirring of Dionysian passions that would be familiar to psychedelic rock fans more than two millennia later. Plato explicitly discussed the influence of music in his dialogues. In *The Republic*, he observed: "A change to a new type of music is something to beware of as a hazard of all our fortunes. For the modes of music are never distributed without unsettling the most fundamental political and social conventions." The Romans undoubtedly were first to deploy music for imperial purposes. We know, for example, that Roman generals used brass instruments in military parades. As Christianity emerged from the ashes of the Roman Empire circa 500 AD, sacred music played a role in the rising power of the Papacy established in Rome.

In modern history, the Romantic movement in the early 19th century was characterized by an intense glorification of heroism and grandeur. Romantic music frequently took inspiration from military battles and imperial conquests. Napoleon in particular was widely hero-worshipped.

Beethoven composed his famous "Emperor's Concerto" as a tribute to Bona-
parte, though scratched the emperor's name from the piece after his
disenchantment with Napoleon's military aggressions. With the emergence
of nation-states in the 19th century, Romantic music became associated
with nationalistic ideals. Composers began turning to myths and legends as
plots for their operas, and to popular folk melodies as inspiration for
symphonies and instrumental music. In this tradition, Franz Liszt wrote his
Hungarian Rhapsodies, and Dvorak composed the *Slavonic Dances*. The
stirring operatic cadences of Wagner became associated with German
nationalism—and, several decades later, inspired the belligerent Germanic
chauvinism of Adolf Hitler.

In Britain, the world's most powerful empire in the 19th century, all forms
of music rendered service to the imperial cause. Popular pride in the British
Empire reached its height in the latter half of the 19th century, when free
trade, economic prosperity, new transportation systems, and technological
innovations fostered the emergence of a mass consumer market. While the
engine of British imperialism was largely economic, the Empire also found
symbolic resources in a complex mixture of national ideologies: monarchism,
Protestantism, and patriotism. Britain's geopolitical challenges also stirred up
imperialistic sentiments at home. The suppression of the Indian Mutiny in
1857; the legendary search for Dr. Livingstone; Britain's acquisition of the
Suez Canal under Prime Minister Disraeli; the Abyssinian and Sudanese
campaigns, the proclamation in 1876 of Queen Victoria as "Empress of India"
—all these events forged surging sentiments of loyalty to the British Empire.
Against this backdrop, the "Rule Britannia" ethos took inspiration from classical music and popular songs. The regal pageants of Sir Edward Elgar—
notably *Pomp and Circumstance*—best characterized this genre. In 1898, Elgar
composed a patriotic cantata, *Caractacus*, about the valiant British race's
resistance, in ancient times, to the Roman invaders. Elgar's most explicitly
imperialist work, of course, was the *Imperial March*. On a different note, the
Savoy Operas of Gilbert and Sullivan also played on imperial themes. *HMS
Pinafore*, for example, is best known for its rousing song, "He is an Englishman." In the popular idiom, the songs of British music halls—such as "Sons
of Our Empire" and "The British Bulldogs (Hail Our Empire's Unity)"—
were fiercely nationalistic and imperialistic. Music in Victorian Britain faithfully served the Empire on every social register—from saloon to salon.[1]

It was in the 19th century that musicians first achieved celebrity status comparable to the fame of today's pop stars. Franz Liszt, a handsome young virtuoso, was worshipped as he dazzled concert audiences throughout Europe and received the kind of adulation and hysteria enjoyed more than a century later by Elvis Presley and Mick Jagger. But Liszt's fame predated the advent of modern recording technology. There were no vinyl records, no tape cassettes, no compact discs, and no radio stations to disseminate his music. It was the advent of recording technology that would confer on popular music its phenomenally powerful attraction to mass audiences.

Recording technology was invented shortly before Liszt's death in 1886. Thomas Edison is generally regarded as the inventor of the first wax-cylinder phonograph machine in the late 1870s, when his first sound recording was a simple recitation of the nursery rhyme, "Mary Had a Little Lamb." After demonstrating his "talking machine" to the staff of Scientific American, Edison formed the Edison Speaking Phonograph Company in 1878. Less than a decade later, Alexander Graham Bell invented his own "graphophone" cylinder. Bell's invention gave birth to the Columbia Graphophone Company, which later would become Columbia Records. By the turn of the century, Columbia had one main commercial rival, Victor Talking Machine Company—later RCA Victor. Both Columbia and Victor sold wax cylinders and discs that were played at fairs and during vaudeville shows. The paying public inserted nickels in phonograph machines—called "nickel-in-the-slot" machines—to listen to Irish songs, brass bands, comic monologues, and other amusements. Another favourite was Negro songs—or so-called "coon songs." By the 1890s, thanks to the popularity of these songs, pay phonographs were a veritable sensation in penny arcades, amusement parks, and ice cream parlours throughout America.

Like motion pictures, sound recording arrived at precisely the moment when the young American republic was beginning to stir with its first imperial aspirations. And, fortuitously, the nascent phonograph industry was ready to capture the blaring trumpets of early American imperialism. Many of the most popular sound recordings of the period were military marches produced by the U.S. Marine Band. Its famous conductor was John Philip Sousa, who previously had conducted Gilbert & Sullivan's *HMS Pinafore* on Broadway. Sousa was also well-connected in Washington. He was intimately associated with the White House, especially after 1880 when he was appointed conductor of the "The President's Own" Marine Band. In that role, Sousa would serve under five U.S. presidents: Rutherford Hayes, James Garfield, Grover Cleveland, Chester Arthur, and Benjamin Harrison. In 1891, Sousa's band—with President Benjamin Harrison's benediction— was the first U.S. musical ensemble to embark on a world tour, performing patriotic works such as his own composition, "The Stars and Stripes Forever." Sousa became so famous for his rousing marches that he was widely known as "the March King." In 1892, Columbia made no fewer than 100 recordings, many of them marches, by the U.S. Marine Band. In 1898, rival Columbia Orchestra recorded a tribute, "The Charge of Roosevelt's Roughriders," celebrating the Spanish-American War exploits that parlayed Teddy Roosevelt to the White House. Sousa's legacy as America's pre- eminent band leader would long be remembered: During the Second World War, a U.S. battleship was baptized the S.S. *John Philip Sousa.*

At the turn of the century, while Sousa was conducting his patriotic marches, Americans were eagerly importing exotic music as the fruits of their nation's early imperial conquests. In the years following the U.S. over- throw of the Hawaiian monarchy in 1893, Victor exploited a sudden surge of interest in the Pacific islands by selling recordings of twangy Hawaiian music. The craze for Hawaiian music continued well after the First World War, and soon other recording companies—notably Columbia and Decca— jumped on the Hawaiian bandwagon.[2] This was also the era of music publishers in New York City's famed "Tin Pan Alley," whose early com- posers included George M. Cohan, Irving Berlin, Cole Porter, and Hoagy Carmichael. In the early years of Tin Pan Alley, music publishers made most of their profits from the sale of sheet music. But they soon realized there was money to be made selling actual recordings of music. In 1909, some 27 million phonograph recordings were sold—either in cylinder form or their new rival, flat discs. The early recording industry peaked in 1921 with gross revenues of $106 million.

The Roaring Twenties was the era of American jazz greats—Bix Beider- becke, Sydney Bechet, Louis Armstrong, Duke Ellington—whose sounds baptized the decade as the "Jazz Age" made immortal by the flappers of F. Scott Fitzgerald. American jazz, in fact, had already followed the U.S. Army to Europe. As early as 1918, the U.S. Army Infantry Regiment—or "Hell- fighters"—had performed jazz in Paris' Tuileries gardens during victory celebrations. By the 1920s, American jazz had caught on fire in Europe, where jazz artists such as Cab Calloway won over audiences with their new sound. It wasn't lost on European audiences that jazz was the music of Negroes, an oppressed American under-class. But in Europe, unburdened by the wrenching legacy of slavery, American jazz musicians were treated as virtuoso legends. There was one dissenting European voice on jazz, however. Oswald Spengler, the German historian whose 1922 book *The Decline of the West* was widely discussed internationally, predicted that Western civilization would soon be overtaken by "coloured" races. The popularity of jazz music, asserted Spengler, was a portent of the West's decline and collapse.

"Jazz music and nigger dances," wrote Spengler, "are the death march of a great civilization."

Spengler proposed a remedy for the West's death throes. "We do not need ideologues anymore," he argued, "We need hardness, we need fearless skepticism, we need a class of socialist master men." Adolf Hitler, who was building his Nazi party in the early 1920s, eagerly picked up Spengler's ideas. When in power a decade later, the Nazis denounced jazz as a prime example of "degenerate art."

In America, the effervescent Jazz Age would be short-lived. In 1929, after more than a decade of soaring prosperity, the Crash plunged America into economic ruin. The impact of the Depression was felt immediately on recorded music in America. True, there were some hit songs, such as the cheerfully ironic "We're in the Money." The reality, however, was that the U.S. recording industry almost vanished in the aftershock of the Crash. In the period from 1927 to 1933, record sales plummeted from 140 million to only 6 million, and U.S. sales of phonograph machines plunged from nearly one million to only 40,000. The recording industry could not count on commercial radio to salvage its declining fortunes. Since the 1920s, radio pioneers had shown remarkably little interest in recorded music. Radio networks such as RCA and NBC preferred to broadcast live performances, from Will Rogers monologues to symphony concerts. By the late 1930s, the main outlet for records was jukeboxes installed in American bars and cafés.

But there were good times ahead. Like television, recorded music took off after the Second World War when America was triumphant, confident, and prosperous. One of the first recording stars of the post-war era was

Frank Sinatra, who had begun his career as a big band singer. Before the war, band leaders such as Benny Goodman and Artie Shaw had been the focal point of widespread adulation. But with the popularity of "swing" in the 1940s, band leaders were eclipsed by their own band singers, who became the new frontmen. Sinatra first gained celebrity during the war when, as a singer for the Tommy Dorsey band, his performances made girls swoon at New York's Paramount Theater. By the late 1940s, Sinatra—dubbed the "Sultan of Swoon"—was making records for Columbia, which marketed the former crooner as a teen idol. Sinatra's fame quickly spread worldwide as thousands of American soldiers were moving through post-war Europe and bringing their musical tastes with them.

Jazz music, too, was conquering the planet in the post-war years. It took some time, however, for the U.S. State Department to acknowledge jazz as an authentically American form of music that could be useful to American foreign policy. In the State Department's senior ranks, jazz had long been dismissed due to its rebellious edge and its association with Negroes. American élites traditionally were attached to the pretensions of "high culture," and consequently disdained artistic trends developing in America's popular culture. But even cultural snobbism—to say nothing of racism—could not long ignore the growing popularity of jazz among foreign audiences. Jazz had become so popular, in fact, that State Department officials could no longer ignore its potential importance in selling America abroad. In the late 1940s, Voice of America and U.S. Army radio stations began playing jazz in Europe to spread America's popular music in tandem with the Marshall Plan's financial largesse. By the 1950s, Voice of America was broadcasting a jazz show called *Music USA*, which quickly became one of VOA's most effective propaganda tools. *Music USA* was so popular, in fact, that host Willis Conover became one of the most famous Americans in Soviet-bloc countries. In 1955, Voice of America told *Time* magazine: "Like it or not, jazz is a valuable U.S. commodity." *Look* magazine, for its part, declared: "Jazz is a door opener everywhere, a Pandora's box full of friendliness that totalitarians won't easily be able to close." *Down Beat*, a magazine read by jazz buffs, put it more bluntly: "Let Hot Jazz Melt Joe's Iron Curtain."

As the popularity of jazz spread globally, the State Department began actively promoting Negro jazz musicians throughout the world. World tours of Dizzy Gillespie and Louis Armstrong, for example, were financed by the State Department. In 1956, *Saturday Review* published an article titled, "Is Jazz Good Propaganda?" The answer was resoundingly affirmative. The magazine was astonished by the impact of Dizzy Gillespie's music on foreign audiences and its power as a conduit for American influence: "It is the old story of finding the bluebird in your own garden. Thus, the concrete example of one good jazz band may communicate more of the sincerity, joy, and vigor of the American way of life than several other American creations inspired by Europe."[3]

Ironically, racial tensions in the United States during the 1950s did little to enhance jazz's reputation in America. In Congress, a proposal to use state subsidies to promote jazz and bebop music around the world met with resolute opposition. Allen Ellender, a Louisiana senator, spoke out with particular vehemence against the export of the Negro music originating in his home state. "I never have heard so much pure noise in my life," said Senator Ellender about the music of Dizzie Gillespie. "To send such jazz musicians as Mr. Gillespie, I can assure you that, instead of doing good it will do harm, and the people will really believe we are barbarians." It is possible Senator Ellender's aesthetic opinions about the virtue of jazz music may have been shaped, at least in part, by his well-known positions in favour of racial segregation.

Jazz was relatively innocuous compared with two other forms of Negro music emerging from the American South: blues and rock 'n' roll. For generations, Negroes working on cotton plantations had alleviated their suffering with soulful songs about their servitude and emotional torment. Gospel—or "Negro spiritual"—music was considered tolerable because it was religious, and piety among blacks was considered desirable. The blues, on the hand, was considered dangerous because it was edgy, salacious, and reputedly inspired by the devil. The 1920s had seen the rise of blues singers such as Bessie Smith, whose "Downhearted Blues" sold nearly 1 million copies in 1923. In the 1930s, many guitar-playing country blues singers, such as Mississippi-born Robert Johnson, emerged from the South. Southern whites, meanwhile, were developing their own brand of "hillbilly" music in the mountains, and a country music style emerged from places like Nashville, famous for the Grand Ole Opry. One of the biggest Opry stars was singer-fiddler Roy Acuff, who shot to worldwide fame with his Smokey Mountains music.[4]

If the colour of their skin was different, southern Negroes and white hill-billies had one thing in common: they were dirt poor. After the Second World War, American blacks and poor southern whites began moving north to find employment as labourers in large industrial cities. They brought with them their manners and ways—including their musical roots in blues and jazz. Willie Dixon, a Mississippi-born blues singer, moved to Chicago as a young man and soon gained a reputation as a gifted blues man. It was in Chicago that, due to the confluence of new influences brought north by Negro musicians, a new musical style known as "rhythm and blues" soon crystallized.

Blues and country music also filtered northward via enlisted U.S. Army soldiers training in southern boot camps. These GIs had listened to southern radio stations that played Negro blues and white country music. Grand Ole Opry singer Roy Acuff was especially popular on U.S. Army camps. Indeed, American soldiers stationed in Europe voted Acuff as more popular than Frank Sinatra. It was even reported that, during the war, Japanese soldiers charged into battle belligerently screaming: "To hell with Roosevelt, Babe Ruth, and Roy Acuff!"

In post-war America, young whites were increasingly coming into contact with Negro music, whose natural rhythm appealed to the rebellious post-war generation. Early pioneers of Negro rock 'n' roll music included Little Richard and Chuck Berry, who quickly found imitators among white musicians in the South, such as Jerry Lee Lewis. A great deal of serious debate has been devoted to the question of rock 'n' roll's birth. But there appears to be a general consensus that Bill Haley—born in Detroit in 1925—was the first white musician to perform rock 'n' roll. As early as 1952—even before Chuck Berry and Little Richard began recording their songs—27-year-old Haley had made a recording of "Rock the Joint." At that time, when Dwight Eisenhower was moving into the White House and Ozzie and Harriet were America's model white-picket-fence television family, the term "rock 'n' roll" had not yet entered the popular lexicon. In 1952, Chuck Berry was an anonymous 21-year-old hairdresser in St. Louis. Little Richard, a 20-year-old kid working odd jobs in Georgia, wouldn't record his first song, "Tutti Frutti," until 1955. Fats Domino's "boogie woogie" sound was still a few years off. Among whites, Jerry Lee Lewis was an unknown Texan playing country music, and Buddy Holly was a 14-year-old high school student in nearby Lubbock. In Memphis, Elvis Presley was an eleventh-grade student whose main goal in life was to become a truck driver. But Bill Haley was already rocking in Detroit. It was Haley who invented the new form of music that would soon conquer the planet.

Rock 'n' roll was officially born on April 12, 1954, when Bill Haley and the Comets recorded "Rock around the Clock" in New York City. Haley's new sound had an immediate impact on America's burgeoning youth culture. Elvis Presley, who had started off as a country singer and debuted at the Grand Ole Opry, soon developed a rock 'n' roll persona with songs such as "Heartbreak Hotel." Other white musicians similarly turned on to rock 'n' roll: Carl Perkins recorded "Blue Suede Shoes," Jerry Lee Lewis gained notoriety for "Great Balls of Fire," and Buddy Holly became famous with "Peggy Sue." Haley, for his part, decided to promote his rock 'n' roll image in Hollywood. In fact, Haley owed his worldwide fame to the movies. In the mid-1950s, the Hollywood studios were keen to produce a movie about the social upheaval triggered by rock music among America's rebellious youth. Marlon Brando had starred as a leather-clad teenager in *The Wild One*, and James Dean would soon become an idolized cult figure as a maladjusted teenager in *Rebel Without a Cause*. Hollywood was developing another picture about youth rebellion called *Blackboard Jungle*, starring Glenn Ford and Anne Francis. Bill Haley was in the right place at the right time when the movie's producers seized on his "Rock around the Clock" as the movie's theme music. When *Blackboard Jungle* opened in 1955, record sales of "Rock around the Clock" soared across America. Haley was suddenly a star. A year later, Columbia Pictures decided to produce its own movie starring Bill Haley and the Comets—and what's more titled it *Rock around the Clock*.

In the conservative 1950s, *Rock around the Clock* whipped around the globe like a tornado. In America and Britain, the movie triggered mass hysteria as young people mobbed movie theatres and danced wildly in the aisles. Hundreds of thousands of British teenagers—including two working-class Liverpudlians called Paul McCartney and John Lennon—watched the movie and took up the guitar to imitate Haley. In Germany, *Rock around the Clock* provoked even more violent reactions. In Hamburg, police resorted to water cannons to control teenagers who had turned over automobiles and vandalized shops after watching the movie. In Holland, where *Rock around the Clock* was banned, young people demonstrated in the streets for the right to see the movie.[5]

In the United States, astonished record executives were taken completely by surprise as rock 'n' roll swept America. Major U.S. record labels—RCA Victor, CBS, Decca—previously had dismissed rock as a marginal, even dangerous, form of popular music. Major radio stations, too, had obstinately refused to play rock 'n' roll. Negative attitudes persisted even as rock songs climbed the charts. Frank Sinatra, the ex-teen idol now crooning his way through the 1950s, resented rock's chart-topping success. Appearing before a U.S. Congressional committee in 1958, Sinatra snorted: "Rock 'n' roll is the most brutal, ugly, desperate, vicious form of expression it has been my misfortune to hear." Many in America agreed. Rock 'n' roll was scorned as "Nigger music" and "devil dancing"—thus rallying it critics behind the combined values of racism and Christianity. In 1956, *Time* magazine observed: "Rock 'n' roll is based on Negro blues, but in a self-conscious style which underlines the primitive qualities of the blues with malice aforethought. Psychologists feel that rock 'n' roll's deepest appeal is to the teener's need to belong; the results bear a passing resemblance to Hitler's mass meetings."

In Britain, meanwhile, post-war teenagers couldn't get enough of American rock 'n' roll. In the 1950s Britain, like America, was experiencing strong economic growth. Young Britons—even from the working classes—were enjoying relatively high disposable incomes to spend on new consumer goods such as cigarettes and cosmetics. The 1950s were also a period of massive "Americanization" in British society through the importation of U.S. lifestyle products—from chewing gum and blue jeans to Hollywood movies and records by Little Richard and Chuck Berry. But there was one important difference. British kids, unlike youth in America, were comparatively untouched by racial divisions. They listened not only to Bill Haley and Elvis Presley, but were equally enthralled by Negro blues, soul, and rhythm and blues. Aspiring guitarists like Jimmy Page, Eric Clapton, Jeff Beck, and John Mayall hero-worshipped American blues guitarists Robert Johnson, Willie Dixon, and Muddy Waters. Mick Jagger, as a teenager growing up in a comfortable London suburb, tuned in to the nearby U.S. Army radio station to listen to American blues. When Jagger and classmate Keith Richard banded together to form The Rolling Stones, their early songs were inspired by the Chicago rhythm and blues sound. Likewise, Eric Clapton formed Cream as a blues group, and Jimmy Page's

Led Zeppelin debuted in the late 1960s with recordings of Willie Dixon songs. After working in obscurity as a session man for years in the United States, in the mid-1960s Seattle-born guitarist Jimi Hendrix arrived in London where he was immediately lionized by the leading names of the U.K. rock scene, including The Rolling Stones and The Who. America produced Hendrix, but Britain discovered him.

After the "British invasion" of the early 1960s—led by groups such as The Beatles, The Rolling Stones, The Animals, and Manfred Mann—American rock bands countered with their own unique sound. Previously, American pop music had produced upbeat vocal groups such as The Beach Boys, or the socially conscious folk music of Bob Dylan and Joan Baez. In the mid-1960s, however, American pop music embraced rock. Many U.S. rock bands of this era hailed from California: Jefferson Airplane, The Doors, The Byrds, and the Grateful Dead. In Detroit, meanwhile, black American artists—Marvin Gaye, Stevie Wonder, The Supremes, Smokey Robinson, and The Temptations—were recording "Motown" songs. This rich mixture of American pop sounds put the United States back on the map following a brief infatuation with U.K. pop.

By the early 1970s, Anglo-American pop music had exploded worldwide. Rock stars of this period included Led Zeppelin, Pink Floyd, Genesis, Alice Cooper, David Bowie, Elton John, Jethro Tull, King Crimson, Electric Light Orchestra, and Cat Stevens. The influence of Anglo-American rock was particularly powerful in Western countries. In culturally proud France, early rockers—Johnny Halliday, Eddy Mitchell, and Dick Rivers—not only modelled themselves on Elvis, but adopted American-sounding names. In the 1960s and 1970s, other French pop stars—Serge Gainsbourg, Jacques Dutronc, Alain Souchon—recorded songs that found obvious inspiration in American and British pop iconography. Gainsbourg, who was arguably France's most ingenious pop songwriter, showed an infatuation with Anglo-American pop culture that was pervasive in his recordings, especially during the psychedelic 1960s when he recorded his classic album, *Comic Strip*. Movie actress Brigitte Bardot, though internationally famous as a French sex kitten, was equally well-known in France as a pop singer and recorded several songs with Gainsbourg. Their songs—such as "Bonnie and Clyde" and "Harley Davidson"—revealed an obvious fascination with American themes, images, and brands. In Greece, in the 1960s young people rejected traditional music as old-fashioned and embraced trendy Anglo-American pop. Greek rock groups actually sang in English, though they quickly learned that Greek youth preferred genuine Anglo-American pop tunes to home-grown ersatz versions. In virtually every other European country, while teenagers listened to pop songs recorded in their own language, they showed a strong taste for the hit tunes of globally famous Anglo-American pop stars.

Behind the Iron Curtain, pop music permeated youth culture by more circuitous channels. Starting in the 1950s, young people in Soviet-bloc countries were able to listen to Western pop music—much to the exasperation of Soviet-backed communist regimes—via Radio Free Europe and Radio Luxembourg. The Kremlin and its puppet states resented rock music because its rebellious messages frustrated efforts to indoctrinate their young populations institutionally through official propaganda and Communist Party youth organizations. In East Germany, the ruling politburo declared in 1965 that rock music was not compatible with the goals of a socialist society. Rock's chief castigator was Eric Honecker, who later would become East Germany's communist leader. Communist regimes failed to understand that pop music's appeal was precisely its status as a forbidden fruit. Official Communist Party tirades against rock music only encouraged East German youths to listen to pop songs from the other side of the ideological divide.

If Soviet-style regimes could not prevent young people from listening to rock 'n' roll, they could prohibit its public performance. Consequently, young musicians living behind the Iron Curtain could not readily become recording artists because Communist Party apparatchiks controlled access to public resources and communications media. For this reason, youth subcultures in Eastern Europe developed a strong orientation towards Anglo-American pop music. In Hungary, for example, punk bands emerged in the 1970s as a subculture disaffected with life under a Soviet-backed regime. These underground bands influenced young people in Eastern Europe more than local youth wings of the Communist Party. In some cases, Soviet-bloc regimes were forced to accommodate the influences of rock music by attempting to capture their energies within party structures. In East Germany, Honecker—as politburo chairman in the 1970s—reversed his earlier position by declaring that "youth dance music" was now permitted as a legitimate form of cultural expression. But it was too late: Soviet communism would not last another decade. And pop music would claim a role in its downfall. In East Berlin, a rock concert in October 1989—ironically celebrating the 40th anniversary of the communist German Democratic Republic—triggered youth protests against Honecker's oppressive regime. And the Berlin Wall came crashing down.

anti American

[Despite these events—or perhaps because of them—the global explosion of Anglo-American pop music emboldened Marxist-inspired diatribe against Western cultural imperialism.] Theorists from the Frankfurt School had argued that the production of "commodified" mass culture was driven by the inexorable logic of standardization and homogenization. Theodore Adorno, in a famous 1941 essay titled "On Popular Music," had asserted that music in commodity form performs an ideological function: passively consumed, it cannot procure authentic cultural pleasure, but rather is exploited to produce fetishistic attachment to songs and the "stars" who sing them. Three decades later, when rock music was a powerful source of social change throughout the world, Frankfurt School theorists were still persisting with Marxist assertions about pop culture as an instrument of the dominant capitalist class, manipulated for its interests, and exploited to neutralize all opposition to the existing social order. In 1972, Adorno published *Introduction to the Sociology of Music*, in which he argued, in essence, that rock music was a mass-culture distraction that served as an opiate that pacified the world's youth.

The Frankfurt ideologues were curiously unaware of the irony of their puzzling postulates. In the years immediately preceding the publication of Adorno's 1972 book on music, pop stars had been in open revolt against the capitalist establishment. In the 1960s, singers such as Bob Dylan, Joan Baez, and many others became poets for a new counterculture opposed to the Vietnam War, corporate America, and sterile middle-class values. The Rolling Stones sang about social revolution in "Street Fightin' Man," and The Beatles recorded "Revolution." A decade later, rock stars were still rebelling against their corporate masters by embracing political crusades—against world hunger, against oppressive regimes, against apartheid. And new technologies—especially satellite TV—could now beam these messages worldwide. In 1985, the "Live Aid" benefit concert to combat Ethiopian famine was broadcast globally on television. The Live Aid message, it is true, did not offend the interests of major Anglo-American corporations that finance global pop music. Ethiopia was ruled by an oppressive Marxist regime.

The Frankfurt School critique, based more on doctrinaire ideology than empirical science, was a gross exaggeration of the alleged homogenizing effects of commercial culture. First, the cultural imperialism critique oversimplified the dynamic between cultural production and its consumption. As with movies and television shows, it cannot be assumed that, merely because Anglo-American pop songs are heard throughout the world, those who listen to them are somehow "Americanized." The Frankfurt critics—with a few notable exceptions—underestimated the capacity of local consumers to filter foreign messages and negotiate their meaning through the prism of their own cultural experience. Critics also assumed that American cultural imperialism was the product of economic imperatives, especially ownership of capital. Frankfurt School disciples frequently asserted that pop music was an instrument of American "hegemony" because the global music industry was controlled by Anglo-American interests. In the 1960s and 1970s, most of the world's major record labels—EMI, CBS, Columbia, RCA, and so on—were indeed Anglo-American. It is true, moreover, that pop superstars such as Elvis Presley, The Beatles, Bob Dylan, Jimi Hendrix, and The Rolling Stones gained international notoriety by making records for these labels. Anglo-American domination of the global pop music industry cannot be disputed, but it brought other cultural influences into what was generally described as "pop" music. For example, George Harrison of the Beatles found inspiration in the Indian sitar music of Ravi Shankar, who subsequently became as famous as most Anglo-American pop stars. By the 1980s, moreover, ownership of the major global labels was markedly more diversified. In 1987, Japanese-controlled Sony bought CBS Records, whose stable of pop stars included Bob Dylan and Bruce Springsteen.

Sony's buyout of CBS Records—followed by its purchase of Columbia Pictures from Coca-Cola—sent a shockwave through America. *Time* and *Newsweek* magazines devoted alarming cover stories to the Sony transactions, and critics claimed that Japanese financial interests had bought "America's soul." *Fortune* magazine, evoking memories of Pearl Harbor, asked ominously: "Where Will Japan Strike Next?" By the early 1990s,

Japanese interests owned an even bigger piece of America's soul: Matsushita, another Japanese electronics giant, bought MCA-Universal. Thus, two major U.S. record labels—CBS and Universal—were now controlled by Japanese consumer electronics giants. Polygram, meanwhile, was owned by Dutch-owned electronics giant Philips, and BMG Music was controlled by German conglomerate Bertelsmann, which also owned RCA. By the 1990s, only two global music giants—Warner Music and Universal Music—remained U.S.-controlled. The latter, in fact, was controlled by a Canadian-based company, Seagram. When Seagram sold Universal to French-controlled Vivendi, that left Warner Music as the only U.S.-based record label among the global giants. In 2003, the so-called "Big Five" were Warner (U.S.), BMG (German), Sony (Japanese), EMI (British), and Universal (French). Only one was American.

Confronted with these facts, critics of cultural imperialism could nonetheless counter that the Big Five, whatever the location of their corporate headquarters, were motivated by a profit-maximizing capitalist logic that compels them to produce mainly Anglo-American music and promote global pop stars whose music reaches a worldwide audience. In other words, risk-reduction strategies forced the Big Five to put musical standardization before cultural diversity. It is true that, in the 1980s and 1990s, the Big Five signed multi-million-dollar, multi-album contracts with a clique of global pop stars—Michael Jackson, Madonna, Celine Dion, Mariah Carey, and Aerosmith. It is also true that the Big Five likely felt compelled to promote these stars, even at the expense of developing local talent, to ensure a return on their investment. But the complex dynamic of cultural influences—especially in music—also demonstrated that something much different, and much less conspiratorial, was at play in global pop music.

Unlike motion pictures and television, pop music is a spontaneous form of cultural expression that does not require massive capital investments. In most industrialized countries, almost any teenager can find a guitar to strum or a drum kit to bang on. Forming a rock band in a suburban garage, or bleak urban ghetto, is not a complicated or financially onerous undertaking. Indeed, many of the world's most successful pop stars began in precisely this manner. What's more, aspiring pop musicians can find inspiration—thanks to the widespread availability of CDs, radio, and the Internet—from virtually anywhere. They are not bound by strictly local or national cultural idioms. Music, in sum, is subject to a complex interaction of styles, forms, trends, and influences that do not obey—and indeed often defy—reductionist theories about one-way cultural "hegemony." In music, there is no centre or periphery.

As the global success of rock 'n' roll has demonstrated, the centre and periphery can sometimes be the same thing.

I Want My MTV

More than two decades after its launch, MTV reaches some 350 million households worldwide. Yet when MTV debuted on August 21, 1981, it was not inspired by boundless optimism about the global appeal of pop music. On the contrary, MTV was born in a climate of economic crisis for the world's major record labels.

At the end of the 1970s, the major labels hit their first slump since rock 'n' roll's earliest days. From the mid-1950s, record sales had achieved spectacular annual growth rates of 20 percent or more. The industry reached its peak in 1977–78 with two monster hit albums: Fleetwood Mac's *Rumours* and the soundtrack from the movie *Saturday Night Fever*. Both records sold more than 20 million copies worldwide. But these spectacular successes concealed a troubling crisis: the music industry was going through a creative dry spell. Disco music, while popular in dance clubs pulsing to the beat of the Bee Gees and ABBA, was detested by rock fans. At the other end of the spectrum, the angry punk rock movement—led by U.K. bands like The Sex Pistols and The Clash—alienated many mainstream fans. Pop music, it seemed, had split into two unappealing camps.

At the end of the 1970s, global record sales were plummeting—from roughly 725 million records and cassettes in 1978 to only 575 million units in 1982. During the same period, revenues for major U.S. record labels dropped from $4.3 billion to $3.6 billion. The global music business was plunged into a severe economic crisis. Even worse, there was no ready supply of hit records or pop superstars on the horizon to pull the industry out of its doldrums.

It was against this backdrop that top executives at Warner Communications came up with a novel solution: record sales could receive a boost from a round-the-clock video channel on cable TV. For Warner, the idea could be implemented without much difficulty. Warner controlled, along with partner American Express, a huge U.S. cable TV empire, including millions of subscribers in the New York area. But, the concept was risky. A wall-to-wall music channel on television was not only untested, it also seemed implausible. Why would teenagers want to listen to music on TV? Still, the major labels were desperate. Disappointed with the radio industry for its inability to generate record sales, they were in no position to resist any possible solution to depressed sales figures.

Warner's experiment, to be sure, was not pop music's first flirtation with television. *American Bandstand* had been airing since 1952, and a few years later Elvis had appeared on television and scandalized network executives with his suggestive hip gyrations. In Britain, *Top of the Pops* debuted in early 1964—just in time for The Beatles. The same year, The Beatles conquered America via national broadcasts on *The Ed Sullivan Show*. In the late 1960s, the short-lived fame of The Monkees was based on a made-for-TV series. By the early 1970s impresarios like Don Kirshner were showcasing pop stars in prime time, while singer Helen Reddy hosted a variety show called *Midnight Special. Saturday Night Live*, too, regularly featured pop singers. As a rule, however, rock stars avoided television because of its inherent constraints. Television, for obvious reasons, was not considered an ideal medium for sound recordings. Rock musicians also felt alienated by mainstream television's conservative morality. But business is business. And since radio was no longer driving increased pop music sales, Warner decided it was worth taking a chance on television as a video jukebox.

Despite misgivings about radio, Warner turned to a young radio executive, Robert Pittman, to launch the new video channel. It was to be called MTV: Music Television. Pittman—who would later resurface as a top executive at the merged AOL Time Warner conglomerate—immediately set about conducting exhaustive research to determine how the new channel should be programmed. Armed with mountains of "psychographic" data commonly used in the radio industry he knew well, Pittman decreed that MTV would target young, affluent, suburban Americans.

Fittingly, MTV debuted with a video called "Video Killed the Radio Star" by British techno-pop group, The Buggles. For MTV, the video undoubtedly contained a combination of sly humour and wishful thinking.

But the video's message would turn out to be prophetic: If MTV didn't kill off radio entirely, it would soon displace radio as the main vehicle for promoting pop music.

"We're now seeing the TV become a component of the stereo system," declared Robert Pittman. "What we're doing is marrying those two forms so that they work together in unison."

Pittman, bringing his radio industry biases to MTV, regarded the channel as a TV-based radio station whose onslaught of visual songs would "flow" uninterrupted day and night.[6]

MTV's immediate challenge, however, was more pragmatic than conceptual: finding videos to put on the air. Because pop stars had long shunned television, there was a paucity of video material featuring the world's most famous rock groups. Also, MTV was controlled by only one major label, Warner. But to succeed, MTV would need the cooperation of Warner's competitors—Polygram, MCA, CBS, EMI, and others—for a constant supply of free videos. Making a pitch to major record labels, Pittman argued that MTV would, like radio, provide a powerful promotional outlet for records.

If the concept was convincing, not everybody bought it. When MTV premiered in 1981, only 1.5 million cable subscribers signed up. Many record executives didn't believe a music video channel would ever catch on. Some labels—notably Polygram and MCA—refused to provide their videos to MTV at no charge. They saw their videos as "programming" that should be sold, not given away free.

MTV also became a victim of its own demographic target group of young, white, middle-class Americans. Black music—whether soul or reggae—was explicitly banned from the channel. Thus confined, MTV's first roster of video stars featured a new generation of white-Anglo pop bands: Madonna, Cyndi Lauper, Pat Benatar, The Pretenders, and Huey Lewis and the News. All had mainstream appeal in white-bread Middle America. Yet MTV still didn't have enough video product to fill its 24-hour schedule. This deficit would have unforeseen consequences for the look and style of pop music, which in the early 1980s fell under the influence of another "British invasion." In Britain, many aspiring pop bands—unlike their American counterparts—were making videos to promote their technopop music on British television. MTV was so desperate for video product that it frantically imported dozens of videos of unknown British pop bands with names like Duran Duran, Human League, ABC, Thompson Twins, Culture Club, Eurythmics, Thomas Dolby, and Flock of Seagulls. Some of these groups undoubtedly would have gained international success eventually, but their fortuitous exposure on MTV in America gave them instant publicity that was wholly unexpected, and greatly appreciated. It was largely due to MTV, in fact, that a "new wave" of British technopop washed over America in the early 1980s.

After the lean years of punk rock, the recording industry was immensely relieved when record sales suddenly began soaring. So did the careers of British pop bands like Culture Club and Duran Duran. Warner's bet had paid off. Within only a year after MTV's launch, the channel was so successful that Polygram was forced to reverse its policy: It would now provide videos to MTV free of charge.

MTV was not without critics, however. The usual suspects among leftist academics coldly dissected the channel's content to marshal evidence that MTV was a pulsing extension of America's global capitalist crusade. MTV was described as a "dream world of mass consumption" that disconnects America's youth from reality. Others observed that MTV was ahistorical, asocial, apolitical, and amoral. MTV's on-air veejays, it was noted, made no references to the date or time in their specific geographical location, New York City. The channel's message was allegedly nihilistic. As one critic observed: "There aren't any problems on MTV." Another commented: "What could be more beautifully, and so completely, capitalistic than a whole channel that programs commercials between the commercials?" There were also complaints that MTV, convinced of its own key position as the music industry's new gatekeeper, was ruthlessly extorting unreasonable terms from record labels and cable TV companies. MTV was also accused of driving rival music video channels out of business.[7]

MTV's more pressing problem, however, was a chorus of criticism about the channel's alleged racism. Since MTV appealed to a young, affluent, white demographic group, its videos excluded, by definition, black music. Consequently, videos made by black pop stars—Michael Jackson, Prince, Stevie Wonder, Marvin Gaye, Smokey Robinson, and Earth, Wind and Fire—were effectively banned from MTV's playlist. The first indignant protest came from funk singer Rick James—famous for the hit song "Super

Freak"—who in 1983 spoke out publicly against his exclusion from MTV. Soon white pop superstars, such as David Bowie, added their voices to the criticism of MTV's whitewashing policy. Bowie even raised the issue during an interview on MTV, pointedly challenging a veejay about the channel's no-black policy.

In damage-control mode, Bob Pittman argued that blacks were not excluded from MTV. It was simply that their music didn't fit into the channel's format. "Our position is that we play rock 'n' roll music," said Pittman. "What we are doing is successful. We hope to find more black musicians doing rock 'n' roll and new music. It's not a colour barrier—it's a music barrier."[8]

Pittman's explanation rang hollow. The controversy reached a boiling point in early 1983, when MTV refused to play superstar Michael Jackson's videos. Jackson's mega-hit album, *Thriller*, had just soared to the top of the *Billboard* charts, but MTV remained adamant in its refusal to play videos such as "Billy Jean." Executives at Jackson's label, CBS Records, were so furious that the company threatened MTV with a scorched-earth boycott *almighty* of all their videos. Facing mounting criticism, MTV finally caved in. In *stroppy* March 1983, MTV put "Billy Jean" on its playlist—and it immediately became a huge hit among the channel's fans. Pittman's radio-oriented research about the need to attract white youths from Middle America seemed like junk science. MTV, embarrassed by the setback, now began promoting other black pop stars, including Prince and Eddy Grant. Ironically, Michael Jackson became MTV's main attraction in its first few years. Prince's songs—especially the movie soundtrack *Purple Rain*—also drove MTV's success in the early 1980s.

MTV was rapidly becoming more than a video channel; it was imposing a new aesthetic on television with its flashy style, quick pace, and pulsing sensuality. Within a couple of years, the MTV look was spilling into American prime-time television. When the stylish cop show *Miami Vice* debuted on NBC in 1983, its fast-paced editing, pulsing music, and trendy settings made the show an immediate hit among young Americans of the new MTV generation. NBC boss Brandon Tartikoff even dubbed the show "MTV Cops." MTV's success was also due to excellent timing. In the early 1980s, the U.S. economy was booming, new consumer products like the Walkman were promoting sales of cassettes and compact discs, and pop stars like

Michael Jackson were driving industry revenues. By late 1983, MTV could boast that 17 of *Billboard*'s Top Twenty records were on its playlist. With this kind of starmaking power, MTV could oblige any rock star to stand before the camera in a promotional clip and cry out: "I want my MTV!"

By 1985, however, MTV was suddenly falling into a ratings slump. Though wildly successful in its first few years, MTV had failed to keep in step with changing musical tastes. Young Americans were getting bored with British technopop and American "soft" rock artists like Lionel Richie and Phil Collins. As its ratings plummeted, MTV found itself going through an identity crisis. The quick-fix solution was to shift away from soft pop music and towards edgier rock and heavy metal bands such as Aerosmith and Def Leppard. But for MTV's corporate parent, Warner-Amex, it was too late. Warner-Amex decided to cut its losses and pull out. In mid-1985, Warner-Amex sold its controlling interest in MTV Networks to media giant, Viacom. Bob Pittman would soon exit, replaced by Tom Freston.

"MTV had become boring," said Freston, who was appointed head of MTV Networks in 1987. Under Freston, MTV abandoned its non-narrative radio style of constantly flowing videos. The channel now attempted to attract audiences with specific "appointment" programs scheduled in fixed time slots—much like traditional network television. Thus, constantly pulsing videos made room for new MTV shows such as *Headbangers' Ball* and *Beavis and Butthead*, which appealed to the young male demographic. Dance shows such as *Club MTV* were tailored for female teenyboppers.

The MTV facelift worked. Within a year, MTV was rejuvenated and revitalized. By the late 1980s, MTV became so identified with youth culture in America that U.S. politicians actively sought out the channel to reach young voters. The interest was reciprocal: MTV embraced politics with a passion. One of the channel's political crusades was its "Rock the Vote" campaign, which exhorted young Americans to exercise their democratic franchise by casting their ballots.

"I'd like to think that MTV is helping making politics cool again," said Freston. In the 1992 presidential election, MTV veejays interviewed President George Bush, Governor Bill Clinton, and Democrat candidate Al Gore. Many believed MTV helped put Bill Clinton in the White House. Al Gore, who became Clinton's vice-president, appeared convinced of the MTV factor.

"Thank you MTV!" hollered Gore at an MTV gala after the 1992 victory. "Thank you for winning this election. You did it!"

With friends in the White House, MTV embarked on a campaign of international expansion. As Freston declared confidently: "Our goal is to be in every home in the world." With its new global mission, MTV's new slogan was: "One Planet, One Music."

MTV's timing was propitious. Throughout the 1980s, many countries had either privatized or deregulated their heavily state-controlled broadcasting systems. At the same time, cable and satellite TV were taking off throughout Europe, in Asia, and elsewhere. The combination of liberalized broadcasting landscapes and multi-channel offerings produced a sudden demand for programs. This was especially true in Europe, where deregulation of state-controlled television was imposed supranationally by the European Commission in Brussels.

Viacom launched MTV Europe in mid-1987 as a partnership with British Telecom and media mogul Robert Maxwell, though Viacom would later take full control. Based in London, MTVE reached some 3 million European homes within a year of its launch—and by 1992 its reach had expanded to 37 million households. MTVE debuted just in time for the collapse of the Soviet Union. As Bill Roedy, MTVE's president, put it: "MTV probably played a very significant part in ending the Cold War. It's a window on the West which came to represent the free flow of expression. When we went into what was then the Eastern bloc, we found that people already knew about us from pirating."

In August 1989, MTV's *Make a Difference* was seen in the Soviet Union, where the program's slogan was "Cool Music, Not Cold War." Roedy liked to recall that, after MTVE hooked up its transmitters in East Berlin in November 1989, the communist politburo resigned within an hour. He was exaggerating only slightly.

Roedy brought interesting credentials to his job spearheading MTV's drive into Europe. A graduate of West Point, he had been a U.S. Army officer based in Europe as part of NATO operations. "Now I'm selling rock 'n' roll to the same audiences we pointed missiles at," he said.

When MTV began broadcasting in post-Soviet Russia, civic leaders in major cities such as Leningrad embraced the channel as a way for young Russians to learn about Western values. MTV was the first cable TV channel from the West to be offered in St. Petersburg. Its arrival was compared to Peter the Great, the czar who had opened up Russia to Western influences.[9]

Bill Roedy, who would later become head of MTV International, made sure MTVE stayed in touch with the pulse of Europe's politically conscious youth. One of MTV's causes was the pan-European bandwagon that was gaining political momentum in the early 1990s. MTV found a natural ally in the political movement behind a supranational Europe. Both regarded Europe as a single commercial and cultural space. And both would learn that the former was more easily accomplished than the latter. MTV nonetheless exercised tremendous power over the European commercial strategies of major record labels. In the past, the major labels had released records at staggered intervals depending on perceived demand in specific countries. But with MTV beaming its signal across the entire continent, labels now felt obliged to release their products in Europe on the same date. MTV also could take credit—or blame—for a new musical style known as "Europop." The Europop sound was associated with Scandinavian pop bands—ABBA, Ace of Base, Army of Lovers, Roxette, and Aqua—who sang lyrics in English and therefore penetrated MTV's video playlist.

Despite MTV's success in Europe, its desire to foster the emergence of a global youth culture soon ran up against persistent criticisms about the channel's neglect of locally produced music. Small European record labels complained that MTVE served chiefly as a video outlet for the same Anglo-American pop stars—Phil Collins, Madonna, Sting, Bon Jovi, Michael Jackson, Aerosmith, and Nirvana—that could be seen on MTV in America. Others noted that MTVE, which featured programs sporting names such as *MTV Coca-Cola Report*, was even more commercial than MTV. MTVE nonetheless won wide appeal throughout Europe as cable and satellite TV penetration grew. MTVE made efforts to devote some airtime to European pop videos, but local colour and flavour were frowned upon by MTV's global advertisers, including Coca-Cola, Nike, and Levi-Strauss. These multinational firms, like MTV itself, wanted to create a global consumer market for their products with as little differentiation as possible. Coca-Cola, for example, bought exclusive sponsorship rights for MTV's World Music Video Awards.

MTV executive Sara Levinson explained MTV's vision in McLuhanesque terms: "Music is the global language. We want to be the global rock 'n' roll village where we can talk to youth worldwide."

Levinson's boss, Tom Freston, confidently announced the existence of a "world pop culture" of young people between 12 and 34 years old. "This is the first international generation," said Freston. "They wear Levis, shop at Benetton, wear Swatch watches, and drink Coca-Cola. This is not to say that there aren't cultural differences, that the French aren't different from the Germans. But a French teenager and a German teenager are much more similar to each other than they are to their parents." → *Kind of thinking that breeds family relationships*

Despite these bold assertions, MTV soon realized that its "going global" strategy was running into trouble. Some of MTV's foreign setbacks were purely business related. In Canada, for example, regulators banned MTV to protect the monopoly of a domestic video channel called MuchMusic—which, as it turned out, ended up importing MTV programs such as *Unplugged* and *Beavis and Butthead*. France, like Canada, imposed severe restriction on radio stations in order to promote *la chanson française*. French hostility to Anglo-American pop was restricted largely to cultural élites in Paris, where the *chanson* enjoyed a quasi-sacred status due to associations with legendary singers such as Edith Piaf, Charles Trenet, Yves Montand, Georges Brassens, Jacques Brel, Juliette Greco, and Serge Gainsbourg. *French hostility again* In Japan, another culturally homogenous Western country, MTV was forced to shop around for airtime on major broadcasters, such as TV Asahi and Tokyo Broadcasting System. The latter cancelled MTV in 1991 due to a contract dispute over MTV's demands for prime-time slots. Another obstacle was Japanese electronics giant Sony, which—besides controlling Hollywood's Columbia Pictures and CBS Records—owned a video channel in Japan called Sony Music TV.

Most foreign hostility to MTV, however, was cultural—or, rather, it was expressed in cultural terms. MTV, it was argued, was a one-way-flow global pop-music channel that played videos produced mainly by the major record labels that controlled global music. By the early 1990s, even American newspapers like the *Christian Science Monitor* were publishing articles with titles like "MTV's Cultural Colonialism."[10]

Ironically, while MTV was promoting its "One Planet, One Music" vision of global pop, some of the world's most famous Anglo-American rock stars were proactively discovering the rich diversity of the world's musical forms. In the late 1980s, Paul Simon was in Africa recording his *Graceland* album with Zulu group, Ladysmith Black Mambazo. Other pop stars—Johnny

Clegg, Stewart Copeland, David Byrne, Ry Cooder—were similarly experimenting with non-Western sounds on their records. Mickey Hart, drummer for The Grateful Dead, recorded *Planet Drum*, inspired by percussion styles from Africa, India, and Brazil. Hart had previously composed the "Rhythm Devils" drum music in Francis Ford Coppola's movie, *Apocalypse Now*. Peter Gabriel—ex-lead singer of Genesis—borrowed from African and Indian percussion sounds to compose the soundtrack for Martin Scorsese's *The Last Temptation of Christ*. Gabriel plunged deeper into non-Western music when he began recording music with Senegal's Youssou N'Dour. Gabriel also played an instrumental role in creating WOMAD—"World Music and Dance"—whose festivals showcased musicians from the non-Anglo-American cultural sphere. Gabriel later launched a record company, Real World, to promote the work of Youssou N'Dour and other artists in the non-Anglo-American musical sphere.

The worldwide commercial success of records like *Graceland* brought exotic musical sounds into direct contact with Western pop fans. Almost overnight, there was a genuine appetite in America and elsewhere for musical styles not normally associated with Anglo-American pop. In 1987, the Bulgarian Women's Choir produced a record that, astonishingly, landed on the *Billboard* charts and won a Grammy Award. On the fringe of the Anglo-American sphere, Celtic music began to attract wide audiences around the world, especially with the global successful of artists such as Enya.

In 1990, *Billboard* officially recognized the importance of non-Anglo-American pop by establishing a "world music" chart. "World music"—sometimes called "worldbeat" or "ethnopop"—can best be described as fusion music, or the blended result of cross-fertilized musical forms from various regions and cultures. The term originally was associated with African music, whose emphasis on rhythm is frequently distinguished from the melodic bias of Anglo-American pop music. Gradually, however, the term "world music" took on a more expansive meaning to encompass all musical forms beyond the Anglo-American sphere. Thanks to the success of "world music," the inter-penetration of global pop sounds is commonplace. Pearl Jam's Eddie Vedder, for example, picked Pakistani pop singer Nusrat Fateh Ali Khan to sing a duet for the soundtrack of the Hollywood film, *Dead Man Walking*.

Predictably, artistic cross-fertilization in pop music has been criticized by denouncers of American cultural imperialism. The burgeoning interest in world music, they claim, was an attempt by Anglo-American pop musicians to "steal" from peripheral cultures in order to reinvigorate their own culturally impoverished obsession with "hit" records. In other words, Anglo-American pop music's appropriation of "world music" was tantamount to cultural pillaging. This critique also asserted that, for major record labels, producing pop music from non-Western regions is merely tokenism that encourages Western fans of "world music" to engage in a self-validating form of cultural fetishism.

A rebuttal to these claims came directly from "world music" pop artists, such as Youssou N'Dour. "In Dakar we hear many different records," he said. "We are open to these sounds. When people say that my music is too Western, they must remember that we, too, hear this music over here. We hear the African music with the modern." French-African funk diva Angélique Kidjo, for her part, remarked: "There is a kind of cultural racism going on where people think that African musicians have to make a certain kind of music. No one asks Paul Simon: 'Why did you use black African musicians? Why don't you use Americans? Why don't you make your own music?' What is the music that Paul Simon is supposed to do?"[11]

MTV at first resisted the exotic allure of "world music"—a second strategic error after its ban on videos by black pop stars. MTV tailored its programming to the world's different regions, but it failed to make cultural distinctions within geographic spheres. When it launched MTV Asia on the Star TV satellite service, for example, the channel was beamed down on a huge region composed of widely different religions, languages, and cultures—such as China and India. Almost immediately, MTV realized it could not compete with other video channels that showcased more local content customized for specific cultural markets. MTV consequently split its Asian service into two separate streams—one aimed at China, the other at India.

Even in America, MTV was under attack. Greg Kot, the *Chicago Tribune*'s rock critic, wrote: "I always thought of MTV as one of the most eclectic radio stations in the world, a place where you could hear Public Enemy alongside Jane's Addiction, Bobby Brown, and R.E.M. Now it is as conservative as the most corporate commercial radio stations, an outlet that promotes expensive videos financed by major labels to the exclusion of almost everything else. The art of the video has become a parade of half-million-dollar copycats, and the underfinanced indie bands or risk-taking artists don't have a chance."

Tom Freston went on the defensive: "MTV would never work if you just took music tailored to the American audience and put it into different countries. It requires some significant changes. Yes, the music is always rock-and-roll based, but the selections are different country to country."

At MTV headquarters in New York's Times Square, the channel's senior executives understood it was time to try another formula. Tom Freston had underestimated the resentment towards MTV's global ambitions. His lesson had already been learned by CNN's Ted Turner: globalization cannot be a Trojan Horse for Americanization.

Now MTV would have to change its tune.

World Music Goes Global

In the mid-1990s, MTV underwent an internal revolution to shed its reputation as a gigantic Anglo-American jukebox for the eyes. Henceforth, MTV would splinter into a multitude of video channels, each one targeting a specific region and culture. More substantively, MTV would endeavour to air roughly 70 percent of local content.

In 1996, MTV India was launched—in Hindi and English—to appeal to youth in India, Bangladesh, Nepal, Pakistan, and Sri Lanka. In China, two distinct services—MTV China and MTV Mandarin—were created. MTV also started a Middle East service spanning the Islamic world from Iran to Morocco, though its programs were featured on Viacom's Showtime channel. In Europe, while MTVE continued to operate, MTV launched separate channels for certain national markets: MTV Italy, MTV Nordic, MTV Spain, MTV France, and MTV Netherlands. MTV Russia went on the air. MTV also launched MTV Brazil as a Portuguese-language channel. These were followed by other local MTV channels: MTV Japan, MTV U.K., MTV Korea, MTV Latin America, MTV Central Europe, MTV Poland.

Freston's new strategy was to combine global hit songs with local music. "There are a few big-name international superstars that everyone relates to," he said. "And there is, simultaneously, a desire among all cultures to see themselves reflected in the media they watch."

As part of its strategy to show cultural sensitivity, MTV expurgated American programs that might offend local sensibilities in some countries.

The irreverent *Beavis and Butthead*, for example, was axed from MTV in parts of Asia. "We make decisions from the bottom up," said Freston.

Today, MTV congratulates itself for creating global pop stars in countries beyond the Anglo-American world. In Russia, pop band Tatu shot to stardom after its videos received airplay on MTV Russia. Taiwanese pop singer Jolin Tsai won a following on mainland China after receiving airplay on MTV Asia. In Latin America, pop singer Shakira, a smouldering blonde bombshell, won a U.S. Grammy and two Latin American Grammy awards after taping an MTV *Unplugged* show that was seen on MTV Latin America. Shakira's song "Whenever Wherever" also shot to the top of the U.K. pop charts and landed in the top slot on *Billboard*'s Hot Latin Tracks chart. Shakira, whose music blends a variety of influences from dance to hip hop, has become one of the world's most successful pop stars to emerge from the non-Anglo-American world. → *rather grave value judgement*

Born to a Columbian mother and Lebanese father, Shakira grew up in Colombia where she absorbed a variety of musical influences, from Donna Summer disco songs to groups like The Cure, Depeche Mode, and Nirvana. Shakira's early records had already won audiences in the United States, but only among Hispanic youths. She remained completely unknown in Middle America. Shakira eventually moved to Miami—though she still didn't speak English—where she signed a contract with Sony Music to make records in English. In the United States, her career came under the guidance of Emilio Estefan, husband of pop star Gloria Estefan, and Freddy DeMann, who previously had managed the careers of Madonna and Michael Jackson.

"I forced the company to record her the way I record Madonna or Lenny Kravitz or Cher or Will Smith," said Emilio Estefan, who like Shakira is part Lebanese. It was Estefan who convinced the singer to mix Latin, Arab, and American musical styles. Her first album in English, *Laundry Service*, soared up the Billboard charts along with hit single, "Underneath Your Clothes." Suddenly, Shakira was a star in America and throughout the world.[12]

In 2002, Shakira's growing fame in America was consecrated with an article in *People* magazine, which noted: "Most Americans are just getting to know Shakira, but she's already a bona fide super-*estrella* in Latin America." Shakira's personal life attracted headlines throughout Latin America when she became romantically involved with the son, and political speechwriter, of Argentine president Fernando de la Rua. *Laundry Service* was banned in Argentina because the raunchy video for "Underneath Your Clothes" featured boyfriend Antonio de la Rua, who had fled to Miami after his father, facing a criminal investigation, left office in disgrace. These scandals, while embarrassing for her boyfriend, provided a surge of publicity for Shakira—and for MTV Latin America.

It was examples like Shakira that made MTV realize, albeit belatedly, that cultural homogenization was bad for business. "We think of our consumers as dual-passport holders," said MTV Asia president Frank Brown. "They wear sneakers and baseball caps, but are equally comfortable in traditional dress with their families."[13]

MTV executives should have understood that, in music especially, local expression is always open to creative influences, whatever its origin. And frequently, musical influences come from the most unexpected sources. In places like China, India, and the Arab world, local pop music is not only thriving, but also has shown remarkable openness to the influences of Anglo-American and other foreign musical trends.

India provides an intriguing example of a country that, while known for its cultural insularity vis-à-vis the West, has shown remarkable openness to foreign pop music. India's first experience with Western music dates to the period of British rule, when local élites tended to regard Western classical music as superior to Indian traditional music. British-controlled Gramophone Company of India, while producing some traditional music, largely neglected music from India's diverse regions. It was the rise of India's movie industry, after the British withdrawal in the late 1940s, that brought traditional Indian music back into the popular consciousness. Songs from Indian movies became popular throughout the country mainly because the price of a movie ticket was infinitely more affordable for most Indians than the cost of a radio. For those who could afford a radio, the songs that received the most airplay were taken from popular Indian movies. The most popular type of movie song was the *ghazal*, an Urdu-language chant associated with India's northern Moslem regions. The widespread popularity of the *ghazal* produced several singing stars in India, notably Talat Mahmood who in the late 1940s was called the "Ghazal King." Mahmood said his own favourite singers were Nat King Cole, Pat Boone, and Bing Crosby.

The *ghazal*'s long reign came to an end in the 1970s, when Indian popular music underwent a profound transformation due to convergence of political, economic, and technological factors. In 1978, India's central government—which had long pursued a policy of non-aligned self-reliance vis-à-vis the West—took measures to liberalize the economy. The positive effects of these policies were higher disposable income and purchasing power—especially for luxury consumer goods such as TV sets, hi-fi stereos, and cameras. It was the arrival of cassette players, in particular, that would have an enormous impact on Indian pop music. Cassette players began flooding into India, many brought home by so-called guest workers returning from temporary jobs in the Gulf states. Recorded music on cassette quickly became a pervasive consumer electronics product among India's middle-classes. By the mid-1980s, the vast majority of Indians—roughly 95 percent—used cassette players to listen to music. The immediate impact of cassette players was the decentralization of the Indian music industry, which had previously been controlled monopolistically by one domestic giant, Gramophone Company of India. It was GCI, in fact, that had sponsored the long popularity of *ghazals*. With the spread of cassettes, however, new forms of music caught on in India—especially disco-based music inspired by the pop music fad sweeping throughout the West at the time.[14]

Western influences intensified at the outset of the 1990s, when India's long-ruling Congress Party was returned to office, after a two-year hiatus, under Prime Minister Narasimha Rao. Rao's government immediately set out to open up India's stagnating economy, including in the media and communications sectors. Within a year of the Congress Party's return to power in 1991, cable and satellite TV was reaching some 50 million households throughout the country. Rupert Murdoch's Star TV satellite service, in particular, was spraying down American and other TV programs from the West. American soap operas, such as *The Bold and the Beautiful* and *Santa Barbara*, were especially popular. It was observed at the time that, in most Indian towns a visitor invariably came across a clothing boutique called "Bold and Beautiful." Thanks to India's new cassette culture and satellite TV, pop stars like Madonna became famous throughout India. Millions of Indian teenagers sang Madonna's tunes in "Hinglish"—a hybrid mixture of Hindi and English. The American pop singer's celebrity also inspired local Madonna clones, though their ritualized emulation remained respectful of local cultural strictures. [While Madonna clones mimicked Madonna's sensual movements, they did so dressed in traditional Hindi female attire covering the entire body.]

imitation ? as flattery

By the mid-1990s, massive exposure to Anglo-American pop via MTV and other foreign television channels inspired young Indian musicians to blend Western pop music rhythms and melodies with their own local sounds. From this fusion was born "Indipop," a mixture of traditional Indian music with Western pop, hip hop, and reggae. A Sikh singer called Daler Mehndi, for example, soared to fame with his unique blend of disco and Indian *bhangra* music. Mehndi's first album, *Bolo Ta Ra Ra*, sold more than 2 million records in 1995. As Mehndi's fame grew in India, Coca-Cola signed him to promote its soft drinks in India. Mehndi soon embarked on an 18-city tour in the United States to win fans from India's diaspora in America, where Mehndi himself had once driven a taxi in San Francisco.

Bhangra also become popular in Britain, where young people born to Indian parents blended pop instruments such as the electric guitar, bass, and keyboard synthesizers with traditional *bhangra* instruments such as the *dholak* and *dholki*. The result was a disco-sounding Indipop fusion known as "*bhangra* beat," which gained a wide following in London's west-end Southall district. Other British *bhangra* bands surfaced in the Midlands and Scotland, where members of *bhangra* group Bombay Talkie were known for their trademark tartan outfits and songs such as "Bonnie Bonnie Banks of Loch Lomond." Some young Asians in the U.K. scoffed at the hybrid *bhangra* beat as a gesture of contempt for its teeny-bopper disco beat—not unlike the "disco sucks" movement in America during the late 1970s. On a deeper level, deriding the *bhangra* beat was a way for some U.K.-born Indian youths to reject their immigrant roots and affirm their British identity. Some U.K.-born Hindi musicians, meanwhile, were blending *bhangra* sounds with other exotic styles to create an altogether new sound. Apache Indian, the stage name of a Birmingham musician born into a Hindi family, found success by mixing *bhangra* sounds with Afro-Caribbean beats.[15]

Today, the diaspora market is hugely successful for Indian pop stars. When Sony Music released the soundtrack from an Indian blockbuster movie, *Kuch Kuch Hota Hai*, the record sold more than 600,000 copies in Britain. Sony has also promoted Indian pop duo, Colonial Cousins, the first

Indipop artists to be given their own MTV *Unplugged* show. Despite the commercial potential of India's diaspora market, major record labels have invested in Indipop because of the huge size of India's population of more than a billion people. One major challenge, however, has been India's anti-quated retail system for the distribution and sale of recorded music. In the past, most Indians purchased cassettes from small mom-and-pop shops. But in the 1990s, major retail chains—such as Bombay's Planet M—began modelling themselves on retail giants like Virgin Megastore and Tower Records. Their main commercial challenge will be to shift Indian consumers away from cheap cassettes towards higher-margin CDs. That transition has been facilitated thanks to the success of certain Indian pop singers, such as Alisha Chinai, hailed as the "Madonna of India" after the release of her record, *Made in India*.

There can be no doubt that pop music has been a powerful mobilizing force in the rapid liberalization of attitudes among India's young MTV generation. But like all pop cultural influences, Indian youth have absorbed Western pop music through the filters of their own cultural experience. As *Business Week* magazine observed in 1999: "India's youth are already having an enormous impact on the economy, on companies hoping to sell them products, on the media, and on the culture … Liberalization's children also differ from their conservative, insular parents in that they proudly mix Indian values with Western packaging. They enjoy wearing saris and still admire Mahatma Gandhi. But they also like wearing blue jeans, drinking fizzy sodas, and watching MTV." Or as Vibha Rishi, marketing director of PepsiCo in India, put it: "The old Brahmanical code of 'lofty thinking and simple living' went out of style, to be replaced by the MTV culture of youth anywhere in the world."[16]

In neighbouring Pakistan, pop music similarly has taken off in a country where concerts were once banned and rock music prohibited from the airwaves due to its allegedly corrupting influence. As in India, pop music in Pakistan went through a period of fascination with disco music, whose apostles were British-born Pakistani musicians exporting the disco beat to their mother country. But Pakistan's disco craze did not survive President Zia's policy of "purifying" Islamization designed to appeal to the country's fundamentalist Moslems. At the end of the 1980s, however, polit-ical reforms brought in by Oxford-educated Prime Minister Benazir Bhutto returned the pulsing sounds of Michael Jackson and Madonna to the streets of Karachi. Bhutto even confessed to being a fan of a Pakistani pop group called Vital Signs.

As in India, in Pakistan the main conduit for pop music in the 1990s was satellite TV—particularly Rupert Murdoch's Star TV and its Hindi-language rival, Zee TV. Facing competition from Western video channels beamed down via high-powered satellites, Pakistan's state-controlled network, PTV, began airing pop videos in shows with names like *Music Channel Charts* and *Top of the Pops*. The latter show was sponsored by Pepsi-Cola. Today, Pakistan boasts its own version of rap music as well as female pop singers, though they tend to sport traditional *shalwar kamees* attire, leaving little skin exposed. Pakistan's most famous pop singer is undoubtedly the late Nusrat Fateh Ali Khan, whose *qawwali* singing has inspired Western pop stars as diverse as Pearl Jam and Peter Gabriel. When he died in 1997, Ali Khan had lived long enough to see the transformation of so-called "Pakipop." In 2001, the United Nations selected Pakistani pop star Salman Ahmad—leader of rock group Junoon—to spearhead its campaign in Pakistan against the spread of AIDS. Junoon had once been banned from performing in Pakistan after the group claimed their music transcended the borders separating Pakistan and India. With satellite TV channels beaming signals onto the entire Indian continent, in pop music those borders no longer existed.

China is not a country that, even today, one normally associates with pop music. In the 1960s Mao Zedong's tragic Cultural Revolution was sweeping through China at precisely the same moment when, in the West, pop music was in full flower—or "flower power." Starting in 1966, Mao's paranoid purges of Communist Party élites and liberal professionals led to the murder of hundreds of thousands, possibly millions, at the hands of his fanatical Red Guards, or so-called "Mao's little soldiers." In the cruel turbulence of those years, China's arts schools were shut down and artistic activity was strictly banned. The Cultural Revolution reinforced Mao's hold on power, but it was a great leap backwards for artistic expression in China.

Two years after Mao's death in 1976, his moderate successor Deng Xiaoping's officially repudiated the state-directed Cultural Revolution with a new "Open Door Policy." For the first time in decades, China began slowly prying open its cultural doors to Western influences. Previously, Western pop music sounds had reached China either secretly, circuitously, or illegally—through mailed packages sent by Chinese visitors in America, through short-wave radio broadcasts from Hong Kong, or via Voice of America. Now, suddenly, Chinese youth were allowed to listen freely to Western pop music. Not surprisingly, the first "foreign" pop music styles officially allowed into China were melodic *gangtai* songs imported from Hong Kong. Also, in the 1980s a musical style known as *xibeifeng*—named after the Xibei region in China's northwest—combined folksong melodies and Western-style disco music. More dangerously, a Chinese form of rock 'n' roll—called *yaogun yingyue*—began catching on among university students.

Chinese tastes in pop music tended to be relatively innocuous, at least compared with rock trends in the West during the 1980s. Among Western pop stars that gained a following in China were John Denver, Karen Carpenter, and Simon and Garfunkel. Some Chinese pop artists nonetheless used their work to make political statements. In 1985, authorities had little reason to be concerned when Cui Jian, a rebellious trumpet player with the Beijing Symphony, recorded a version of "Say Say Say" by Paul McCartney and Michael Jackson. They took notice, however, when Cui Jian began performing songs of political protest. In March 1989, when Cui Jian performed at Beijing's Concert Hall, the 2,000 young Chinese in the audience leapt from their chairs and began dancing and chanting to songs such as "I Have Nothing" and "Rock 'n' Roll on the New Long March." Several months later in Tiananmen Square, when Taiwanese pop singer Hou Dejian joined the demonstrations that ended in massacre, he was promptly deported and his music was banned from sale in China. For the ruling Communist Party, lip-synching the syrupy tunes of Karen Carpenter was permitted, but defiantly chanting edgy rock 'n' roll anthems would not be tolerated. Taiwanese pop star Chang Hui-mei learned that when in 2000 she sang Taiwan's national anthem at the inauguration ceremonies of the country's new president, Chen Shui-bian. In China, the communist regime reacted immediately by banning all her songs and records from the mainland Chinese market, where she was so famous that Coca-Cola had signed her up to promote its soft drink, Sprite, on Chinese television. But after the pop star publicly sang the national anthem of Taiwan—which China regards as a breakaway province—the Sprite ads were banned from Chinese television.[17]

When Hong Kong was under British rule, so-called "cantopop" stars—who sang in the local Cantonese dialect—rallied to the pro-democracy cause in mainland China, often with songs that were openly contemptuous of China's communist regime. Prior to Tiananmen Square, cantopop was similar to Anglo-American "soft rock" songs whose themes invariably deal with love, rejection, and heartbreak. After Tiananmen Square, however, cantopop took on a political tone. In 1989, about 150 Hong Kong pop singers recorded a song called "All for Freedom" to show their solidarity with Beijing student protestors. At the same time, a well-known cantopop star, Danny Summer, released an album called *You Awaken My Soul,* which featured several songs about the pro-democracy movement in China. But not all Hong Kong pop stars joined the political protest movement against China. Some Hong Kong singers continued to sing non-political songs in Mandarin, thus reaching a wider audience in mainland China. By rejecting Mandarin, Hong Kong's cantopop stars were marking their opposition to the Chinese regime in Beijing where Mandarin is spoken. The Hong Kong pop singers who continued singing in Mandarin—known as "mandopop" stars—tended to be teeny-bopper heart-throbs with little interest in embracing political causes. Two of Hong Kong's most famous mandopop stars in recent years have been Andy Lau and Jacky Cheung. Lau, a former kung fu film actor with chiselled good looks, got his start in Hong Kong television series. Cheung, for his part, won fame in the mid-1980s after triumphing at a Hong Kong singing contest, where he sang a patriotic Chinese song, "Fatherland." Both Lau and Cheung, ironically, had begun their careers singing cantopop love songs, but as their fame spread switched to Mandarin to reach a larger market beyond the Cantonese region surrounding Hong Kong.

More recently, Hong Kong pop stars have modelled their images and careers with explicit Anglo-American references. One is pop diva, CoCo Lee, who frequently is compared with American pop singer Mariah Carey. Lee, who makes records for Sony, was actually raised in San Francisco after moving to the United States at age ten. But besides English, she sings in Mandarin and Cantonese. When she recorded her debut album in English, *Just No Other Way,* Lee had already made 14 records in Chinese that sold nine million copies. *Just No Other Way* sold one million units worldwide in 2000. One song from the album, "Before I Fall in Love," was the theme song for the Hollywood movie, *Runaway Bride.* Lee also recorded a love duet, "When You Tell Me That You Love Me" with Julio Iglesias, and sang "A Love before Time," which was featured on the soundtrack of the Chinese movie *Crouching Tiger, Hidden Dragon.*

⌈In Washington, a persistent source of Sino–U.S. diplomatic irritation over the past several years has been China's role as a producer, and importer, of pirated American pop music.⌋In the mid-1990s, China and the United States reached an agreement to stamp out counterfeit intellectual property in China. The accord, which narrowly averted a trade war between the two countries, seemed promising at first. But after two years, Washington remained unconvinced Beijing was keeping its anti-piracy promises. In 1997, the value of pirated music, movies, and other software in China was estimated at nearly $3 billion. China was making some progress, however, in reducing levels of pirated music CDs. This was accomplished, to a large degree, by opening the Chinese market to legally produced CDs from foreign countries, especially the United States. In 1997, some 1,200 foreign record titles were imported—ten times the import level only two years previously. Chinese authorities also seized production facilities illegally mass-producing CDs, CD-ROMS, videocassettes, and other software products. But these measures have only displaced the problem, as Chinese software pirates simply moved to other locations, such as Taiwan and Macao. After China joined the World Trade Organization in 2001, American trade officials were still complaining about China's ringleader role in international software piracy.

Unlike China, Japan's infatuation with Anglo-American pop music has not produced a major piracy problem. Since Japan is a global leader in hardware and software production—including Sony and Nintendo—its commercial trade policies are more readily allied to American positions on issues such as piracy. But if relations between Japan and the United States have been harmonious on some fronts, they have been more fractious on others.

From the earliest days of rock music, Japanese youth were transfixed by Anglo-American pop stars. But as in other parts of Asia, locally promoted Japanese talent tended to emulate bubblegum American groups, such as The Monkees. In the 1970s, however, a Japanese youth subculture emerged with a strong identification with Anglo-American rock music. Many Japanese rock musicians were *ronin*, or high school students, who had failed to gain entry into university and consequently drifted into the less respectable world of pop music. Yosui Inoue was the first Japanese pop star—and *ronin*—to produce a record, *Kohri no Sekai*, that sold a million copies. Released in 1973, *Kohri no Sekai* was the Japanese equivalent of early David Bowie records such as *Hunky Dory* and *Ziggy Stardust*. Bowie himself was going through a "Japanese" phase in the early 1970s with his Ziggy persona. Among other Anglo-American pop stars that enjoyed immense success in Japan in the 1970s were glam rocker Marc Bolan of T-Rex fame and Cheap Trick. Many Japanese pop bands of the period were inspired by Anglo-American rock band of the decade. Yellow Magic Orchestra, for example, emerged as Japan's first major synthesizer band with an Anglo-American look and style.

When Japan began rising as an economic superpower in the 1980s, many believed America was falling into permanent decline as Japan emerged as a new global hegemon. In the entertainment industries, Sony purchased CBS Records and Columbia Pictures—thus grabbing control of not only a Hollywood studio but also a major record label. In pop music, Japan boasted the second-biggest market in the world, after the United States. The combination of industrial strength via giants like Sony and a large domestic market provided advantageous conditions for a burgeoning Japanese pop music industry. It was during this period that the so-called "J-pop" phenomenon produced a constellation of local Japanese pop stars. Many of them—like Japanese pop diva Namie Amuro—became famous throughout Asia. Japanese pop singers could successfully compete with Anglo-American rock stars because their songs conveyed culturally specific Asian nuances, even when influenced by Anglo-American pop music styles. Some Japanese pop groups—Boredoms, Ruins, Melt Banana—sported English names and showed a variety of Anglo-American influences, from grunge to hip hop. Melt Banana recorded a record with producer Steve Albini, famous for producing the albums of Seattle-based grunge super-group Nirvana.

Japan's sudden decline in the 1990s—and the reaffirmation of American power—put an end to speculation about Japanese global domination. Still, Japan's cultural influence continued to expand. As Daniel McGray wrote in *Foreign Policy*: "Instead of collapsing beneath its political and economic misfortunes, Japan's global cultural influence has only grown. In fact, from pop music to consumer electronics, architecture to fashion, and food to art, Japan has far greater cultural influence now than it did in the 1980s, when it was an economic superpower."[18]

Despite the diversity of Japanese rock music, the country's most famous pop stars have been so-called "concept" bands of the teeny-bopper variety.

Japan has proved adept as faithfully replicating the appeal and success of Anglo-American bubblegum groups like Backstreet Boys and Spice Girls. Though fabricated by the dictates of marketing, Japanese concept bands are obliged to obey local cultural conventions. Lipless X Sister, for example, is an all-girl Japanese pop group whose members are in their early twenties. Their attraction to corporate image-makers would seem puzzling in the Anglo-American world: All are mothers of small toddlers. The band's producer explained the appeal of Lipless X Sister: "You can like them. But they're mothers, so you can't kiss them." After their debut in early 2000, Lipless X Sister quickly became famous throughout Japan for their "Pada Pada" dance, which featured the band's female members, dressed in denim jeans and skimpy tops, pushing their kids in strollers on stage while chanting, "Pada Pada mama, Pada Pada mama." Their act may be ersatz Spice Girls, but it has a distinctly Japanese cultural twist.

Japanese pop stars are immensely popular in many parts of Asia, but in some countries bitter memories about Japan's role in the Second World War have lingered painfully. Taiwan didn't end its restrictions on Japanese cultural imports until 1994. In South Korea, where officially sanctioned hatred for all things Japanese had been particularly intense, in the late 1990s the government finally liberalized—for the first time in more than 50 years—its cultural relations with Japan. In October 1998, Korean President Kim Dae Jung adopted a policy of openness towards Japanese culture, including Japanese movies and live performances of Japanese rock groups. Yet strict censorship remained in force on all songs with Japanese lyrics. When Japanese pop singer Tomoe Sawa performed in the Korean city of Kwangju, she sang two songs in Japanese that had to be pre-approved by the Korean government. Tomoe Sawa was a logical choice to thaw the cultural ice between the two countries: She was born to a Japanese father and Korean mother, spent her childhood in Korea, and was the granddaughter of a famous Korean poet.

In the Islamic world, pop music aspirations have been even more fraught with cultural and political tensions—and indeed have sometimes resulted in assassination. Following the rise of Islamic fundamentalism throughout the Moslem world, Arab pop stars have become targets due to their connection with an essentially Western form of music. In 1996, Moroccan pop singer Bechiri Boujemaa—known as "Cheb Aziz"—was brutally murdered by Islamic guerrillas. His sin was to have chosen a musical style—known as "*raï*"—that blends traditional Algerian music with Western pop sounds. The roots of *raï* stretched back to the 1920s, when female singers, called Shikhas, performed at weddings, cabarets, and brothels in the Algerian port city of Oran. Thematically, *raï* songs were generally about youthful love. As *raï* evolved over the following decades, however, it absorbed influences from Western pop music, especially the throbbing disco beat. By the 1980s, Algerian *raï* singers had become national heroes. But the timing of their glory was tragic. As Islamic fundamentalism spread throughout the Maghreb, *raï* was denounced by Moslem spiritual leaders for allegedly promoting "immoral" values, notably liberal attitudes about love and sex. Algeria's Islamic leaders issued a *fatwa* calling on Moslems to kill all pop singers whose music offended Islam.

Algeria's so-called "*raï* wars" began in 1990, when Islamic fundamentalists won stunning victories in the country's elections. A year later, a group of young Islamic fundamentalists torched a theatre in Algeria to prevent a *raï* concert. In 1994, guerrillas calling themselves the Armed Islamic Group assassinated *raï* singer Cheb Hasni outside his parents' home in Oran. The following year, Algerian pop music producer Rachid Baba Ahmed was gunned down. In 1996, the Islamic guerrillas who kidnapped and murdered Cheb Aziz justified their crime by claiming that his music was turning Moslem youth away from the Koran. He was the fourth *raï* singer to be murdered by Islamic guerrillas in the Maghreb. After Cheb Aziz' murder, several famous Algerian *raï* singers—such as Cheb Mami—fled their native country for Paris, where *raï* music is popular among France's large Arabic population. Algerian pop star Khaled—the so-called "king of *raï*"—had already moved to Paris, where he enjoyed superstar status among France's Arab population. Khaled, who recorded for Polygram, had a hit record in the early 1990s with his song, "Didi," whose producer Don Was had previously worked with Bob Dylan and The Rolling Stones. Khaled subsequently recorded an album, *Kenza*, which featured a number of songs—including his version of John Lennon's "Imagine"—that sent a message to his Islamic critics. In 1997, Algerian filmmaker Mahmoud Zemmouri featured Khaled and Cheb Mami in his movie *100 Percent Arabica*, which portrayed *raï* music as the main force of resistance to Algeria's mad mullahs. Three years later, pop star Sting featured the vocals of Cheb Mami in his hit song "Desert

Rose." In 2000, Sting recorded *The Two Tenors of Arab Music*, featuring Lebanon's Wadi al-Safi and Syrian vocalist Sabah Fakhri, who is known as "the Frank Sinatra of Syria." But the tragic events of September 11, 2001, seriously affected the growing appetite in the West for Arab music. Khaled, for example, had been booked on a U.S. tour to begin on September 14, 2001, but the entire tour was cancelled at the last minute after the Islamic terrorist attacks on America three days earlier.

The world's most famous Islamic pop star is undoubtedly Yusuf Islam—formerly known as Cat Stevens. As Cat Stevens, Yusuf Islam had topped the Anglo-American charts in the 1970s with songs such as "Morning Has Broken" and "Oh Very Young." By the end of the decade, London-born Stevens had sold 25 million records worldwide, but he was searching for something more meaningful than material success. In late 1977, Stevens converted to Islam at a London mosque, and immediately changed his name to Yusuf Islam. Shocked, his record label A&M hastily released his latest album, *Back to Earth*, before news of Stevens' religious conversion became widely known. Many believed Stevens' Islamic infatuation would be short-lived; but it turned out to be enduring. What's more, he became an outspoken Islamic activist. He provoked a storm of controversy when he publicly suggested that the Islamic *fatwa* against writer Salman Rushdie was justified. Today, many of Cat Stevens' millions of fans prefer to forget the singer's religious crusades and continue to enjoy his old hits. → willful deniability

Elsewhere in the Islamic world, the appeal of Western pop music has confronted profoundly paradoxical reactions. Regimes in some Moslem-dominated countries—such as Malaysia and Indonesia—have resolutely opposed the allegedly poisonous influence of Western pop music, though at the same time these countries have energetically embraced Western-style capitalism. In Malaysia, President Mohatir Mohamad denounced the noxious effects of Western cultural imperialism, yet his government sponsored the careers of Islamic "boy bands" modelled on Anglo-American groups like the Backstreet Boys. The main difference is that Malaysia's boy bands sing the praises of Allah. The most famous Malaysian boy band, Raihan, has sold millions of records in Malaysia and Singapore with lyrics such as "God is great" and other phrases lifted directly from the Koran. Following in Raihan's footsteps, Malaysia now boasts a Spice Girls-style girl group, called Huda, whose female members promote family values and urge women to be submissive towards their husbands. The packaging of these kinds of pop groups is based on a simple formula: Western image, Islamic message.

In Iran, the ayatollahs who led the 1979 revolution banned satellite television dishes carrying MTV. They soon realized, however, that they were powerless against Iranian youths who were secretly installing dishes on their windowsills in the slums of Tehran. It took many years, but the ayatollahs finally conceded defeat. In the early 1990s, Iran's theocratic rulers began liberalizing their anti-satellite TV laws. Even more surprisingly, in 1999—twenty years after the revolution—Islamic authorities gave permission for a pop concert to be held in Tehran. The decision was taken by Iran's moderate president, Mohammad Khatami, as part of his policy to bring meaningful reforms to Iranian society. In a country where youth make up more than half of a population of 65 million people, this gesture was inevitable. President Khatami was not indifferent to the fact that Iran's youth had overwhelmingly supported him against hardline Islamic fundamentalists. The Tehran pop concert nonetheless was billed as a 20th anniversary celebration of the overthrow of late Shah, Mohammad Reza Pahlavi. Still, the concert was a radical departure from twenty years of Islamic orthodoxy, when only traditional Iranian music was allowed to be performed in public. For many Iranian pop artists, however, it was too late. The revolution had triggered the exodus of many of Iran's most accomplished musicians. Persian pop groups, such as Black Cats, had moved to the United States. Some Iranian pop groups recorded in America but had their music—sometimes millions of copies—smuggled back into Iran to reach their fans. Among Persian pop icons who stayed in Iran was diva Googoosh, whose fame in Iran was akin to Madonna's notoriety in America. But Googoosh stopped making records after the ayatollahs took power.

In Iraq, Saddam Hussein's oppressive regime, while fiercely anti-American, nonetheless showed remarkable indulgence towards American pop music. Before the U.S. invasion of Iraq in 2003, a foreign visitor riding in a Baghdad taxi could hear an FM disc jockey denounce President George W. Bush as a "criminal" before making a zippy intro for a song by Madonna. This bizarre paradox could be reconciled only upon learning that the FM station was owned by Uday Hussein, the eldest—and most unpredictable—

son of Saddam Hussein. It was believed that Uday Hussein, who was also a member of the Iraqi parliament, was idly looking for a hobby farm when he launched the FM station and youth television channel called Youth TV. The radio station captured a 95 percent audience share at peak listening hours. Youth TV, for its part, showcased pirated Hollywood movies starring action heroes such as Sylvester Stallone, Arnold Schwarzenegger, and Jean-Claude Van Damme. Some believed Uday Hussein's interest in media outlets was part of his ill-conceived campaign to position himself as his father's successor. It was known that Uday had been engaged in a bitter rivalry with younger brother, Qusai, who headed the country's Republican Guards and oversaw the secret service. If Uday Hussein wished to succeed his father, he had many enemies. He survived an assassination attempt in 1996, but was critically wounded when Iranian agents used rocket-propelled grenades to assault his sports car. In the end, the toppling of his father's despicable regime in 2003 put an end to Uday's putative ambition to become a power broadcaster in the Arab world. The U.S. Army didn't neglect to launch a soft-power assault on Iraq in the run-up to its "shock and awe" campaign. As part of the Pentagon's "psyops" campaign—for "psychological operations"—Western pop songs such as Celine Dion's "My Heart Will Go On" were part of an American-backed Arabic station's attempt to promote American values in Iraq. American pop songs were mixed with Arabic music and speeches by President George W. Bush denouncing the regime of Saddam Hussein.

Latin American pop stars, meanwhile, have been burning up the international charts—Gloria Estefan, Shakira, Ricky Martin, Marc Antony, and Enrique Iglesias, to name only a few. These pop singers are modern-day versions of Latin music's early sensations, such as Perez Prado, Carmen Miranda, and Xavier Cugat. For decades, Latin music vibes—tango, conga, rumba, salsa, samba, mambo, and bossa nova—were entrenched in world's popular imagination. Today, Latino pop is hot.

In some respects, today's Latino pop phenomenon is not unlike early British rock: it began emulating American pop music, and then invaded the United States with its own American-influenced brand of pop music. From its earliest days, American rock music spread into Mexico and into South America. In most cases, local rock musicians began by imitating Anglo-American pop stars, but gradually found their own idiom with fusion sounds. In the late 1960s, Brazilian rockers created *tropicalia*, a hybrid form of rock that mixed Anglo and local musical styles with a counterculture edge provided by electric guitars and rebellious lyrics. In Argentina, *rock naçional* concerts rallied young people against the military dictatorship that took power in 1976. When Argentina's military regime invaded the Falkland Islands in 1982, the ruling *junta* banned the transmission of pop music in English. But after the Union Jack was planted on Falklands soil again, the British pop invasion of Argentina continued—and was embraced. Throughout Latin America, as military regimes were successively toppled and the values of liberal democracy took hold, a new generation of musicians and pop singers emerged as cheerleaders for these profound social changes.

[handwritten margin note: not democracy, so pop music]

But not all Latino pop stars have championed political causes. Latin America's biggest star in recent years has been sex symbol Ricky Martin. Like other Latino pop stars, Puerto Rican-born Martin grew up with one foot in Latin America and the other in the United States. After leaving the Latino boy band Menudo, Martin shot to international stardom when he sang "La Copa de la Vida" at the 1998 World Cup soccer final. Besides his good looks and hip-grinding sensuality, Martin's success was also owed to good timing. His career was taking off just as Spanish-language radio stations were being launched in major U.S. cities—New York's La Mega 97, Chicago's WOJO, and L.A.'s La X. At the same time, *People* magazine was desperately searching for Latino stars for its new Hispanic edition, *People en Español.* MTV Latino, meanwhile, had been launched in 1993 and was growing increasingly popular as cable and satellite TV subscriptions soared throughout Latin and South America. Also, the tragic death in 1995 of pop singer Selena, and her posthumous hit records, made major record labels wake up to the potential of Latino pop. In May 1999, *Time* magazine put Ricky Martin on its cover under the headline: "Latin Music Goes Pop!"

Martin was the most famous face among a new generation of Latino pop stars. Another was singer Thalia, a Mexican beauty who graduated from television soap operas to pop records produced by Gloria Estefan's husband, Emilio Estefan. In Brazil, Max de Castro gained fame with the release of his album, *Sambo Raro*, whose fusion sound blends Latino samba and bossa nova with American hip hop and soul. "Most Brazilian musicians are labeled international artists," said de Castro. "I will be very glad when I enter an American record store and find *Samba Raro* not in the world-music section but beside people I admire like Prince and Stevie Wonder."

Another Castro—Fidel Castro—has been decidedly less enamoured of his namesake's samba sounds. In communist Cuba, pop music has long been suspect for ideological reasons. Before Castro took power in the late 1950s, Havana was a culturally rich cosmopolitan city where the Latin salsa provided a constant musical backdrop to a moveable feast of effervescent social activity in the city's Mafia-controlled hotels and casinos. But that swirling world of music, dance, and moral corruption abruptly came to an end when Castro closed the casinos, kicked out the Mafia, and nationalized Cuban industries. Many Cuban musicians and singers moved to Miami or elsewhere in the United States to pursue their careers.

In recent years, pop singer Gloria Estefan has been the world's most famous Cuban pop star. Born in 1957, Estefan left Cuba with her family as a toddler. In 1961, her father had taken part in the embarrassingly unsuccessful U.S.-backed Bay of Pigs invasion to overthrow Fidel Castro. Estefan moved with her family to Miami and grew up in the city's Cuban ghetto. After achieving fame with the Miami Sound Machine, Estefan shot to superstardom as a solo pop diva with songs like "Conga" and "Everlasting Love." Despite her global stardom, Estefan didn't forget her roots. Indeed, Estefan has worked tirelessly—and sometimes controversially—as an anti-Castro pop emissary speaking for Cuban-American exiles. Her song "Go Away" was a taunt directed at Castro.

"People don't have a lot of information and when they ask me about it," said Estefan, "I tell them about the drama of the exiles, the repression, the firing squads, the horror of communism. I'm very clear about that. I left Cuba when I was two years old. They took away my country, they stole the most intimate thing a human being can have. How could I forget that Fidel Castro was the person who did me so much harm?"

Fidel Castro understood early that pop music was a natural adversary to his Soviet-backed regime, and therefore banned all pop songs from Cuban radio stations. But that didn't stop American pop music from reaching Cuba from southern Florida via U.S. state-financed broadcasters such as Radio Martì. These Washington-sponsored broadcasters have been a constant source of irritation to Castro's regime. The Cuban dictator has been more effective with other measures, such as restrictions on Cuban musicians seeking to perform abroad. It was this policy that triggered violent protests among Cuban-Americans, though with an ironic twist.

In October 1999, the popular Cuban group Los Van Van embarked on a 28-city tour of the United States with Castro's official permission. One stop was Miami, but there was one problem. Los Van Van's concert had been prohibited by a city ban on any performance by Cuban musicians. The municipal interdiction against performances by Cuban musicians had been passed by Miami's powerful Cuban-American elected officials. The ban provoked an outcry in the musical community, who claimed there is no such thing as "communist music." Cuban-American supporters of the ban, on the other hand, dismissed Los Van Van as the "official Communist band of Fidel Castro." They maintained that Miami should not subsidize, with taxpayer dollars, any performance by a Cuban musician because the Castro regime insists that musicians share their earnings with the government.

Gloria Estefan sided with Cuban-American protestors. "I cannot imagine how we could explain to the people of Cuba, who have suffered so much oppression, that the very freedoms that they so desperately desire and deserve are being annihilated in their name," she said.

As the controversy heated up, the American Civil Liberties Union threatened to sue the City of Miami for prohibiting a public performance. Fearful of a full-blown scandal in the national media, the city finally relented and the concert went ahead. But the city got a full-blown media scandal just the same when the concert degenerated into violent scenes resembling a riot.

During the concert, Los Van Van's bandleader, Juan Formell, shouted out to about 2,500 fans in the audience: "To us, you represent millions of people; there are more of you who love us than don't love us."

After the concert, Los Van Van's fans were confronted in the street with an angry mob of anti-Castro protestors, who pelted them with bottles and eggs. The controversy was particularly embarrassing in Miami, capital of the billion-dollar Latin American pop music industry—and, what's more, headquarters of MTV Latino. The impact of this incident was immediate. Another famous Cuban musical band, the Buena Vista Social Club, cancelled its Miami engagement. Also, the Latin Academy of Recording Arts and Sciences—sponsor of the Latin Grammy Awards—decided to move its annual awards event from Miami to Los Angeles.

Today, not even Castro's brutal regime has been able to silence American pop music in Cuba. In Havana, the rebellious chanting of American hip hop—sung by Cuban *raperos*—enliven the dreary streets where Cuba's dispossessed youth congregate and search to assign a meaning to their lives. One of Cuba's best-known rap groups is Orishas. When Orishas' fame began to spread through the island, Castro summoned them to his presidential palace for a private tête-à-tête.

"So you are the ones who have been making so much noise," snapped Castro.

Following Orishas' success, Castro began showing some indulgence towards Cuban pop music. When rap producer Pablo Herrera wanted to record Cuban hip-hop songs, he sought the permission from Castro's Ministry of Culture—and obtained it. Herrera produced the very first Cuban rap record, *Cuban Hip-Hop All Stars Vol. 1*, that was released commercially in the United States.

In many respects, it was inevitable that American rap music would eventually catch on in Cuba, a country with a large Afro-Cuban population. While Cuba's youth had access to American pop music on cassettes, CD, and on the radio, most could not afford to buy stereo systems, download songs on the Internet, or make songs in high-tech recording studios.

Like urban blacks in the Bronx twenty years ago, young Afro-Cubans have taken their music to the streets. The rhythms are from America, but the message is their own. → *America as tool of liberation*

We Are the World

More than a half century since the birth of rock 'n' roll, theories about American cultural imperialism in pop music find little support in the economic realities of the music industry—or, more importantly, in the cultural realities of music preferences. If anything, America is awash in pop music sounds from beyond its borders. American music is no longer a one-way export to the world. World music has come to America. *not our way*

Few would have predicted that a blind Italian operatic singer, Andrea Bocelli, would win millions of fans in America—selling nearly 7 million copies of his 1997 record, *Romanza*. More unimaginable, the hit song from that album—an operatic duet with Sarah Brightman—bore a title in Italian: "Con Te Partiro." Following the success of that song, Bocelli became a bona fide international pop star. The global success of *Romanza* powerfully illustrates the dynamic nature of musical expression: It is spontaneous, unpredictable, open, and constantly cross-pollinating. In music, cultural centres cannot durably dominate marginal peripheries; and "high" culture cannot prevail long over "low" culture. Music at the margins inevitably ends up dominating the centre; and "high" and "low" culture inexorably become interpenetrated and fused in a creative alchemy that results in new musical forms. Rock 'n' roll, it should be remembered, emerged from the soulful music of Negro slaves. One of the world's most famous pop icons, Paul McCartney—who started in the 1950s imitating Little Richard and Chuck Berry—today is composing symphonies.

As Steve Silberman observed, ironically, in *Wired* magazine: "It would seem that the kind of gluttonous cultural imperialism described by Marx's *Manifesto* has reached its apotheosis in music. Any sound that's ever been recorded or imagined, anywhere on Earth, can be heard or imitated, and bred with any other sound—on equipment affordable even by musicians whose incomes firmly locate them in the proletariat ... Marx had it right, and wrong. Economic forces determine who has the time to devote their lives to music, who gets the advertising push and the Peter Gabriel 'Real World' treatment, who sings their schlock in state-of-the-art studios, and who's hot on the cover of *Rolling Stone* this month. But the patchwork history of the world's music stands as testimony to the fact that, even when there's no profit in it, human beings have an insatiable desire to steep themselves in the sounds, tastes, jargon, and ways of cultures other than their own. And the most useful thing the arbiters of cultural purity can do is dance out of the way."[19]

The Big Five global music giants now understand this, and deploy their resources accordingly. Only a generation ago, Anglo-American rock dominated the world. Today, even in the United States rock music is a commercial and cultural force in decline. Whereas in the early 1990s, the "rock" and "pop" music represented, respectively, roughly 35 percent and 12 percent of total sales, a decade later those figures had dropped to 25 percent and 11 percent. During the same period, previously marginal forms of music—such as rap and hip hop—soared in popularity. At the same time, so-called "world music" gained a growing audience in America and internationally. What's more, the Big Five labels—responding to these trends—were increasingly investing in local recording artists. In 2001, seven out of ten records produced by the Big Five were by local artists—not global Anglo-American pop stars. In the decade from 1990 to 2000, sales of domestic music rose from 58 percent to 68 percent.

"The recording industry in the past decade has emerged as a major investor in local culture worldwide," says Jay Berman, chairman of IFPI, the global music industry's umbrella organization. "The industry continues to develop creative talent in all regions and countries of the world, and it is contributing more than ever to the success of local artists and to the development of national music cultures."

It would be naïve, to be sure, to assert that Anglo-American pop records are no longer the main engine of the global music industry. In 2001, the world's biggest-selling pop stars were: Britney Spears, Santana, The Beatles, Eminem, Red Hot Chili Peppers, Bon Jovi, U2, Madonna, Moby, Backstreet Boys, and Enrique Iglesias. Only one—Enrique Iglesias—was not Anglo-American. Still, major record labels are increasingly looking for alternatives to the old model of promoting a select group of Anglo-American megastars who demand colossal sums and cost millions more in marketing and promotional campaigns. Recent tensions between Anglo-American pop stars and their record labels are symptoms of a major shakeout in the global music industry. In early 2002, pop diva Mariah Carey was dumped by her record label, EMI Group, who paid the singer $49 million merely to go away. Other established pop stars—Rod Stewart, Sinead O'Connor, David Bowie, and Van Halen—similarly were dropped from their labels.

Today, global music giants—EMI, Universal Music, Warner Music, BMG, and Sony—have been frantically attempting to respond to threats beyond their control. First, sales have been declining. Second, music tastes have been fragmenting across a wide range of genres as Anglo-American rock's traditional dominance is eroded by hip hop and other forms of music. Third, young people have been downloading songs on the Internet and listening to music on MP3 players. Confronted with these realities, big record labels feel they no longer can keep a large stable of fading rock stars on their payrolls in the hope that, some day, they may produce another hit record. Global music giants are increasingly driven by short-term results.

Younger pop stars—Creed, Ja Rule, Shakira, Linkin Park—produce more profits for the major labels than older stars like Rod Stewart, David Bowie, and Elton John.

Whatever its commercial fate, pop music inspires feelings, stirs emotions, mobilizes beliefs, and even calls to action. For those reasons, pop music is, and will continue to be, a potent soft power resource—as the White House's Radio Sawa project in the Arab world demonstrates.

Some pop stars, impressed by the power of their music on global audiences, have attempted to project themselves onto the stage of global geopolitics. Irish rock star U2 lead singer Bono, embarked on a tour of African countries with U.S. Treasury Secretary Paul O'Neill during the spring of 2002. Their mission was to seek solutions to Third World poverty. When the press dubbed their fact-finding trip the "O'Neill-Bono Africa Tour 2002," they could have been describing a concert in America by U2 or The Rolling Stones. *Time* magazine remarked: "Africa hasn't seen a celebrity road show like this since Stanley met Livingstone … Like heroes in a buddy movie, opposites attract." In Ghana, O'Neill and Bono posed for the international media sporting traditional Ghanian outfits, including striped headdress that resembled a jester's cap. O'Neill eagerly boasted that Bono, sporting Romeo Gigli sunglasses, was his "very good friend." On their 10-day trip, the two men visited four African countries—Ghana, South Africa, Uganda, and Ethiopia—travelling on a chartered jet called "Great Expectations" and accorded full U.S. secret service protection. They were also followed by reporters from media outlets as varied as the *New York Times*, *Financial Times*, *Rolling Stone*, and MTV.

Bono, in fact, was already familiar with the corridors of global power. In February 2002, the pop singer had stolen the spotlight at the World Economic Forum in New York, where he met with world leaders and senior U.S. administration officials. A few weeks later, Bono was in Washington meeting with President Bush in the Oval Office, where the singer took his "Drop the Debt" campaign to the U.S. President. It worked. After their meeting, President Bush made a speech announcing an additional $5 billion in U.S. aid to the Third World. Bono also met with top Bush administration officials including Colin Powell and Condoleezza Rice. White House critics noted that the Bush administration was suffering from a psychological condition known as "Celebrity Envy."

Bono's mingling with top White House officials was ironic for a pop star who once—in songs like *Bullet the Blue Sky*—railed against American cultural imperialism and U.S. big business. Bono clearly had changed his tactics: Instead of protesting in the streets, he was penetrating the inner sanctums of global power to make his views known. As Bono said when standing next to his friend Paul O'Neill in Ghana: "He's the man in charge of America's wallet and I am looking to open it."

Bono shrewdly understood the publicity-generating value of schmoozing with the world's most powerful men and women at the White House. He undoubtedly was canny enough to understand that he, too, was being exploited for publicity. American political leaders, who face elections, are always keen to seem sympathetic to the concerns of young people. Even unelected U.S. leaders, like Secretary of State Colin Powell, have appealed to the world's pop fans to get U.S. foreign policy messages to the planet's youth.

During his globally televised MTV appearance on Valentine's Day 2002, Powell was defensive only once, when a 19-year-old Norwegian woman asked him frankly how it felt to represent a nation frequently decried as a "Great Satan."

"Far from being a Great Satan," Powell replied, "I think we are the Great Protector."

That message, it should be hoped, will be embraced by the world's MTV Generation.

→ proves the point the music as a whole is liberating, and because of US economic domination + the ability for music to make money, US brings music to world, however liberating qualities are not just US attributes + US sends out much more than it receives of "World music influence"

→ Pop music argument has been strongest so far but mostly b/c of economic advantages not cultural sensitivity.

four

Fast Food

Coca-Colonization and McDomination

IN JUNE 1945, General Dwight D. Eisenhower triumphantly returned to America as the hero of the Second World War. Fascism had been defeated in Europe, and victorious America was the undisputed leader of the free world. In Washington, one of the most lavish victory celebrations was a sumptuous dinner in honour of General Eisenhower at the Statler, a grand hotel two blocks from the White House.

After enjoying a copious meal, General Eisenhower was asked if he wished anything else.

"Could somebody get me a Coke?" he replied.

When a bottle of Coca-Cola was produced, Ike promptly polished it off. He had one more request, he said. Nervous attention fixed on the four-star general, awaiting his behest.

"Another Coke," he snapped.

Eisenhower wasn't the only U.S. military hero of the Second World War addicted to Coca-Cola. General George Patton always kept a cache of Coke, his favourite beverage, which he liked to mix with rum. During the war, General Patton once barked with characteristic gruffness: "Hell, we ought to send the Coke in first, then we wouldn't have to fight the bastards!"

By the end of the war, Coca-Cola had become synonymous with America throughout the world. In the decades that followed, Coke was joined by an arsenal of other American "fast food" icons—McDonald's, Burger King, Kentucky Fried Chicken, Pepsi, Taco Bell, and Starbucks—which would, like Coca-Cola, be regarded with a mixture of envy and suspicion as symbolic extensions of U.S. imperialism. For Americans—the inhabitants of "Fast Food Nation"—the corporate logos of these products have become a banal part of everyday life. But beyond America's borders, Big Macs and Coca-Cola provoke powerful reactions.

When America retaliated against Osama bin Ladin's terrorist attacks on the United States, the U.S. bombings in Afghanistan triggered violent counter reprisals throughout the Islamic world that seized on McDonald's, Coca-Cola, and KFC as targets. Eighteen months later when the U.S. Army invaded Iraq, anti-American violence flared up again throughout the Moslem world. In Indonesia, members of the Moslem Students Alliance picketed McDonald's while shouting "God is great!" and "USA go to hell!" Anti-American protests also erupted in Asia and throughout the West. In South Korea, anti-war demonstrators wearing George Bush masks brandished M-16 rifles while scaling the Golden Arches of McDonald's restaurants and chanting "No to war!" In Athens, the cradle of Western civilization, demonstrators splashed red paint outside two targeted locations: the U.S. embassy and a nearby McDonald's. Another McDonald's outlet in Athens was destroyed in a grenade attack. Violent assaults against McDonald's erupted in many other Western countries—Spain, Argentina, Bulgaria, and Ecuador—where protestors burned effigies of George Bush, smashed apart Golden Arches, and chanted "killer capitalism."

For America's most strident adversaries, McDonald's and Coke are interchangeable with America itself. Coca-Cola and Big Macs are regarded, and resented, as potent symbols of American global power—or "Coca-colonization" and "McDomination."

Coca-Colonization

Coca-Cola and Hollywood share an intriguing historical experience. Like motion pictures, Coke had the good fortune of being invented, and rapidly commercialized, at the outset of the 20th century just as America was emerging as a global power. Also, the early promoters of Coke, like the first Hollywood moguls, emerged triumphant after facing, and defeating, fierce rivalry from a formidable soft-power adversary: France.

Coca-Cola was invented in the 1880s as a "nerve tonic" during a period in America that has been described unflatteringly as the Golden Age of Quackery. Coke's inventor, a Southern "root doctor" called John Pemberton, concocted his beverage at a time when battalions of patent medicine salesmen were shamelessly flogging their dubious elixirs throughout America. Besides Coca-Cola, very few of these patent medicines survived commercially. One early Coke rival that did endure was Hires Root Beer, which in the late 19th century promised to "purify the blood and make rosy cheeks." Another, Dr. Pepper, claimed to "aid digestion and restore vim, vigor, and vitality." Coca-Cola, for its part, produced an even more potent effect on its early enthusiasts, thanks mainly to one of its ingredients: cocaine.

Dr. Pemberton was not unaware of the beneficial effects of cocaine in his Coca-Cola syrup. "The use of the coca plant," he wrote in 1885, "not only preserves the health of all who use it, but prolongs life to a very great old age and enables the coca eaters to perform prodigies of mental and physical labor."

The French had already understood the wonders of cocaine in liquid form. The forerunner of Coca-Cola was a French drink called Vin Mariani, named after a Corsican wine merchant, Angelo Mariani, who in 1863 had begun selling his Bordeaux products with a novel twist: infusions of coca leaves. Today, Vin Mariani has been erased from the annals of oenology. In the Victorian era, however, Vin Mariani was a spectacular success, especially among the upper classes known for the refinements of their ritualized libations. Queen Victoria herself was addicted to Vin Mariani—and therefore was, de facto, a cocaine user. Pope Leo XII awarded Vin Mariani a gold medal "in recognition of benefits received from the use of Mariani's tonic." In America, among the many famous personalities who happily gave promotional testimonials to the therapeutic benefits of Vin Mariani were Thomas Edison and President William McKinley. Another U.S. president, Ulysses Grant, owed a great debt to Vin Mariani. During his retirement, Grant suddenly fell ill in 1885, but his physicians managed to prolong his life by administering Vin Mariani. Thanks to the cocaine-infused French drink, Grant's life was extended long enough for him to complete his memoirs. At the height of Vin Mariani's popularity in the late 19th century, the French drink was being produced in Paris and New York and counted distribution centres in London, Montreal, Brussels, Geneva, Saigon, and other cities.

In his hometown of Atlanta, Dr. Pemberton was among Vin Mariani's first imitators with his own product, which he called "French Wine Coca." Pemberton himself was a drug addict hooked on morphine. It is believed, in fact, that he seized on cocaine as an ingredient for his French Wine Coca as a potential alternative to morphine. During the 1880s, morphine addiction—known as "morphinism"—was creeping into American society. At the time, however, alcoholism was actually regarded as a much more dangerous evil, especially by the powerful Temperance movement in the United States. It was the Temperance movement, in fact, that drove Pemberton out of the wine business. It mattered little whether cocaine was mixed into his wine. The problem was the wine. Ironically, Pemberton's company, after he sold out, eventually came under the control of a Methodist called Asa Candler, who began flogging with religious zeal a non-alcoholic version of the cocaine-infused beverage. The drink was rebaptized "Coca-Cola."

By the early 20th century, Coca-Cola was rapidly becoming a widely popular drink throughout America, despite concern in some quarters about its cocaine content. Asa Candler, Coke's chief salesman, received his missionary zeal from his brother, Warren, a Methodist bishop who preached a combination of Protestant evangelism and American imperialism. In his 1904 book, *Great Revivals and the Great Republic*, Bishop Candler predicted that America would lead the world thanks to its combined virtues of religion and capitalism. Thus inspired, Asa Candler vowed to conquer the world with Coca-Cola. The timing was propitious. In the aftermath of the Spanish-American War, the United States was starting to emerge as an imperial power. The first commercial opportunity Candler seized was Cuba, a strategically important market for a drink manufacturer that depended on predictable, low-cost supplies of sugar.

In 1916, Coca-Cola was so powerful economically in Atlanta that Asa Candler was well-positioned to become mayor of the city. His political coronation was the beginning of a long and prosperous relationship between Atlanta and Coca-Cola, which funded the city's Emory University. Following Candler's entry into politics, Coca-Cola found a new corporate leader in another charismatic figure, Robert Woodruff. A tall, elegant southern gentleman, Woodruff moved quickly to standardize the product so every hobbleskirt bottle looked and tasted exactly the same wherever it was sold. It was Woodruff who pushed Coke into the worldwide market. Woodruff shrewdly realized that the new movie industry in Hollywood could be exploited as a promotional vehicle for his drink. By the 1930s, Coke had enlisted a glittering roster of Hollywood's biggest names—Clark Gable, Cary Grant, Carole Lombard, Johnny Weissmuller, and Greta Garbo—to promote the soft drink. One Coke slogan of the era was: "If it's good for the stars, it's good for you." The entire cast of George Cukor's movie *Dinner at Eight*—including Lionel Barrymore and Jean Harlow— gathered on the MGM lot to pose for a Coca-Cola advertisement in which they each sipped the beverage from a straw.

In the early 1930s, the Coca-Cola label appeared on 20,000 walls, 160,000 billboards, and 5 million soda fountain glasses throughout the United States. Coke's appeal in Middle America was strengthened and deepened by ads featuring quaint Norman Rockwell images. A major publicity coup for Coke came in 1931, when an ingenious adman created the "Coca-Cola Santa Claus"—thus assimilating the appeal of Coke and the good cheer of Christmas.

The only threat to Coke's dominance of the beverage market was Pepsi. Like Coca-Cola, Pepsi had been invented as a patent medicine at the end of the 19th century. Originally known as "Brad's Drink," in 1898 the drink was renamed "Pepsi-Cola." After several near bankruptcies, Pepsi was reborn during the Depression thanks to the popularity of its radio jingle, *"Pepsi hits the spot!"* This was only the first shot in a long, nasty war between Coke and Pepsi that would reach the highest echelons of American politics— including the White House.

When the United States entered the Second World War after Pearl Harbor, Coke's corporate mission became boldly patriotic. Robert Woodruff issued the following order: "We will see that every man in uniform gets a bottle of Coca-Cola for five cents, wherever he is and what- ever it costs the company." While Woodruff's patriotism could not be doubted, he was not indifferent to more bottom-line considerations. By positioning Coke as part of the war effort, the company would be exempted from the U.S. government's sugar-rationing measures. The exemption was duly obtained, and U.S. military bases were soon awash in Coca-Cola. The top U.S. Army brass was particularly fond of Coke. General Patton's affection for rum-and-Coke was well-known. General Omar Bradley, for his part, had a predilection for ice cream and Coke. But the biggest Coca-Cola addict was Eisenhower. In North Africa in 1943, Eisenhower cabled home the following shorthand message: "On early convoy request shipment three million bottled Coca-Cola (filled) and complete equipment for bottling, washing, capping same quantity twice monthly ... Also sufficient syrup and caps for 6 million refills. Syrup, caps and sixty thousand bottles monthly should be an automatic supply."[1]

Ike later explained the rationale behind his Coca-Cola command: "I had them make a survey to see what the men wanted, and more of them voted for Coke than beer."

The U.S. war effort also became part of Coke's advertising campaigns in America. One ad, showing U.S. sailors gathered at a bar buying Cokes, featured the caption: "Wherever a U.S. battleship may be, the American way of life goes along. So naturally Coca-Cola is there, too."

When the historic Normandy invasion was in its planning phase, Coke desperately wanted to be part of the operation by crossing the English Channel with Allied Forces. This would be inconceivable, however, without first getting substantial shipments of Coke into England—a difficult task during wartime rationing. Attempts to seduce Winston Churchill with cases of Coca-Cola failed when 10 Downing Street shunned the entreaties of Coke's agents in London. Finally, Coke executives prevailed upon General Eisenhower. He ordered a payload of Coca-Cola to be shipped to England and brought across the English Channel in the wake of the invasion in June 1944. Following the Normandy landings, Allied troops throughout northern France could be seen grabbing Cokes off the backs of two-ton trucks.

In Nazi Germany, meanwhile, Coke had been branded as a symbol of American decadence. As one Nazi official put it: "America has never contributed anything to world civilization but chewing gum and Coca-Cola."

Coke faced a competitor in Germany: an imitation drink called Afri-Cola that was manufactured by Germans with Nazi connections. To undermine Coke's brand in Germany, Afri-Cola executives spread the rumour that Coca-Cola was a "Jewish-American" company. It appears, however, that top Nazis—including the Führer himself—enjoyed a refreshing Coke. Hitler is said to have drunk Coca-Cola while privately screening *Gone with the Wind*. Herman Göring, for his part, was photographed sipping a Coke. This was not necessarily an endorsement that Coke wanted, however. Coke boycotted Germany, though the company continued to do business in Germany by marketing another soft drink, Fanta. Yet the Coke brand was still strong in Germany and throughout Europe after the war. Coke executives liked to tell the story of the German prisoners taken to Hoboken, New Jersey, after the Allied victory. Upon their arrival in America, the German soldiers reacted with curious excitement when they spotted a huge Coca-Cola billboard. Asked to explain their interest in the Coke logo, one of the Germans blurted out: "We're surprised that you have Coca-Cola here, too!"

The Allied victory was a commercial bonanza for Coca-Cola. When international leaders gathered in San Francisco to hammer out a founding charter for a United Nations, Robert Woodruff dispatched his top men to the city to promote Coke among the delegates. In 1948, Coke shrewdly seized on a global branding opportunity with a massive corporate presence at the Olympic Games in London. The same year, Coca-Cola held its first international bottlers convention in Atlanta. The Cold War had already begun and anti-Communism was in the air. One placard at the Atlanta convention read: "When we think of Communists, we think of the Iron Curtain. But when they think of democracy, they think of Coca-Cola."

By the early 1950s, Coca-Cola was established well beyond the Americas and Europe. Among nations conquered by Coke were Egypt, Tunisia, Kenya, Morocco, India, Congo, Lebanon, and Iraq. *Time* magazine, whose publisher Henry Luce was a strident anti-Communist, was happy to toast Coca-Cola as America's global ambassador. In May 1950, *Time*'s cover featured a smiling globe holding a bottle of Coke above the caption: "WORLD & FRIEND—Love that piaster, that lira, that tickey, and that American way of life." Luce happened to be a hunting companion of Robert Woodruff.

Not everybody was Coke's friend. When Mao Zedong's communists took over China, he promptly nationalized Coca-Cola's bottling plants. In Europe, most countries were desperate to benefit from the Marshall Plan's economic aid, but their gratitude was attenuated by the constant sight of cocky American soldiers living on nearby U.S. military bases, which became pejoratively known as "Coca-Cola towns." Coke got its most hostile reception—not surprisingly—in culturally proud France.

France's Fourth Republic, whose unstable governments dissolved with alarming frequency, was generally in favour of the Atlantic Alliance because the Marshall Plan was helping the country emerge from economic ruin. But the French Communist Party—the largest faction in the country's fractious parliament—remained virulently anti-American. Louis Aragon, the famous French poet known for his Communist affinities, dismissed America as "a civilization of bathtubs and Frigidaires." These sentiments—which appeared to provide indirect revelations about the state of French hygiene and standards of living in the post-war years—were widely shared among Parisian intellectuals. Aragon, enraged by the site of a Ford automobile that, for some reason, was placed on the spot of a missing statue of France's great writer Victor Hugo, publicly fulminated: "The Yankee, more arrogant than the Nazi iconoclast, substitutes the machine for the poet, Coca-Cola for poetry, American advertising for *La Légende des siècles*, the mass-manufactured car for the genius, the Ford for Victor Hugo."[2]

The real source of French anti-American hostility was not cultural, but economic and political. The Marshall Plan was desperately needed, but French Communists resented dependency on capitalist America and hence denounced *marshallisation*. Others on the French left believed France was dangerously flirting with the Atlantic Alliance and should adopt a neutralist foreign policy. In 1949 the leftist paper *Le Monde* ran a series of articles under the rubric "Imperial America." Some French intellectuals—such as Raymond Aron, François Mauriac, and André Maurois—were openly pro-American. But they were in a minority. Most, including Jean-Paul Sartre, gravitated towards Soviet Communism. Many French intellectuals liked American jazz music, but politically they embraced the slogan: "Yankee Go Home!" For the French, America was at once fascinating and repugnant.

It was in this climate that France's Coca-Cola Affair erupted at the end of the 1940s. In 1948, Coca-Cola obtained a bottling licence in France as part of a more concerted campaign to market the beverage in a country where it had been largely ignored during the 1920s and 1930s. But Coca-Cola's commercial plans in France did not sit well with the French Communist

Party, which was quick to seize on a convenient pretext to combat capitalist America. Many French Communists were aware of a Coke executive's controversial remark describing Coca-Cola as the "essence of capitalism." France's Communist-controlled newspaper, *L'Humanité*, quickly warned against "Coca-Colonization." Another Communist rumour claimed that Coke distributors in France were actually American spies. According to an even more ludicrous whisper campaign, Coke was planning to erect huge "Coca-Cola" advertising billboards on the gothic spires of Notre Dame Cathedral. *Le Monde* joined the anti-Coke chorus by comparing, somewhat facetiously, the soft drink's invasion of France to Hitler's annexation of Danzig. In an article titled "To Die for Coca Cola," *Le Monde* observed: "We have already stood by silently as American chewing gum, Cecil B. DeMille, *Reader's Digest*, and be-bop music invaded our shores. Now a conflict has erupted over a soft drink. Coca-Cola seems to be a cultural Danzig in Europe. After Coca-Cola moves in and takes over, what next?" In another article, *Le Monde* inveighed against "the dangers that Coca-Cola represents for the health and civilization of France."[3]

Jim Farley, one of Coke's most powerful executives, inflamed the controversy when he snapped: "Coca-Cola was not injurious to the health of the American soldiers who liberated France from the Nazis so that Communist deputies could be in session today."

Incensed, the Communist Party attempted to push a bill through France's National Assembly banning Coke on the grounds that its potentially poisonous ingredients were unknown. The bill's political sponsor claimed Coke was a threat to public health. In truth, the Communists' propaganda war on Coke was sponsored by French union interests in the domestic wine and mineral water industries. Coke was hardly a health threat to French citizens. Cocaine had been removed from the beverage many years before. Nor was the drink a gastronomic threat to French culture. In truth, Coke posed a commercial threat to the interests of powerful French unions that controlled France's Communist Party.

Coke nonetheless faced a serious diplomatic problem in France that called for high-level intervention. The company's chief lobbyist in Paris was a White Russian prince called Alexander Makinsky, an anti-Communist who had joined Coke in 1945 after working for the Rockefeller Foundation. Fluent in French and English, Makinsky was a legendary figure who was well-known for his close ties to U.S. intelligence services. In Paris, he was famous as an impeccably well-dressed bon vivant with a tidy mustache and predilection for slender cigars, champagne, and chic social circles that included Coco Chanel. Well-connected throughout Europe, he was friendly with several reigning monarchs, including King Farouk of Egypt.

Makinsky was given the difficult task of defusing Coke's political troubles in France. The Communists' backroom campaigns had been indisputably effective. By 1950, five French government ministries were conducting investigations into Coca-Cola. Also, French customs suspended Coke's import licence and criminal charges were brought against the company's bottlers. In the streets of Paris, Coke trucks were being overturned by angry mobs. Makinsky followed these events in horror, and even feared for his safety. He was convinced that France's secret police were following him and tapping his telephone.

"The best barometer of the relationship of the U.S. and any country," observed Makinsky, "is the way Coca-Cola is treated."

Makinsky got bad news from the French parliament, where the Communist-sponsored anti-Coke bill was passed in both houses. Fortunately for Makinsky, he had support in the highest levels of the Washington political system. Secretary of State Dean Acheson sent a memo to the U.S. ambassador in Paris, David Bruce, ordering him to inform the French government that the United States was "disturbed" by the anti-Coke legislation. Acheson also warned, through his ambassador, that French hostility to Coke would provoke U.S. reprisals against French commercial interests—notably wine, champagne, and perfume. In the United States, the press had gotten wind of the Coke kerfuffle in France. Some U.S. editorialists angrily urged Washington to cut off Marshall Plan aid. The *Philadelphia Inquirer* remarked: "This is worse than Marie Antoinette. The Commies won't even let 'em drink Coke." Another commentator noted: "You can't spread the doctrines of Marx among people who drink Coca-Cola."

At Coke's head office in Atlanta, the company's top executives were determined not to back down in France. A capitulation would send a message to other countries where local beverage and winemaking interests would similarly use their political clout to keep Coca-Cola out of their markets. It was now time to play hardball. Makinsky's gentlemanly Old World touch, while endearing, was not working. Coke parachuted into

Paris an executive called Steve Ladas, who arrived in early 1950 and immediately began meeting leaders of France's splintered parliament. It didn't take long for Ladas to understand that French political leaders were less concerned about "Americanization" than they were about appeasing the commercial interests of their national wine and beverage industries. French politicians who met with Ladas also expressed their dissatisfaction with U.S. tariffs on French wine imports. Ladas went to the U.S. embassy on Place de la Concorde to meet with ambassador David Bruce to enlist his help in untangling Coke's legal battles in the French courts. Ambassador Bruce was sympathetic, but the issue was complicated by high-level talks with the French government over NATO. Also, France's centrist government under Prime Minister Georges Bidault feared stinging criticism from Communists and Socialists that it was an American puppet.[4]

Fortunately, anti-French diatribe in the U.S. media had succeeded in getting the attention of French leaders. The implied threat of a trade war with the United States could not be casually ignored in France, a country that still depended on Marshall Plan credits. Officials at the French embassy in Washington were eager to defuse the crisis. It was finally agreed that the French government would restore Coke's import licence in France. But Coke did not escape significant damage to its brand and reputation in the Fourth Republic. In 1953, a poll taken in France discovered that only 17 percent of the French claimed to like Coca-Cola. More than 60 percent said they didn't like Coke at all.

As in France, Communist Party apparatchiks throughout Europe were targeting Coca-Cola as a symbol of American capitalism. Compared with the French Communists' anti-Coke crusade, in other countries Communist-inspired propaganda campaigns were preposterous. In Italy, the Communist Party spread a rumour that Coke turned your hair white and caused a disease called "Coca-Colitis." In Austria, it was rumoured that Coca-Cola was planning to market cuckoo clocks whose birds burst out of their little door clucking, "*Coca-Cola! Coca-Cola!*" In Cyprus, Communists defaced Coca-Cola signs with graffiti-like images of the hammer and sickle. In Switzerland, an organization calling itself the Defence Center against Coca-Cola warned that the Swiss population was in danger of becoming Americanized by Coke, ballpoint pens, and nylon stockings. Anti-Coke propaganda in Switzerland became so preoccupying for Coca-Cola executives that they hired public relations firm Hill & Knowlton to put a positive spin on Coke's image. Hill & Knowlton came up with the idea of offering free tours of Coke bottling plants to local hairdressers and barbers, who were known as strategic conduits of local gossip. In Germany, wine and beer lobbies formed a group called the Office for German Beverages, which distributed a pamphlet, "Coca-Cola, Karl Marx, and the Imbecility of the Masses," which claimed that Coca-Cola, not religion, was the opiate of the masses. In some countries, local taboos and national vanity were exploited to engender ill feelings towards Coke. In Egypt, it was claimed that Coke contained "pig's blood"—thus offending the Moslem religion's aversion to pork. In Brazil, Coke's enemies claimed that the drink caused male impotence—thus striking terror into the hearts of Latin macho men. In Morocco, Coke's competitive battles with Pepsi spread to the turbulent political landscape: Moroccans loyal to mother France drank Pepsi and sometimes physically assaulted Coke drinkers, who were regarded as activist agitators in favour of national independence.[5]

Despite the political potency of its brand, or perhaps because of it, figures? Coca-Cola remained immensely popular in most of these countries. That was precisely the problem for Coke's adversaries. Even where Coke was deeply resented, it was nonetheless widely consumed. Political leaders belonged to an international elite with cosmopolitan tastes—including Coca-Cola. Even outdated monarchs and despicable despots were fanatical Coke addicts. Egyptian King Farouk ensured that his favourite restaurants always kept a supply of Coke in case he showed up. Young King Hussein of Jordan loved Coca-Cola, as did another boy king, Faisal of Iraq. One reason for Coke's success among the world's rulers was the company's corporate emissary, Jim Farley, who counted among his friends many kings, princes, presidents, prime ministers, and dictators. In some non-Western countries, local potentates enriched themselves by doubling as owners of local Coke bottling operations. Still, Coke's commercial success posed a serious problem for governments concerned about their balance of payments. Antipathy towards Coke was invariably linked to the commercial interests of local beverage industries.

Back in America, General Eisenhower was installed in the White House in the early 1950s. One of President Eisenhower's close friends was none other than Robert Woodruff. It was even believed Woodruff played a key role in

Ike's pre-election image makeover to give him popular political appeal at home and abroad. Ike enjoyed playing his favourite sport at Augusta National Golf Club in Georgia, which not only was on Woodruff's home turf but was also where Coke's headquarters were located. Ike and Woodruff frequently played golf together, and the President was often a guest at Woodruff's plantation-style residence in Georgia. One day when the two were on the links together, someone asked President Eisenhower his handicap. His reply: "Woodruff." In 1955, Woodruff announced the appointment of his own successor as Coca-Cola president. The new man was Bill Robinson, who happened to be another close friend of President Eisenhower.

Woodruff, who continued to hover powerfully over the company's affairs, had less affectionate relations with Eisenhower's vice-president, Richard Nixon. Ike himself detested Nixon, so there was no particular reason for Woodruff to like him. Woodruff was infuriated at Nixon following the Vice-President's official trip to the Soviet Union in July 1959 when Nixon had his famous "kitchen debate" with Soviet leader Nikita Khrushchev. Coke, known for its anti-Communist corporate culture, had refused to sponsor the U.S. Trade and Cultural Fair in Moscow's Sokolniki Park where the two leaders were scheduled to meet. Top executives at Pepsi shrewdly saw a branding opportunity. Don Kendall, head of Pepsi's international division, convinced Nixon to plug Pepsi during his walkabout with Khrushchev.

"I went to Nixon the night before, at the embassy, and told him I was in a lot of trouble at home because people thought I was wasting Pepsi's money coming to a Communist country," recalled Kendall. "I told him that somehow, I had to get a Pepsi in Khrushchev's hand."

Nixon kept his promise. At the trade fair, Nixon gave Khrushchev a guided tour of a model of the American kitchen. Their impromptu exchange gave Nixon an opportunity to boast about the material comforts of American capitalism. Soon Nixon and Khrushchev were engaged in tense verbal jousting as each attempted to convince the other of the superior achievements of their own economic systems. Don Kendall, meanwhile, had ensured that Pepsi-branded dispensers were installed at the exhibit. And, true to his word, Nixon led the Soviet leader to a Pepsi booth and—before a phalanx of photographers and TV cameras—cajoled Khrushchev into take a sip of the beverage. When the Soviet leader obliged, the camera bulbs started flashing frantically. Headlines around the world the following day reported that Pepsi had sold Khrushchev on the virtues of capitalism. At Coke headquarters, Robert Woodruff was furious. For Pepsi, the "kitchen debate" was a publicity coup that Don Kendall could never have imagined. Kendall would be richly rewarded six years later by becoming Pepsi's president.

Nixon, for his part, lost the 1960 presidential election to John F. Kennedy. After his electoral defeat, Nixon looked like a political loser. For Woodruff, Nixon's misfortune was good news for Coke. Nixon was identified with Pepsi. JFK was a known Coke drinker, and Woodruff shrewdly got close to President Kennedy. It was even said that Kennedy offered Woodruff the post of ambassador to the United Kingdom, but the Coke boss declined. Two years later, Nixon ran for the governorship of California—and lost again. This time, Nixon was desperate for employment and, to Woodruff's amazement, he approached Coke for a job.

"No, we don't want that son of a bitch on the payroll," snapped one top Coke executive. Woodruff agreed. Nixon got the cold shoulder.

This snub turned out to be a strategic error that Woodruff would regret. Spurned by Coke, Nixon went to Pepsi and was hired in the company's outside law firm on a $250,000-a-year salary, an enormous pay package in the 1960s. Pepsi also helped restore Nixon's shattered self-confidence by sending him around the globe as Pepsi's commercial emissary. In the shorter term, Woodruff could be indifferent to Nixon's sore feelings. After President Kennedy's assassination in late 1963, Lyndon Johnson just happened to be an old pal and drinking buddy of Woodruff. Like JFK, President Johnson was a Coke man. During the 1964 presidential election campaign, President Johnson told journalists that Coke was the official soft drink on Air Force One.

One day, President Johnson was being whisked through Washington in his motorcade when he spotted a familiar face on the sidewalk. It was Ovid Davis, Coke's lobbyist in the U.S. capital.

"Hey, there's Bob's boy!" shouted Johnson. LBJ ordered his motorcade to stop and hollered out to an astonished Davis, "You tell Bob I said hey, you heah?"[6]

Coke's bitter rivalry with Pepsi grew intense, and sometimes acrimonious, during the turbulent 1960s in America. Coke had concocted its winning slogan, "Things go better with Coca-Cola," but Pepsi was gaining ground with a buzzword that seemed to capture the spirit of the times: "The Pepsi Generation." A Pepsi jingle also deliberately appealed to young people: "You've got a lot to live, and Pepsi's got a lot to give." It seemed, indeed, that young people preferred Pepsi. Coke was for old folks. To counter its fusty image, Coke hired a roster of pop singers—including Petula Clark and Neil Diamond—to sing Coca-Cola jingles.

The 1960s was also the era of political protest in America as the U.S. Army was sinking deeper into the quagmire of the Vietnam War. Writer Tom Wolfe suggested that the United States should attempt to "seduce its way to victory" by bombing North Vietnam with Coca-Cola. After 1967, U.S. foreign policy became fixed on the Middle East where tensions between Israel and its Arab neighbours had triggered a war. Coke found itself embroiled in a diplomatic crisis in the region after the company refused to grant a franchise to an Israeli bottler. The Anti-Defamation League accused Coca-Cola of complicity with the Arab League's boycott of Israel. Immediately, powerful Jewish interests in the United States called for a boycott against Coke. In New York, Mt. Sinai Hospital complied by removing Coke from its cafeteria. Coke defended its position by reminding its critics that the company had attempted to gain access to the nascent Israeli market in the late 1940s but had been thwarted by pervasive anti-American attitudes. Coke nonetheless agreed to grant a franchise to an Israeli bottler. This gesture, predictably, triggered a boycott threat from the Arab world. Coke frantically dispatched Prince Makinsky, the company's legendary lobbyist in Paris, to conduct shuttle diplomacy with Arab leaders. But his efforts failed. Not even a discreet intervention from President Johnson helped defuse the situation. The Arab boycott began in August 1968. Coke's business in the region dried up overnight. Thus, a new market opened up for Pepsi.

In 1968, Richard Nixon, after an eight-year exile in the political wilderness, won the White House by promising Americans that he would end the Vietnam War. Nixon immediately forgot his election promise, but he didn't forget his snub from Coke. Pepsi, not Coke, had reached out to Nixon at his most desperate hour. Nixon had a long memory—and a long arm. Coke executives learned that when, under the Nixon administration, the Federal Trade Commission suddenly stepped up its anti-trust actions against Coca-

Cola. Also, when Coke and Pepsi began competing to gain market access to the Soviet Union, discreet interventions from the White House were not unrelated to the Kremlin's decision, in 1972, to award Pepsi a ten-year franchise. President Nixon was helping his old friend Don Kendall, who was still running Pepsi-Cola. In the Nixon administration, Coke was out and Pepsi was in.

After President Nixon's humiliation and downfall in the wake of Watergate, Coke returned triumphant to power when Jimmy Carter won the White House in 1976. Not only was Carter a former governor of Coke's home state of Georgia, he was a close friend of Coke's president, Paul Austin. This surprised no one in Georgia, where Coke had long enjoyed tremendous clout with state politicians. Georgia governors routinely made foreign trips using Coca-Cola corporate jets. In 1974 when he was still governor, Carter was remarkably candid about Coke's influence: "We have our own built-in State Department in the Coca-Cola Company. They provide me ahead of time with penetrating analysis of what a country is, what its problems are, who its leaders are. And when I arrive there, they provide me with introductions to their leaders."

When Carter entered the White House, despite his image as a humble peanut farmer he immediately appointed to key posts a clutch of powerful Coca-Cola insiders: Charles Duncan as deputy Secretary of Defense (and later Energy Secretary), Griffin Bell as Attorney General, and Joseph Califano as Secretary of Health, Education and Welfare. Known as the "Georgia Mafia," these White House insiders were a Coca-Cola clique. And, not surprisingly, Pepsi was banned from the White House and replaced with what one Carter advisor called "a good old Democratic drink, Coke." When President Carter used his presidential powers to block a legislated tax on imported sugar—a product vital to Coke's business—observers claimed the White House was showing undue indulgence towards Coca-Cola's business interests. When the amended piece of legislation went through Congress, it was even dubbed the "Coca-Cola bill." News also leaked that Coke president Paul Austin had held secret, and ultimately unsuccessful, talks with Cuban dictator Fidel Castro to facilitate Coca-Cola's commercial return to the island to secure cheap sugar cane. Columnist William Safire—a former White House speechwriter for Richard Nixon—remarked with a witty allusion to Coke's slogan: "The Carter-Coke-Castro sugar diplomacy is not merely a potential conflict of interest, it's the real thing."

Thanks to Jimmy Carter's geographical proximity and gastronomic affinity for Coca-Cola, the company prospered in many foreign countries during the Carter administration. When Portugal opened its market to Coke, the gesture was not indifferent to $300 million in badly needed loans from President Carter's Treasury Department. Coke also gained entry into Egypt, China, and the Soviet Union during the Carter presidency. In China, Coke's permission to enter the market was timed precisely with the U.S. State Department's successful negotiations with Mao Zedong in 1978 to normalize relations between the two countries. Coke was less fortunate shortly afterwards in Iran, where Ayatollah Khomeini's fanatical mullahs seized Coca-Cola plants, which were taken over by the Association of the Oppressed and shut down.

In India, Coke left the country in 1977 after the government demanded to know the precise contents of the drink's ingredients. Coke's retreat from India was so acrimonious that the company ground up all its glass bottles and abandoned its bottling factories. In 1990, the Indian government offered to allow Coke back into the country, but only as a minority partner with a local firm. Coke eventually invested in an Indian company, Parle Exports, which bottled the country's best-selling soft drink, Thums Up. Coke attempted to use that investment to leverage more marketing efforts behind the Coca-Cola brand, but Indians still preferred Thums Up. In fact, Coke lagged not only behind Thums Up, which had a 40 percent market share, but also behind Pepsi's 30 percent. Coke's market share in India was only 20 percent.

In China, Coke's challenges were both commercial and diplomatic, especially in the 1990s when politicians began denouncing Coca-Cola as a foreign cultural influence. Chinese hostility towards Coke was becoming so preoccupying that, in 1995, Coca-Cola chairman Robert Goizueta visited China to meet with President Jiang Zemin. After the meeting, Goizueta announced: "We are now very much welcomed, very much liked, and not only by the consumers but also by government officials. They view us as American, but also as local. Coca-Cola is ours, but to them it's also a symbol that to become more like Americans they consume Coca-Cola."[7] Coke faced yet another diplomatic nightmare in China in 1999 when American warplanes bombed the Chinese Embassy in Belgrade during Yugoslavia's bloody civil war. While the United States claimed the bombing had been an accident, the incident triggered a wave of anti-American sentiment and protests throughout China. And, not surprisingly, the two main targets were Coke and McDonald's.

At the end of the 1990s, Coke entered its third century well-established as one of world's most famous brands. Coke dominated the global carbonated soft drink market with roughly half of total sales. In Europe, however, Coke was the victim of its own global success. In Brussels, the European Commission ordered raids on the offices of Coke and its bottlers under suspicion of monopolistic practices. Coke had irritated European regulators with a takeover attempt on Cadbury Schweppes' beverage brands without seeking clearance from the European Commission. In Europe, Coke's move was regarded as a sign of the American company's arrogant, high-handed attitude towards foreign markets. To make matters worse, Coke was at the centre of a contamination scare in Belgium after some 200 people, including schoolchildren, complained that drinking Coca-Cola had given them severe headaches and nausea. The claims were actually based on fearmongering, but the scare hurt Coke's image.

Coke faced its biggest diplomatic controversy in France. In the late 1980s, Coke had become increasingly frustrated with its French-based bottling franchise, Pernod Ricard, which was also marketing its own soft drink, Orangina. Coke believed, correctly, that Pernod was neglecting Coke sales in order to maximize revenue from Orangina. In 1989, Coke took action by ending its contract with Pernod. Coke wanted a divorce from Pernod in order to launch a blitzkrieg commercial effort in the run-up to the winter 1992 Olympics in Albertville and the much-anticipated opening of EuroDisney outside Paris. A decade later, in 1999, Coke took an even more aggressive attitude by attempting to buy Orangina outright. But French anti-trust officials quickly moved to block the deal. One concern cited by French authorities was that Orangina, still owned by Pernod Ricard, also distributed Pepsi in France. Thus, Coke would have been in a position to thwart its biggest global rival in the French market. For Coke executives, it seemed like the company was reliving its French diplomatic blunders of a half century earlier. Contamination fears and anti-trust incident actions in Belgium and France left Coke with a black eye in Europe. And once again, Coke's misfortunes were a commercial boon for Pepsi.

Much of the blame for Coke's sudden troubles was laid at the door of the company's chairman, Doug Ivester, who had succeeded Robert Goizueta after the latter's death in 1998. Unlike the charming and diplomatic Goizueta, Ivester was regarded as arrogant and abrasive, and this approach did not work in Europe. Coke was even described as a "fallen icon," and its débâcle led to predictions about the "decline of global brands."

Coke needed to change its approach. Soon Ivester was out. He was replaced by Australian-born Douglas Daft, who immediately took a more conciliatory approach towards foreign governments with a "think local" strategy. Daft's calculation was simple: Since Coca-Cola accounted for 51 percent of the world's carbonated soft drink sales, and derived 80 percent of its profits from overseas markets, Coke had no choice but to become more diplomatic in foreign markets.[8]

"The mistake we made was we saw only what was legally acceptable in the U.S.," said Daft. "You've got to be able to look at things through their eyes." Daft called Coca-Cola's new commercial diplomacy a "world citizen policy." In the future, he said, "we need more of a balance between global and local brands."

Coke's lesson had already been learned by McDonald's, and not without controversy. If "Coca-Colonization" evoked the dominating ambitions of the American Empire, the term "McDomination" implied a coercive force that was not always welcome.

Global McDomination

Basketball superstar Michael Jordan is the most powerful product endorser in the history of sport. *Fortune* magazine once estimated that Jordan's commercial endorsements produced a $10 billion economic impact on the U.S. economy. Half of that amount benefited Nike, the sportswear giant whose products the Chicago Bulls star tirelessly promoted during his phenomenal career.

Jordan's other favourite brand was McDonald's. In 1992 when the Bulls were playing a championship series against the Phoenix Suns, Jordan's 41 points-per-game average set an NBA record. In the last game, when the final buzzer sounded, a McDonald's SWAT team quickly descended onto the court with a television crew to shoot a spontaneous commercial featuring Jordan. As the crowd cheered, an announcer's zippy voice asked

Jordan over the loudspeaker: "Michael, you've just won your third straight NBA championship. Are you hungry for a fourth?"

Jordan, taking his cue, replied: "I'm hungry for a Big Mac."[9]

Within 24 hours, the impromptu McDonald's advertisement was edited and fed by satellite to broadcasters around the world, including MTV and ESPN.

By the end of the 1990s, Jordan's fame had spread throughout the entire planet. Even in Communist North Korea, dictator Kim Jong-il idolized Michael Jordan. Jordan was more than a sports superstar; he was now a transnational corporation[Michael Jordan Inc., who embodied a form of U.S. cultural imperialism that was at once revered and reviled.]

In October 1997, Jordan's global appeal was put to the test in France. Despite French resistance to American culture, when Jordan and his teammates came to Paris to play in the McDonald's Championship, more than 13,000 fans wearing Bulls warm-up jackets showed up to cheer their hero at Bercy Stadium. A thousand sports journalists were also on hand to cover the Bulls, who were playing a Greek team, Olympiakos Piraeus. One fan in the audience was France's socialist prime minister, Lionel Jospin.

When a French journalist asked Jordan whether he was a god, the Bulls star replied: "I play the game of basketball. I could never consider myself a god."

Jordan, voted the most popular athlete in France that year, was nonetheless treated like a demi-god everywhere he went in Paris. He could not leave his hotel room without being mobbed by a crush of media and fans. One day Jordan was at the foot of the Eiffel Tower posing for publicity shots featuring Nike products and McDonald's burgers.

What Jordan did not know, however, was that the Golden Arches were a highly controversial symbol in France. Proclaiming his hunger for a Big Mac in America was one thing. In France, however, the famed "Big Mac attack" was taking on a new meaning. In mid-1999, just as Jordan was retiring from basketball, the most celebrated act of aggression on a McDonald's restaurant occurred in a normally quiet corner of southwestern France. On August 12, a French farmer called José Bové and nine comrades led a guerilla assault on a local McDonald's in the town of Millau, nestled in the verdant Tarn Valley famous for its Roquefort cheese. The perpetrators ransacked, vandalized, and partially demolished the McDonald's outlet using tractors, crowbars, and chainsaws. They tore off a large piece of the fast-food outlet's roof, and a slogan was painted on one wall in giant orange letters: *McDonald's Get Out, Let's Keep Our Roquefort!*

Bové and his accomplices proudly confessed their crime. That was the point. Their gesture had been a publicity stunt to protest the ill effects—including Big Macs—of globalization. Bové surrendered to police and, to maximize media coverage of his stunt, opted to spend three weeks in jail instead of posting bail.

A year later, Bové and his comrades were hauled into the Millau court-house for trial. They each faced maximum five-year prison sentences and $100,000 fines. The media-savvy Bové had attracted support throughout France for his violent attack against the global scourge of American fast food. News of Bové's trial spread beyond France and captured the imagi-nation of the worldwide anti-globalization movement. On the day of Bové's court appearance, Millau was transformed into a veritable Mecca where more than 30,000 protesters from around the world—ecologists, union organizers, small farmers, Communists, anarchists, Catholic traditionalists, anti-capitalists, and assorted other revolutionary groups—converged to denounce McDonald's, Coca-Cola, Disneyland, and other symbols of American cultural imperialism. The seemingly spontaneously show of support for Bové clearly had been well-organized. Rock bands were setting up their instruments for a concert. Some were calling the event an "Anti-Globalization Woodstock." In the crowd, hundreds of tie-dyed teenagers and pot-smoking acrobats were chanting, *"Non à la McDomination!"* Protesters held up placards that read, "Multi-nationals Don't Make the Law!" and "No to Savage Capitalism!" Dozens of Bové supporters wore T-shirts emblazoned with the slogan: *"Le monde n'est pas une marchandise."* Their living martyr, and man of the hour, was José Bové.

Millau had never before seen such agitation in its quiet streets. Fearing that Bové's trial might provoke riots, the town's mayor asked the French government to send in 800 police officers. Local schools were closed, parking lots were made inaccessible, and traffic was banned in the town's centre. The targeted McDonald's outlet, now rebuilt, was shut down, boarded up, and blockaded by two dozen police vehicles. CNN, another symbol of American imperialism, rented rooms and set up cameras in apartments overlooking the Palais de Justice, which was ringed by riot police.

Bové, recognizable by his handlebar moustache and pipe hanging from his mouth, finally made his long-awaited appearance. In the jubilant, carnival-like atmosphere, the crowd cheered their hero. Like unjustly condemned men during the French Revolution, Bové and his nine co-defendants greeted the roaring mob from a creaky wooden tumbrel pulled by a giant tractor rolling down the Rue de la République. Following behind, a cortège of farm vehicles was festooned with giant wheels of Roquefort cheese. Suspended from Bové's tractor was a drum featuring a message to the President of the United States: "Clinton, gardez votre malbouffe!" Roughly translated: "Clinton, keep your lousy junk food!" When the cortège finally reached the Place du Mandarous in the town's centre, a crush of cameras and press photographers encircled Bové as he descended from the open cart, fist raised triumphantly in the air, and pushed through the crowd to the courthouse.

"This is no longer a movement with one single idea, but lots of different movements that have united," declared Bové. "The fight against junk food, multinationals and the ultra-liberal ways of the World Trade Organization has now clearly become a planetary struggle."

Bové was by now well accustomed to the hot glare of media attention. In France, he had become an instant media celebrity, hailed as a "living saint of the world's anti-globalizers." Charismatic and media-friendly Bové was lauded in the French press as a modern-day incarnation of the mythical French hero, Astérix, the plucky Gaul who had stood up to the invading Romans. Bové's attack against McDonald's was portrayed as a defensive assault against the American Caesar. Some compared his vandalism to the storming of the Bastille—an historic moment in France's struggle for freedom and democracy against the autocratic Bourbon kings.

In truth, Bové's highly publicized attack against the Golden Arches claimed less lofty inspiration. It was only one incident in a wave of aggressions against McDonald's throughout France in the late 1990s. While McDonald's enemies in France claimed to be against the noxious effects of American *malbouffe* on traditional French cuisine, the real issue was the commercial threat of U.S. agricultural imports. French farmers, in particular, were becoming increasingly exasperated over the importation of genetically modified foods from the United States. The use of hormone-fed U.S. beef to make Big Macs in France was a particular irritation. The European Union finally banned hormone-treated American beef, but the move immediately provoked retaliation from Washington. The U.S. struck back by slapping a 100 percent tariff on targeted agricultural products from European countries. The French products affected were Dijon mustard, truffles, *foie gras*—and the pride of Millau, Roquefort cheese. The U.S. tax on Roquefort was precisely what had provoked the ire of José Bové. The goats he raised on the Larzac plain produced milk used to make the cheese. He may not have liked Big Macs, but Bové's assault on McDonald's had been a symbolic reprisal against U.S. trade measures that threatened his livelihood. [Bové was just one of many French farmers who exploited the high-minded language of cultural sovereignty to mask the real issue: commercial protectionism.]

[handwritten margin note: commercial protectionism]

Anti-American protests by French farmers had begun in a relatively civilized manner. At first, the chosen weaponry against U.S. culinary hegemony was traditional French cuisine. French farmers entered unsuspecting McDonald's outlets and, in the hope of reminding their countrymen of their traditional values, offered patrons gorging themselves with Big Macs an assortment of baguettes, pungent raw-milk cheeses, and *foie gras*. But after the World Trade Organization approved the punitive U.S. tax, angry French farmers took a more aggressive approach. They began dumping manure, mountains of apples, and other rotting fruit and vegetables at the doorstep of the nearest McDonald's. Their anger quickly spread to other global brands that, in France, had long symbolized U.S. imperialism. In Paris, farmer's unions plastered signs on university campuses that shouted slogans like: "Boycott America! Not one more penny spent on McDonald's, Coca-Cola, and Disney!" In the French seaside resort town of Deauville, local farmers disrupted the annual festival of Hollywood movies. Café owners throughout France showed their solidarity by boycotting Coca-Cola beverages. The French media provided coverage of this well-orchestrated campaign organized by powerful French unions. However, the media showed particular interest in the colourful figure of José Bové. His highly publicized ransacking of McDonald's reinforced a deep-seated hostility in France, and throughout Europe, towards what elites spurned as American junk culture.

Back in the United States, Senator Richard Lugar, a Republican from Indiana, expressed bewilderment at the frenzy of anti-Americanism spreading through Europe. "Europe seems to be gripped right now by a kind of collective madness," he said, "and we don't want that to spread to the rest of the world."

It wasn't long before the mainstream American media took an interest in José Bové. Prestigious newspapers such as *The New York Times*, *Washington Post*, and *Wall Street Journal* published lengthy accounts of the genial, mustachioed Bové's anti-American crusade. It was soon discovered, however, that Bové was no ordinary French farmer. In fact, he was hardly a "peasant," as he liked to portray himself. Born in Paris, Bové's parents were well-educated scientists. And, ironically, Bové had spent part of his childhood in California, where his parents were conducting research at Berkeley. Back in Paris as a youth in the 1970s, Bové embarked on a career as a skilled political organizer, union activist, and self-proclaimed anarchist. In those days, Bové's radicalism wasn't particularly focused on *la malbouffe*. He first gained notoriety while protesting the French government's nuclear testing in Polynesia. In 1985, Bové was aboard Greenpeace's *Rainbow Warrior* to protect France's nuclear tests in the south Pacific. When French secret agents blew up the *Rainbow Warrior*, the incident destabilized the French government. Some claimed that Bové had spent time at one of Muammar el-Quaddafi's "direct action" training camps in Libya. Later, when Bové and his family moved to the Tarn Valley, they had no experience in farming. They had come at the behest of local farmers, who were seeking Bové's political skills to protest against the French military's plans to extend its army base onto the Larzac plain. Bové arrived and squatted in a deserted 16th-century farmhouse that was supposed to be razed to make way for the military base. Bové won the case, and continued to live on the same farm, where he began raising his sheep just outside Millau. Just before his guerilla attack on McDonald's, Bové had received a suspended sentence for destroying a stock of genetically modified seed corn owned by the Swiss pharmaceutical giant Novartis. Bové had also helped organize the destruction of a field of transgenic rice at a research laboratory in the southern French city of Montpellier. In short, Bové was no peasant; he was an activist union leader and head of France's Confédération Paysanne.

In his interviews with the international media, however, Bové shrewdly disparaged symbols of American-style capitalism, like McDonald's, that he claimed were destroying France's traditional way of life. "Firstly, McDonald's represents globalization, multinationals, the power of the market," he said. "Then it stands for industrially produced food, which is bad for traditional farmers and bad for your health. And lastly, it's a symbol of America. It comes from the place where they not only promote globalization and industrially produced food but also unfairly penalize our peasants."

[In truth, Bové's main adversary wasn't America. His real enemies, surprisingly, were his fellow French farmers—or, at least, the big French agribusiness interests that had pushed aside small, rural farmers like himself. Bové had attacked McDonald's not to protest American *malbouffe*, but to attract the attention of the French government.] Bové's Confédération Paysanne union had long been disaffected because the French government recognized only one farmer's lobby, the powerful Fédération Nationale des Syndicats d'Exploitants Agricoles, which represented the big, rich, and conservative landowners who controlled France's agribusiness industry. Bové and his fellow "peasants" were outraged that roughly 80 percent of France's farm subsidies went to the large-scale agribusiness sector, not to the small farmers who belonged to the more radicalized Confédération Paysanne.

But the French media glossed over Bové's real agenda, preferring to play up his heroic image as a "Robin Hood of Roquefort." Riding high on a crest of media adoration, Bové was accorded an audience with France's conservative president, Jacques Chirac, who saw in Bové a political opportunity to reinforce his own appeal as a man of the people. After meeting with Bové, President Chirac declared: "I am in complete solidarity with France's farm workers. And I detest McDonald's."

Chirac also used the occasion to send a political message to America. "It would be in nobody's interests to allow one single power, albeit a respectable and friendly one," he said, "to rule undivided over the planet's food markets."

Bové, now a bona fide media celebrity, was accorded a place of honour at high-level negotiations with the French government on agricultural matters. Bové's fame, while an embarrassment for McDonald's, was intensely annoying for Luc Guyau, head of the powerful Fédération Nationale des Syndicats d'Exploitants Agricoles. Guyau claimed to speak for all French farmers, even though in reality he represented mainly the interests of big French agribusiness. But he now had to share the spotlight with the canny publicity seeker, José Bové, who was quoted more frequently in the press—and, moreover, was now a *copain* of President Chirac. Bové was no fool: His coup against McDonald's had worked magnificently to promote his union agenda. While fabricating the mythology of José Bové as the Robin Hood of Roquefort, the French media neglected to point out that, in fact, millions of their compatriots seemed to like wolfing down Big Macs and French fries. McDonald's operated 240 outlets in France, where the company employed some 30,000 workers directly or indirectly. And what's more, McDonald's bought 80 percent of its ingredients in the French market.

Bové, meanwhile, had taken his crusade to another level. His battle wasn't just against Big Macs, he said, but against the entire onslaught of American mono-culture. McDonald's, he said, was just a symbol for the ill effects of U.S.-dominated global capitalism. Bové was now jet-setting around the world as a leading figure in the radical ranks of the anti-globalization movement. In November 1999, he showed up in Seattle to join the noisy protests against the World Trade Organization meeting in the city where the head offices of Boeing and Microsoft were located. Once again, Bové proved his shrewd instincts for effective publicity stunts. He arrived in Seattle with large quantities of smuggled Roquefort cheese, which he distributed freely in front of a downtown McDonald's before a crush of television cameras. Later, he led a march in the Seattle rain, chanting, "throw the multinationals into the sea!" The violent anti-globalization protests that erupted in the streets of Seattle turned the WTO meeting into an international embarrassment.

Bové was now as famous in America as he was back home in France. Naomi Klein, a radical voice of the anti-globalization movement through her book *No Logo*, lauded Bové's image as "a cheese-making Che Guevara." Some called him a "French Ghandi." Even *Business Week* magazine praised Bové. In a cover story for its international edition called "The Stars of Europe," *Business Week* selected Bové as one of Europe's "50 leaders on the forefront of change." The magazine observed: "Our agenda setters are redefining architecture, labor relations and—like France's farming radical José Bové—even the way people protest." The *Wall Street Journal* noted that Bové had been transformed from "small French farmer to big world player." Soon Bové was off to Brazil to attend an "anti-Davos" summit called the World Social Forum, where he was cheered for his courageous defiance of the American Empire. Other prominent figures attending the event included movie star Danny Glover, anarchist Noam Chomsky, and Aleida Guevara, daughter of Che Guevara.[10]

While Bové was being lionized by the international glitterati, his aggression against Millau's McDonald's had set off a series of shockingly violent acts against other McDonald's outlets. In April 2000, a bomb exploded in a McDonald's outlet in Quevert, a small town in France's northwestern region of Britanny. The blast killed a 28-year-old female employee whose tattered body was thrown into the parking lot. The bomb had been planted by the pro-independence Breton Revolutionary Army. A month earlier, the same group had fired three bullets into another McDonald's in the nearby town of Dinan. The Breton separatists—like Corsican and Basque terrorists—had long been fighting the central French state for political independence. Britanny, whose population traditionally spoke the Celtic language, had been an independent dukedom until the 16th century and lost all its autonomy during the French Revolution in the 1790s. Separatist groups in France usually planted bombs on the premises of French government buildings. McDonald's, it seemed, had become a convenient target for any form of protest or disaffection—whether political, ideological, or commercial.

"Behind all this lies a rejection of cultural and culinary dispossession," observed Alain Duhamel, a French political commentator. "There is a certain allergy in Europe to the extent of American power accumulated since the Cold War's end, and the most virulent expression of that allergy today seems to be food."

Bové, to be sure, had exploited the crusade against American cultural imperialism to fight a strictly local battle within the French union movement. Yet on a deeper level his protests successfully tapped into pervasive anxieties sweeping Europe. Many Europeans were worried about health threats from "mad cow" disease transmitted through British beef. Also, the introduction of a new European currency, the transfer of political power away from national governments towards "Eurocrats" in Brussels, and a general feeling of powerlessness against the forces of global commerce and transnational corporations were the source of growing malaise in many European countries. In some respects, anti-Americanism was a convenient scapegoat for these powerful trends transforming European society.

There was some irony in French concerns about American-led global capitalism. French multinationals, in fact, were adapting exceedingly well to the pressures of globalization. While Bové was railing in the media about global "McDomination," a French industrial champion called Vivendi SA— a century-old water utility turned media giant—made a spectacular $34 billion takeover bid for Hollywood's Universal Studios and all its related entertainment companies. At the same time, France's Publicis bought the world-renowned British advertising firm Saatchi and Saatchi. Other globally oriented French companies—Michelin, L'Oréal, Carrefour, Rhone-Poulenc, Alcatel, Axa—were world-beating giants who earned the lion's share of their profits in global markets. Even José Bové's own Roquefort cheese, an expensive delicacy, was largely exported to the world's richest countries.

But Bové, emboldened by his global media celebrity, did not let facts obstruct his crusade. When he returned to Millau to face magistrates for his attack on the local McDonald's, a throng of supporters cheered as he triumphantly marched into the Palais de Justice. His court appearance was dubbed the "trial of globalization." Others called it the "Millau Trade Round" and "Seattle-sur-Tarn." In the courtroom, it almost seemed as if prosecutors were on Bové's side. They asked for a lenient one-month jail term and a suspended sentence. But Judge François Mallet shocked Bové's supporters by denouncing his conduct and sentencing him to three months in prison.

"Our combat must continue," declared Bové, who went to prison in June 2001. Within a month, however, his friend Jacques Chirac came to his rescue. On Bastille Day—July 14—the French president invoked his powers to pardon Bové and secure an early release from prison. Out of jail, Bové immediately returned to his international publicity stunts. He showed his solidarity with Palestinian leader Yasser Arafat, for example, by meeting with Arafat in the West Bank town of Ramallah as Israeli soldiers were surrounding his compound. When Bové was promptly deported, the international media covered his travails.

In November 2002, Bové got bad news in France. The country's highest court sentenced him to 14 months in prison for a pre-McDonald's incident in which Bové led an attack on genetically modified rice fields. Stunned, Bové again appealed to his friend Jacques Chirac to use his presidential powers to overturn the decision. He called on the French head of state to "make a clear declaration that the place of union leaders is not in prison." Outraged by the court's sentence, in January 2002 a group of French movie stars—including Lambert Wilson and Anémone—destroyed a crop of genetically modified rapeseed northeast of Paris to show their support for

Bové. The rapeseed field raid was led by the leader of France's Green Party, Noël Mamere.

Bové, meanwhile, was already protesting the imminent U.S. invasion of Iraq while awaiting to be hauled off to prison. In February 2003, the ABC television network aired a feature interview with Bové that, once again, played up his image as a folkloric peasant. "Here in the European country which is most resistant to war against Iraq, José Bové is in that most fortunate position—he's highly political but he's no politician," said an ABC newsman. "So Jose Bové can speak with impunity from the heart and what he says and what he stands for tells you a great deal about why so many French people are opposed to the United States and its war plans."

On cue, Bové looked into the ABC camera lens and, in impeccable English, criticized President Bush and imperial America. "People say why does the United States want to go into Iraq—the only reason is oil and everybody sees this," he said. "What's happening now in Iraq is just the next step for the United States to control the production of oil. So people think that this war is only a war for oil."

Bové was asked about those who compared him to Astérix. Flattered by the comparison, Bové replied: "Astérix was in his little village surrounded by the empire. We try to do it from the other way. We want to surround the empire. That's the new way to make resistance. So we need millions of Astérixes all over the world."

McDonald's, meanwhile, was already beginning to respond to the dangers inherent in its status as a global cultural icon and ubiquitous symbol of American domination. In April 2002, McDonald's issued a "social responsibility" report to soften criticism by anti-globalization and environmental activists.

"Our brand can sometimes be used as a symbol for these kinds of issues," said McDonald's chairman Jack Greenberg. "Although we may not always agree on every issue, we want to be responsive and more transparent." In the 46-page corporate report, McDonald's promised not to buy beef from rainforest lands, to improve animal welfare, and to test new packages made from recyclable potato starch rather than plastic.[11]

McDonald's was going through a corporate revolution, especially beyond America's borders. In a radical departure from company founder Ray Kroc's Fordian vision of uniform standards throughout the Golden

Arches empire, McDonald's was now eager to cater to local tastes. In France, McDonald's made a concerted effort to win over customers by adding local themes to each restaurant. Today, some McDonald's outlets in France feature faux marble surroundings, espresso coffee, and "premiere" sandwiches such as "McChicken Première." The McDonald's on the Champs Elysées features music booths, CD players, and walls of video screens that blast pop music through the restaurant. The trendy "Music McDo" outlet attracts Parisian teenagers who congregate at the restaurant in the same way their upscale elders lounge on armchairs and read newspapers at Starbucks. The *Wall Street Journal* dubbed the fast food chain's new French strategy as "McHaute Cuisine."[12]

Even more surprisingly, the bellicose cartoon character, Astérix, has switched camps. One can only imagine the reaction of Jose Bové—once hailed as an "Anti-McDonald's Astérix"—when McDonald's announced it had enlisted the services of the Gallic cartoon hero himself to promote Big Macs throughout the Fifth Republic. In early 2002, McDonald's replaced Ronald McDonald with Astérix as the fast-food chain's official mascot in France to induce modern-day French consumers to switch from baguettes to Big Macs by distancing the Golden Arches from their corporate roots in America.

McDonald's was adopting similar localized commercial strategies in other foreign markets. In the Netherlands, McDonald's began selling a vegetable burger called *groenteburger.* In Uruguay, McDonald's unveiled a "McHuevo," a hamburger with a poached egg, as well as toasted cheese sandwiches called "McQuesos." In Thailand, Samurai pork burgers can now be ordered at McDonald's. And in Japan customers can buy a Chicken Tatsuta sandwich under the Golden Arches. In the Philippines, McDonald's offers "McSpaghetti" to cater to the local taste for the Italian dish. In Norway, McDonald's sells a new sandwich called "McLaks," featuring grilled salmon with dill sauce on multi-grain bread. The so-called "McAfrika" burger—garnished with lettuce, tomato and cheese and served in pita bread—met with less success in Norway after a barrage of criticism for insensitivity to the African continent's famine and starvation crises.

One of McDonald's most successful international conquests has been the Soviet Union, where in 1990 the chain opened its first restaurant in Moscow shortly after the fall of the Berlin Wall. On opening day, more than

5,000 Muscovites gathered in front of the McDonald's restaurant to order their first Big Mac and fries. By the end of the Moscow McDonald's first day of operation, some 30,000 customers had been served. The Moscow restaurant has consistently been one of McDonald's busiest outlets worldwide. It took many years for McDonald's to get a foothold in the Soviet Union, where American fast-food imperialism was once labelled "Snickerization" after the famous candy bar that was popular throughout Russia. McDonald's had been negotiating with the Kremlin for a decade before Mikhail Gorbachev's *glasnost* finally opened the door. In 1997, Gorbachev himself—who by now was making television commercials for Pizza Hut—described McDonald's in the following terms: "The merry clowns, the Big Mac signs, the colourful unique decorations and ideal cleanliness in and around the restaurants, the welcoming smiles and helpful service—all of this complements the hamburgers whose great popularity is well-deserved."[13]

McDonald's also inspired imitators in Russia. The opening of a Russkoye Bistro chain appeared to be a nationalistic reaction to the Big Mac's global domination. At Russkoye Bistro, patrons are offered traditional Russian nosh such as *pirogi* (meat and vegetable pie), *blini* (thin pancakes) and Cossack apricot curd tarts—and, of course, vodka. Still, Russkoye Bistro adopted American-style management and service techniques used by McDonald's. In the former Yugoslavia, McDonald's served Big Macs throughout the bloody civil war even though its restaurants were frequently the target of violent attacks. After one series of air strikes on Belgrade, mobs of youths wearing Nike sneakers and Levi's jeans vandalized McDonald's outlets in Belgrade, Jagodina, Cacak, and Zrenjanin. These hostile acts dealt a troubling blow to McDonald's, whose Golden Arches curiously had long been a source of pride in Serbia. In fact, at soccer matches between Serb and Croatian teams, Serbian fans were known to taunt Croats by hollering, "We have McDonald's and you don't!" Now that NATO bombs were raining down on Belgrade, however, the local population began turning against McDonald's as a symbol of America. Anxious to placate their Serb customers, McDonald's pandered to local tastes by serving a "McCountry" pork burger with paprika garnish. McDonald's, somewhat paradoxically, also handed out free cheeseburgers at anti-NATO rallies.

McDonald's faced a more difficult commercial challenge in India, where the Hindu taboo against beef was an insurmountable obstacle to an invasion of Big Macs and Quarter Pounders. In a country with strong aversion to foreign cultural influences, the fast-food chain has been forced to radically reshape its menu. Thus, McDonald's began offering a vegetarian pizza called "McPuff" and a "McChicken" sandwich made with mint mayonnaise and Indian spices. Soon a "McAloo Tikki" burger—combining potato patties with green peas, carrots, coriander, and cumin—was added to the menu. Today, a "Maharaja Mac"—made with lamb patties instead of beef—is McDonald's signature sandwich in India. McDonald's willingness to show flexibility has worked in India, where other American fast-food chains—notably Kentucky Fried Chicken—have had more difficulty with their fixed formulas. In fact, some KFC outlets in India have been vandalized due to fears that the Colonel's secret recipe is carcinogenic because of high levels of monosodium glutamate. For the most part, however, hostility towards American fast food has generally been motivated by Indian economic nationalism targeting specific U.S. brands. One anti-American campaign fixed on Lays potato chips. Its slogan—"microchips, not potato chips"—made it clear that the motive was commercial, not cultural.

In China, the Communist regime has sometimes looked upon McDonald's with suspicion, but Big Macs nonetheless have been popular with Chinese consumers since 1992, when the first McDonald's opened not far from Beijing's Tiananmen Square. Ironically, in a Communist country McDonald's has become a status symbol conferring social distinction: wealthy Chinese frequent the Golden Arches as a sign of conspicuous consumption. It is precisely the "Western" appeal of McDonald's that has made the fast-food chain so popular in China, where the Golden Arches enjoy a positive association with modernization. The same phenomenon has been observed at KFC and Pizza Hut outlets in China. Customers do not necessarily go to KFC to munch on crispy chicken, but rather to hang out, preferably near the windows, to have superior social status conferred on themselves in the eyes of passersby. Patrons of McDonald's, KFC, and Pizza Hut wish to be regarded as trendy Chinese who appreciate Western values.[14]

McDonald's nonetheless has been careful to show sensitivity to local Chinese customs. Mascot Ronald McDonald, for example, has a female companion in China called "Aunt McDonald." In many McDonald's outlets in China, there are numerous "Aunt McDonald" figures whose function is to interact in a helpful, nurturing manner with children. Ronald McDonald, for his part, is known affectionately in China as "Uncle McDonald"—thus appealing to Chinese values of kinship. Today, Chinese university students sporting Nike baseball caps, Mickey Mouse T-shirts, and Ray-Ban sunglasses congregate at McDonald's in the same way American students hang out at suburban malls. Starbucks, too, has come to China—a major achievement in a country of tea drinkers. When a Starbucks opened in the Forbidden City, the American brand's arrival provoked a controversy in the local media that made the Chinese regime nervous. The kerfuffle quickly blew over, however, and today the Chinese are getting used to the powerful effects on their nervous systems from syrupy espressos and pungent lattes.

McDonald's arrived in Hong Kong in 1975, more than two decades before the city returned to Chinese rule. In Hong Kong, as in China later, the Golden Arches became an "in" place for young people who saw McDonald's as an escape from traditional Asian values. In Taiwan, where the regime had long been pro-American and where the U.S. Army counted several bases, McDonald's didn't open a restaurant until the mid-1980s. At first, upper-class Taiwanese frequented McDonald's as a sign of their openness to American values. At the same time, however, there were persistent tensions between traditional Taiwanese values and the invasion of American fast-food culture. In April 1992, bomb blasts destroyed McDonald's outlets in Tapei and Kaohsiung, killing a police officer and injuring employees. At first, it was believed the bombings were violent reactions to American cultural imperialism. It was soon discovered, however, that local racketeers were behind the incidents. McDonald's main challenge in Taiwan was culinary: the local population spurned Big Macs, preferring traditional rice-based lunch boxes sold in convenience stores. In 2002, McDonald's responded by offering rice dishes throughout Taiwan as part of its "local" strategy.

In South Korea, McDonald's entered the market cautiously—in 1988 during the Seoul Olympic Games—by partnering with local entrepreneurs who branded the restaurants with their own names: "McAnn," "McKim," "ShinMc" and so on. When genuine McDonald's restaurants opened, South Korean customers initially were attracted by the idea of eating a "real"

American hamburger as opposed to Korean versions sold in ersatz chains such as Lotteria and Uncle Joe's Hamburger. But as in Taiwan, McDonald's had failed to understand the symbolic importance of rice in South Korea as a staple food that represents national self-sufficiency. In the early 1990s when the Korean government was involved in trade negotiations with its main commercial partners, it insisted on banning rice imports to protect local agricultural interests. Thus, McDonald's unwittingly found itself caught in the cross-fire of a bilateral dispute between South Korea and the United States when the Korean government launched a publicity campaign whose slogan was: "Healthy eating = eating our rice." On one poster, a healthy grain of rice was juxtaposed with a greasy hamburger.

In Japan, McDonald's food, curiously, enjoys "snack" status. The Japanese do not regard McDonald's food as whole meals. It is believed that the Japanese—who traditionally regarded meat-eaters as barbarians—treat McDonald's nosh as snacks because of the absence of rice. As in many Asian countries, the Japanese prefer lunch boxes served with rice. While the Japanese are open to McDonald's and American-style fast food, hostility sometimes surfaces in unusual ways. In the early 1970s, shortly after the first McDonald's appeared in Tokyo, there was a widely reported rumour that McDonald's burgers were made with cat meat. The success of McDonald's in Japan can nonetheless be measured by its impact on deeply entrenched cultural habits. The ritual of gobbling down a Big Mac and fries, for example, has broken Japan's time-honoured taboo against using one's hands when eating. The Japanese taboo against standing up while eating has also been effectively challenged by McDonald's. Still, McDonald's made cultural concessions to the Japanese market. In 2001, McDonald's Japanese operations, now a separate publicly traded company, began offering teriyaki burgers.

Big Macs may be popular throughout Asia, but the culinary imperialism of Asian cultures should not be neglected. The worldwide appetite for Chinese food is not open to dispute. And Japan, while conquering the global consumer electronics and videogame markets with Nintendo and Playstation, also caters to a global predilection for sushi. Many regional foods—from the Mexican tortilla and Italian pizza to Moroccan couscous and the Arab falafel—also enjoy global popularity thanks to their unique local flavour. Even greasy British fish and chips, soaked in malt vinegar, are popular far beyond the shores of the United Kingdom. And yet American fast-food imperialism is the object of constant criticism. The reason is not difficult to discover: America is an imperial political and economic power, too.

Critics of American fast-food imperialism sometimes focus on its nutritional deficiencies, which are marshalled as evidence of America's corruption and decay as a civilization. Some anti-American extremists have, somewhat ludicrously, denounced U.S. fast food as a form of global "bioterrorism," which they claim is even more noxious in its effects than American cultural imperialism.[15] But the nutritional merits of Big Macs and Coke versus chicken fried rice misses the point. As the global popularity of McDonald's, KFC, and Coca-Cola demonstrates, what is important is not calories, but the symbolic connection with everything America represents. The followers of Osama bin Laden are indifferent to the nutritional merits of cheeseburgers and French fries. For them, McDonald's is synonymous with America.

Golden Arches Conflict Prevention

No two countries that boast a McDonald's will ever declare war on each other. That, at least, is the basic assumption of the "Golden Arches Theory of Conflict Prevention."

Posited by Thomas Friedman in his book *The Lexus and the Olive Tree*, the Golden Arches Theory of Conflict Prevention has the intriguing appeal of a seemingly ludicrous notion that nonetheless should be taken seriously. As Friedman puts it: "When a country reaches the level of economic development where it has a middle class big enough to support a McDonald's network, it becomes a McDonald's country. And people in McDonald's countries don't like to fight wars any more, they prefer to wait in line for burgers." Friedman's theory finds support in the optimism of classic liberalism, which asserts that peace among nations would be promoted by international trade because commerce requires stability. As the use of blockades and embargoes demonstrate, war and trade are difficult to conduct simultaneously.[16]

The Golden Arches Theory of Conflict Prevention may not be as fatuous as it appears. When President Bush employed the term "axis of evil" to describe Iraq, Iran, and North Korea, the phrase provoked considerable controversy. On the surface, these three countries had little in common, despite being despicable authoritarian regimes. Iraq was ruled by an oppressive secular regime, Iran was an Islamic theocracy, and North Korea was a Stalinist communist state. But all three shared one common characteristic: none had a McDonald's. After the U.S. toppled Saddam Hussein's dictatorship in Iraq, America's attention turned towards another brutal dictatorship on Iraq's border: Syria. Like the three "axis of evil" countries, Syria too had no Golden Arches. Neither was Osama bin Laden fond of Big Macs. When the U.S. Army put an end to Taliban rule in Afghanistan, there was no McDonald's in that country.

When America's liberation of Afghanistan provoked a groundswell of anti–U.S. violence throughout the Moslem world, protestors predictably staged violent assaults on the most powerful symbols of American fast-food culture: McDonald's, Pizza Hut, KFC, and Coca-Cola. A McDonald's was torched in Saudi Arabia, and a bomb ripped through a McDonald's in Beirut. Three people died in a bombing of a McDonald's in eastern Indonesia. When Islamic militants were arrested in Pakistan for bombing the U.S. embassy in Karachi, it was discovered they were also planning to blow up a McDonald's. By late 2002, America's war on global terrorism had provoked a series of well-organized boycotts in the Islamic world. And, once again, they targeted powerful U.S. brands. Stores and supermarkets throughout the Middle East began pulling American products from their shelves. McDonald's was forced to close two of its six outlets in Jordan, and Burger King outlets were attacked in Lebanon, Oman, Bahrain, Egypt, and Qatar. Burger King had already provoked indignation throughout the Middle East when it announced plans to open a restaurant on the West Bank. Those plans were hastily cancelled after boycott threats in the Arab world. In Egypt, anti-American boycott organizers targeted all products manufactured by Procter & Gamble because of one of the company's soap powders, called Ariel. The Moslem boycott organizers claimed, absurdly, that the soap powder had been named after Israeli prime minister Ariel Sharon.

Hostility towards American fast food in the Moslem world sometimes has produced unintended consequences—and timely business opportunities for Moslem entrepreneurs. In late 2002, a newfangled soft drink called Mecca Cola was launched in France to appeal to that country's large

Moslem population. Mecca Cola, invented to fill a void left by widespread Moslem boycotts of American brands, quickly caught on in Britain and throughout the Moslem diaspora. Tawfik Mathlouthi, a French businessman who launched Mecca Cola, was explicit about its marketing campaign: "It's all about combatting American imperialism and Zionism by providing a substitute for American products and increasing the blockade of countries boycotting American goods."

In Britain, another ersatz Coke product called Qibla Cola was already on shelves. Its slogan: "Liberate Your Taste!" Qibla Cola's inventor, Zahida Parveen, stated unequivocally that his product was inspired by anti-Western values: "The Qibla brand offers a real alternative for people concerned about the practices of some major Western multinationals who support causes that oppress Muslims." Qibla Cola was not the first soft drink thus inspired. In Iran, a soft drink called Zam Zam Cola had been on the market since the overthrow of the pro-Western shah and the triumph of the ayatollahs in 1979. Zam Zam, named after a holy spring in Mecca, saw its sales soar throughout the Persian Gulf region after Iran's ruling ayatollahs declared Coke and Pepsi to be "un-Islamic." Zam Zam was thus an "Islamic" soft drink that, paradoxically, had coopted and integrated the commercial values and cultural tastes of American-style cola. Zam Zam is especially popular in Saudi Arabia, but the drink is also sold in distant Moslem countries such as Pakistan.

Amirah Ali, a spokesperson for the London-based Islamic Human Rights Commission, explained the success of Islamic colas by pointing to widespread hostility towards America. "It makes us feel like we can do something," she said. "Coca-Cola has become a big symbol of America. It's a tangible symbol at a time when there is increasing unhappiness about U.S. foreign policy."

That unhappiness was quickly transformed into virulent opposition after the U.S. invasion of Iraq in early 2003. In Saudi Arabia, authorities arrested a fanatic who was planning to firebomb a McDonald's in the eastern city of Dammam. Attacks against McDonald's and other American symbols were not limited to the Moslem world. In India, an organization called the People's War Group attacked Coca-Cola and Pepsi warehouses. In Berlin, where the German government opposed the U.S. invasion of

Iraq, restaurants and other commercial establishments boycotted Coca-Cola, Budweiser, and Marlboro cigarettes. In many German restaurants, waiters told patrons: "Sorry, Coca-Cola is not available any more due to the current political situation." In France, with its long history of anti-Americanism, many French restaurants joined the boycott against Coca-Cola. They were galled that "French Fries" in America had been renamed "Freedom Fries" after the French government's refusal to support the U.S. military intervention in Iraq. Throughout France, anti-war protestors vandalized McDonald's restaurants. Yet when the United States triumphed in Iraq and overthrew Saddam Hussein, the governments of France and Germany suddenly showed a curious eagerness to win favour with imperial America. Astérix was munching on Big Macs again. *We really didn't win!*

In the Middle East, meanwhile, the defeat of Saddam Hussein signalled a new era for the entire region. America finally seemed determined to bring liberal democracy to the Arab world, even if it meant toppling authoritarian regimes. Was it therefore inevitable that Iraq, Iran, and Syria would soon boast their own McDonald's? Would Coke and Pepsi soon be fighting for market share with Zam Zam and Mecca Cola? *America loving liberal democracy*

One shrewd Kuwaiti businessman was betting on this eventuality even before the U.S. Army stormed Baghdad. Loay Sami Fahad al Ibrahim, who owned the popular Shrimpy's fast-food chain in Kuwait, believed a U.S. victory would open up a new market for his fried seafood snacks. "The Iraqi market will be very hungry for fast food," he said. "Right now, there is no McDonald's in Iraq—also no Burger King, no Domino's pizza, no Baskin Robbins, no nothing. Most Iraqis have never even seen a Starbucks. The regime has denied the people these simple pleasures of life. I remember when McDonald's first came to Kuwait. You had to wait an hour in line for your cheeseburger. Some day soon, it will be the same for Shrimpy's in Iraq."

It's a safe bet Shrimpy's will find itself competing with McDonald's for Iraqi customers. But when the first McDonald's opens in Baghdad, the site of the Golden Arches in that city will carry more symbolic importance. American hard power had been necessary to overthrow a ruthless tyrant. Now American soft power is needed to bring liberal democracy and market capitalism to the Arab world. And Big Macs and Coke will play a powerful role in that process. → *point that is never explicitly stated*

Conclusion

So, all things considered, do things really go better with Coca-Cola? Would the world be a better place if Disneyland theme parks were constructed in Baghdad and Damascus? Would global stability be less precarious if Big Macs were sold with a smile in Pyongyang and Tehran?

These questions, as we have seen, are not as facetious as they seem. And the easy answer is a resolute yes. Supported by historical analysis presented in the preceding chapters, we persist in the affirmation that American soft power—movies, television, pop music, fast food—promotes values and beliefs that, while contentious, are ultimately good for the world. American entertainment—Hollywood, Disneyland, CNN, MTV, and Madonna—conveys values that have made America great, such as an abiding belief in democracy, free enterprise, and individual liberties. What's more, much of the world's population has embraced America as a model society that has championed these values. Whatever America's shortcomings, there are many more people seeking to emigrate to the United States than are actively engaged in Jihad against it.

The values of American pop culture are penetrating even the most stubbornly resistant societies where despotic regimes rule with the iron fist of tyranny and oppression. In communist North Korea, Kim Jong-il idolizes Michael Jordan, and his eccentric heir Kim Jong-nam is fascinated by Mickey Mouse. True, weapons of mass distraction cannot triumph over weapons of mass destruction. But they can temper the pernicious values and beliefs that build them.

The deployment of American soft power, as we have seen, has played a role in U.S. foreign policy for nearly a century. From Woodrow Wilson to George W. Bush, the White House has been acutely aware of the strategic importance of pop culture as a powerful conveyor of American values and ideals throughout the world. As we noted at the outset of this book, for most of the 20th century American soft power was marshalled to promote the national interests of the United States. Pop culture was, in effect, an extension of U.S. trade policy, which of course served the interests of American capitalism. At the same time, however, American soft power took inspiration from fundamental values commonly associated with the "American way." The Cold War brought those values into focus, and for nearly half a century U.S. soft power was driven by the dictates of geopolitical realism and the loftier goals of moral idealism. In the post-Cold War world, as America asserted its imperial ambitions, soft power has become an overarching frame of reference for the entire Western world bonded by common cultural values and strategic interests. It is not insignificant that the Golden Arches can be found nowhere in countries—Iraq, North Korea, Iran—whose regimes have been hostile to everything America represents. The absence of Golden Arches in certain countries tells us more about geopolitics than about gastronomical predilections.

Today, communications technologies such as the Internet and satellites have intensified the ubiquity, velocity, and impact of American soft power. Local cultures cannot build electronic Berlin Walls against foreign influences; if they do, they quickly discover that these ramparts are hopelessly porous. MTV's signals are beamed down from geostationary orbit, while CNN's Web site can be accessed on computers in virtually any country on the planet. In the Information Age, soft-power resources have become strategic resources and America's adversaries know this. For this reason, the threat of cyberterrorism has become increasingly preoccupying in the United States, especially in the wake of Al Qaeda's attacks on the World Trade Center and Pentagon. In an era when *realpolitik* has been superceded by *cyberpolitik*, those who control information resources will possess enormous strategic advantages. The U.S. military interventions in Iraq and Afghanistan demonstrated the critical importance of information technologies in the conduct of warfare. Gunboat diplomacy of the 19th century has been replaced by smart bombs in the 21st century.[1]

We have asserted that soft power has led to the emergence of an American Empire. We do not deny, however, that U.S. imperial domination has relied on the superiority of America's hard power and the strength of the American economy. Make no mistake, the American Empire is a military and economic superpower. The United States boasts a defence budget greater than the combined military spending by the next 14 nations. What's more, the American economy is three times larger than its four largest rivals— Japan, Germany, Britain, and France—combined. Given these awesome advantages, America is now regarded as a unipolar superpower with no likely rival in the foreseeable future. It has been our contention, however, that the American Empire, like all empires, is essentially a *cultural* construction. The role of American soft power consequently has been crucial to the extension and maintenance of American imperial power.

Only a few years ago, the notion that America was becoming an imperial power was casually dismissed. Today, it has become commonplace. It has even become fashionable—in newspapers, magazines, and scholarly journals—to describe the United States as an empire ruling the world much like the ancient Romans. In early January 2003, Michael Ignatieff published an essay in the *New York Times Magazine* titled, "American Empire: Get Used to It." Ignatieff described American imperial power today as "empire lite." At the same time, *U.S. News & World Report* published a cover story titled "The New American Empire?" The British economist Niall Ferguson contributed a more extended analysis in a new book, *Empire*, in which he compared the British Empire of the 19th century with the American Empire of the 21st century. Ferguson's book, made into a BBC television documentary, concluded that empires are a good thing. Further support for the virtue of empires came in the spring of 2003 from a series of essays in *The National Interest* under the title, "Empire?" Against this backdrop, there appears to be a growing acceptance of empire—or at least an American Empire—as a desirable form of political organization.[2]

Much discussion about American Empire has been focused on the *formal* attributes of U.S. imperialism—in other words, the deployment of U.S. hard power and economic resources in the assertion of America's global dominance. Less attention has been given to the *informal* attributes of U.S. imperialism that have been underscored in the preceding pages—in other words, the deployment of U.S. soft power. As James Kurth put it in

The National Interest: "If there is now an American empire, it is best defined by the 'soft power' of information networks and popular culture rather than by the hard power of economic exploitation and military force. It is an empire representative of the information age rather than the industrial age." We agree—indeed, the ambition of this book has been to demonstrate, through historical analysis, that very assertion.[3]

America is a benevolent hegemon, especially when compared with previous imperial powers. But what about the alleged dangers of American hegemony? So far, the only dangers are to America itself. The cost of maintaining a global empire is great, especially since America borrows more than it lends. True, there is a persistent claim that American soft power promotes a barren global monoculture, and anti-globalization protestors continue to denounce corporate America and rail against the World Trade Organization as the handmaiden of global capitalism. They can even find support among insurgent nationalists, like the anti-American demonstrators in Serbia who trashed a McDonald's in Belgrade and brandished placards shouting: "Stop NATO-Cola!" Some claim America, labelled as a global "brand bully," is undermining its own influence by aggressively promoting the expansion of Disney, Coca-Cola, and McDonald's. As *Business Week* put it in a headline: "Cultural imperialism is no joke." Why? Because American imperialism could potentially backfire if other societies become unstable due to social and cultural ruptures produced by its effects. *Business Week* added: "From the Roman to the Soviet empires, superpowers have aimed to spread their cultures, and from Lorenzo de Medici to Michael Eisner, there has always been a link between commerce and culture. Still, while America's lifestyle and ideas can be liberating and uplifting, they are also often destabilizing abroad. Movies and music frequently glorify violence and rebellion. Darwinian capitalism requires societies to uproot traditional structures without adequate regulation, safety nets, or education. The U.S. legal system encourages confrontation, not conciliation."[4]

Even among American neo-liberals—who call themselves conservatives —the ambitions of an imperial America are disputable. Patrick Buchanan, a right-wing candidate for the U.S. presidency, published a book titled *A Republic, Not an Empire*. But other conservative voices in the United States insist that America has the best model to offer the world as a humane and just society. Many argue that America must demonstrate active leadership throughout the world. In 1996, Joshua Muravchik, of the American Enterprise Institute, published *The Imperative of American Leadership*, in which he wrote that "aside perhaps from the French, the only people averse to American leadership are Americans." Henry Kissinger, in a 2001 essay entitled "America at the Apex: Empire or Leader?," warned that if post-Cold War America does not pursue a policy of "enlightened national interest" the result will be "progressive paralysis, not moral elevation." David Rothkopf, a former top official in the Clinton Administration, chimed in with an apology for American hegemony called "In Praise of Cultural Imperialism." Rothkopf asserted: "The United States should not hesitate to promote its values. In an effort to be polite or politic, Americans should not deny the fact that, of all the nations in the history of the world, theirs is the most just, the most tolerant, the most willing to constantly reassess and improve itself, and the best model for the future." This conviction was taken up by conservative columnist Charles Krauthammer, who in early 2001 made the following statement in *Time* magazine: "America is no mere international citizen. It is the dominant power in the world, more dominant than any since Rome. Accordingly, America is in a position to re-shape norms, alter expectations and create new realities. How? By unapologetic and implacable demonstration of will."[5]

Advocates of an American Empire, to be sure, have their contradictors. Lewis Lapham, writing in *Harper's*, attempted to debunk the notion of America as a "virtuous empire" with the following observation: "Unlike their overlords in Washington, the American people have never been infected with the virus of imperial ambition; nor have we acquired an exalted theory of the state that might allow us to govern subject peoples with a firm hand and an easy conscience."[6] Others argue however that, far from a hated Ugly American, the United States has become an "empire by invitation." In many parts of the world, the slogan is not "Yankee Go Home!" but rather a pleading "Yankee Stay!" American leadership today is convinced that the world's problems are America's problems. Strobe Talbott, former U.S. deputy Secretary of State, asserted that America has convergent interests in domestic peace and global stability: "In order to keep our streets safe, we must attack sources of crime at the far ends of the Earth." Echoing this view, Dominique Moisi, deputy director of France's Institute for International Relations, noted: "Europeans don't know what to fear most—to be abandoned by the United States or to be dominated by it."[7]

Samuel Huntington, the author of *Clash of Civilizations*, has asserted: "A world without U.S. primacy will be a world with more violence and disorder and less democracy and economic growth than a world where the United States continues to have more influence than any other country shaping global affairs." [8] This moral assertiveness has been taken up aggressively in the White House under President George W. Bush. In the Bush administration, conservatives such as the Pentagon's top official Paul Wolfowitz championed a muscular U.S. foreign policy that, driven by moral absolutes, sees the world in terms of good and evil. Wolfowitz was associated with the "Project for the New American Century," which gathered a constellation of conservative thinkers including Robert Kagan, William Kristol, and Thomas Donnelly. They were united in the belief that America is now an imperial power and therefore can behave unilaterally in the assertion of American global leadership.

But how long can an American Empire endure? The Roman Empire collapsed, and so, in like manner, will the American Empire vanish some day. But that day is a long way off. Like the Roman Empire, the American Empire of the 21st century is both a formal imperial system and an informal empire of values and beliefs and meaning. Unlike the Roman Empire, the American Empire possesses the advantage of powerful communications technologies that export, distribute, and transmit cultural messages with awesome efficiency. Even the culturally proud French are increasingly Americanized. Following the shocking events of 9-11, the leftist Parisian newspaper *Le Monde* declared on behalf of France: "*Nous sommes tous Américains*"—we are all Americans.

We know that the Roman Empire fell after constant attacks from belligerent barbarians. Today, the American Empire, too, is similarly under attack. America's adversaries are terrorist cells motivated by fanatical ideals that are antithetical to Western values. Not surprisingly, these threats represent the most serious challenge to U.S. foreign policy. In the fight against terrorism, American soft-power resources have become important cultural antidotes to prevent the growth of attitudes and values that foment hatred and incite violence. If terrorism triumphs, our fate could be that of Rome— a collapse leading to a chaotic neo-medieval order with no central authority. America would become a latter-day Holy Roman Empire, struggling to contain violence and establish order in a world fraught with constant peril, disease, and disorder. At the dawn of the 21st century, there are already ominous signs of an emerging world overrun with private armies, terrorists, and drug cartels. The moats and drawbridges of the Middle Ages could well be replaced by a world order where the distinction between public and private property becomes blurred; where the centres of authority are uncertain; where Visigoths and Vandals are Islamic fundamentalists in hijacked jetliners; where, in short, the center cannot hold and frightening passions are unleashed upon the world. As Zbigniew Brzezinski puts it: 'The only alternative to American power is global anarchy.'

Given these hard realities, it is surprising that American cultural imperialism has been so persistently challenged as a destructive force. We have attempted to demonstrate that America's weapons of mass distraction are not only necessary for global stability, but also should be built up and deployed more assertively throughout the world. The world needs more MTV, McDonald's, Microsoft, Madonna, and Mickey Mouse.

Yes, things really do go better with Coke.

Endnotes

Introduction

[1] For Madeleine Albright's visits to China and North Korea, see "Oscar night," *Financial Times*, 30 November 2000; and Elisabeth Rosenthal, "In Beijing Students' Worldview, Jordan Rules," *The New York Times*," 16 June 1998.

[2] Aidan Foster-Carter, "Fat Bear: No Meeting Mickey Mouse Any Time Soon," *Asia Times*, 11 May 2001.

[3] See Joseph S. Nye, "The Power We Must Not Squander," *New York Times*, 3 January 2000. Nye elaborated on his "soft power" concept in *The Paradox of American Power* (New York: Oxford University Press, 2002).

[4] See David Gress, *From Plato to NATO: The Idea of the West and Its Opponents* (New York: The Free Press, 1998), p. 3. See also John Tomlinson, *Cultural Imperialism*, (London: Pinter, 1991); and Edward Said, *Culture and Imperialism* (New York: Vintage, 1993).

[5] Paul Kennedy, *The Rise and Fall of the Great Powers* (New York: Random House, 1988), see ch. 8.

[6] See Henry Nau, *The Myth of America's Decline: Leading the World into the 1990s* (New York: Oxford University Press, 1990); Francis Fukuyama, "The End of History," *The National Interest*, n. 16, summer 1989; and Joseph S. Nye Jr., *Bound to Lead: The Changing Nature of American Power* (New York: Basic Books, 1990).

[7] Among the rich literature on empires, see Michael Doyle, *Empires* (Ithica: Cornell University Press, 1986), and a more recent book by Michael Hardt and Antonio Negri, *Empire* (Cambridge MA: Harvard University Press, 2000).

[8] Edward Gibbon, *The Decline and Fall of the Roman Empire* (New York: Heritage Press, 1946), see Volume I, ch. 2.

[9] On Westphalia, see Steven Krasner, "Sovereignty," *Foreign Policy*, January 2001. See also Steven Krasner, *Sovereignty: Organized Hypocrisy* (Princeton: Princeton University Press, 1999).

[10] See Kevin O'Rourke and Jeffrey Williamson, *Globalization and History: The Evolution of a Nineteenth-Century Atlantic Economy* (Cambridge: MIT Press, 1999).

[11] See Fareed Zakaria, *From Wealth to Power: The Unusual Origins of America's World Role* (Princeton: Princeton University Press, 1998). See also Richard Pells, *Not Like Us: How Europeans Have Loved, Hated, and Transformed American Culture Since World War II* (New York: Basic Books, 1997), p. 7. For American brands circa 1900, see Emily S. Rosenberg, *Spreading the American Dream: American Economic and Cultural Expansion 1890–1945* (New York: Hill and Wang, 1982), ch. 2.

[12] For an excellent book on globalization, see David Held et. al., *Global Transformations: Politics, Economics and Culture* (Stanford: Stanford University Press, 1999).

[13] See Alain Minc, *Le Nouveau Moyen Age* (Paris: Gallimard, 1993). See also Stephen Kobrin, "Back to the Future: Neomedievalism and the Postmodern Digital World Economy," *Journal of International Affairs*, Spring 1998; and Robert O. Keohane and Joseph S. Nye Jr., "Power and Interdependence in the Information Age," *Foreign Affairs*, September/October 1998.

[14] See Robert D. Kaplan, *The Coming Anarchy* (New York: Random House, 2000). See also Stephen Kobrin, op. cit. See also Zbigniew Brzezinski, *The Grand Chessboard* (New York: HarperCollins, 1998). Brzezinski is quoted in Charles William Maynes, "The Perils of (and for) an Imperial America," *Foreign Policy*, Summer 1998.

[15] Benjamin Barber, "Jihad vs. McWorld," *Atlantic Monthly*, March 1992. See also Barber's book, *Jihad vs. McWorld: How Globalism and Tribalism are Reshaping the World* (New York: Ballantine Books, 1996), see Introduction.

[16] Samuel P. Huntington, "Clash of Civilizations," *Foreign Affairs*, Summer 1993. See also Huntington's book, *Clash of Civilizations and the Remaking of World Order* (New York: Simon and Schuster, 1996).

[17] See *Bound to Lead*, ibid., p. 191. Also see Joseph S. Nye Jr. and William A. Owen, "America's Information Edge," *Foreign Affairs*, March–April, 1996; and Robert O. Keohane and Joseph S. Nye Jr., "Power and Independence in the Information Age," *Foreign Affairs*, September–October 1998. On cyberpolitik, see David J. Rothkopf, "Cyberpolitik: The Changing Nature of Power in the Information Age," *Journal of International Affairs*, Spring 1998.

one

Movies: The Power and the Glamour

[1] See Richard Abel, *The Red Rooster Scare: Making Cinema American 1900–1910* (Los Angeles: University of California Press), ch. 5.

[2] See Tino Balio, *The American Film Industry* (Madison: University of Wisconsin Press, 1985), ch. 17.

[3] See Kerry Seagrave, *American Films Abroad: Hollywood's Domination of the World's Movie Screens* (Jefferson: McFarland & Company, 1997), p. 59.

[4] See Ian Jarvie, *Hollywood's Overseas Campaign* (Cambridge: University of Cambridge Press, 1992), ch. 2.

[5] See Ronald Brownstein, *The Power and the Glitter: The Hollywood-Washington Connection* (New York: Pantheon Books, 1990), p. 35.

[6] David Puttnam, *Movies and Money* (New York: Alfred A. Knopf, 1998), p. 159.

[7] See Paul Swann, *The Hollywood Feature Film in Postwar Britain* (London: Croom Helm, 1987), p. 101.

[8] Puttnam, *Movies and Money* (New York: Alfred A. Knopf, 1998), p. 165.

[9] See Richard Pells, *Not Like Us: How Europeans Have Loved, Hated, and Transformed American Culture Since World War II* (New York: Basic Books, 1997), p. 215.

[10] Dennis McDougal, *The Last Mogul: Lew Wasserman, MCA, and the Hidden History of Hollywood* (New York: Crown Publishers, 1998), p. 320. See also a fascinating portrait of Jack Valenti in *The New Yorker*, "The Personal Touch," *The New Yorker*, 13 August 2001.

[11] Quoted in a portrait of Jack Valenti by Connie Bruck, "The Personal Touch," *The New Yorker*, 13 August 2001.

[12] See David Puttnam, *Movies and Money* (New York: Alfred A. Knopf, 1998), p. 214.

[13] "At 80, Valenti rates an R for resilient," *Variety*, 16–22 July 2001, p. 1.

[14] See Steven Watts, *The Magic Kingdom: Walt Disney and the American Way of Life* (New York: Houghton Mifflin, 1997), ch. 12.

[15] See Eric Smoodin (ed.), *Disney Discourse: Producing the Magic Kingdom* (New York: Routledge, 1994), ch. 10.

[16] For a Marxist interpretation of Disney fiction, see Julianne Burton-Carvajal, "Surprise Package: Looking Southward with Disney," in Eric Smoodin (ed.), *Disney Discourse: Producing the Magic Kingdom* (New York: Routledge, 1994), ch. 9. See also Eleanor Byrne and Martin McQuillan, *Deconstructing Disney* (London: Pluto Press, 1999).

[17] See Steven Watts, *The Magic Kingdom: Walt Disney and the American Way of Life* (New York: Houghton Mifflin, 1997), pp. 287–88.

[18] Steven Watts, *The Magic Kingdom: Walt Disney and the American Way of Life* (New York: Houghton Mifflin, 1997), p. 392.

[19] See Mitsuhiro Yoshimoto, "Images of Empire: Tokyo Disneyland and Japanese Cultural Imperialism," in Eric Smoodin (ed.), *Disney Discourse: Producing the Magic Kingdom* (New York: Routledge, 1994), ch. 12.

[20] "Welcome to bankruptcyland," *The Economist*, 20 April 2003.

[21] Michael Eisner, *Work in Progress* (New York: Random House, 1998), p. 269.

[22] Kerry Seagrave, *American Films Abroad: Hollywood's Domination of the World's Movie Screens* (Jefferson: McFarland & Company, 1997), p. 227.

[23] See David Bordwell, *Planet Hong Kong: Popular Cinema and the Art of Entertainment* (Cambridge MA: Harvard University Press, 2000); and Stefan Hammono, *Hollywood East: Hong Kong Movies and the People Who Make Them* (Chicago: Contemporary Books, 2000).

[24] For an account of Sony's troubles in Hollywood, see Nancy Griffin and Kim Masters, *Hit and Run: How Jon Peters and Peter Gruber Took Sony for a Ride in Hollywood* (New York: Simon and Schuster, 1996).

[25] "Indonesians Finally See Film Banned 17 Years Ago," *New York Times*, 12 November 2000.

[26] Joanne Slater, "Bollywood Tries to Go After Mainstream American Cinema," *Wall Street Journal*, 27 March 2002.

two

Television: Lotusland as Global Empire

[1] See Peter de Jonge, "Television's Final Frontier," *New York Times*, 22 August 1999.

[2] See Martin Meyer, *Whatever Happened to Madison Avenue?* (Boston: Little, Brown, 1991).

[3] See Kerry Seagrave, *American Television Abroad: Hollywood's Attempt to Dominate World Television* (Jefferson, NC: McFarland & Company, 1998), ch. 1.

[4] David Held *et al.*, *Global Transformations: Politics, Economics, and Culture* (Stanford: Stanford University Press, 1999), p. 358.

[5] For a critique of the global advertising industry, see Armand Mattelart, *Advertising International* (London: Routledge, 1991).

[6] Rhonda J. Crane, *The Politics of International Standards: France and the Color TV War* (Norwood NJ: Ablex, 1979), ch. 3.

[7] "British TV Goes U.S.," *U.S. News & World Report*, 20 July 1956.

[8] See Albert Moran, Copycat TV: *Globalisation, Program Formats and Cultural Identity* (Luton: University of Luton Press, 1998); and Hugh O'Donnell, *Good Times, Bad Times: Soap Operas and Society in Western Europe* (London: Leicester University Press, 1999).

[9] See Roberto Mader, "Globo Village," in Tony Dowmunt (ed.) *Channels of Resistance* (London: British Film Institute, 1993).

[10] See Hugh O'Donnell, *Good Times, Bad Times: Soap Operas and Society in Western Europe* (London: Leicester University Press, 1999).

[11] See Joseph Turow, *Breaking Up America: Advertisers and the New Media World* (Chicago: University of Chicago Press, 1997), ch. 3.

[12] See John B. Thompson, "The Globalization of Communication," in *The Global Transformations Reader*, David Held and Anthony McGrew (Cambridge: Polity Press, 2000). See also Jeremy Tunstall and Michael Palmer, *Media Moguls* (London: Routledge, 1991) ch. 3.

[13] See "Unsnoozing the continental news," *The Economist*, 20 November 1997; and "Stop Press," *The Economist*, 2 July 1998.

[14] See "The Network's Not Working," *The Economist*, 2 August 2001.

[15] For an upbeat, book-length account of Al-Jazeera's rise to international fame, see Mohammed El-Nawawy and Adel Iskandar, *Al-Jazeera: How the Free Arab News Network Scooped the World and Changed the Middle East* (Cambridge MA: Westview, 2002).

16 See Thomas L. Friedman, "The Hidden Victims," *New York Times*, 1 May 2001.

17 See Naomi Sakr, "Optical Illusions: Television and Censorship in the Arab World," *Transnational Broadcasting Studies*, Fall 2000.

18 John Burns, "Arab TV Gets a New Slant: Newscasts Without Censorship," *New York Times*, 4 July 1999.

19 William Shawcross, "Rupert Murdoch," *Time*, 25 October 1999.

20 See John Cassy, "Murdoch Seals TV Deal with China," *The Guardian*, 20 December 2001; and Geraldine Fabrikant, "Western TV May be Nearer for Chinese," *New York Times*, 5 September 2001.

21 See Lynne Schafer Gross, *The International World of Electronic Media* (New York: McGraw-Hill, 1996), ch. 8.

22 See Jack Shaheen, *The TV Arab* (New York: Popular Press, 1976). See also Shaheen's *Reel Bad Arabs: How Hollywood Vilifies People* (Northampton MA: Interlink Books, 1984).

23 See Abdoul Ba, Télévisions, paraboles et démocraties en Afrique noire (Paris: L'Harmattan, 1996).

24 See Hussein Amin, "Egypt and the Arab World in the Satellite Age," in John Sinclair et al. *New Patterns in Global Television: Peripheral Vision* (Oxford: Oxford University Press, 1996).

25 Alice Rawsthorn, "Hollywood Turns Focus to Europe," *Financial Times*, 16 February 1998, p. 19. See also Martin Dale, *The Movie Game: The Film Business in Britain, Europe and America* (London: Cassell, 1997), p. 242.

three

Music: Pop Goes the World

1 See Jeffrey Richards, *Imperialism and Music: Britain 1876–1953* (Manchester: Manchester University Press, 2001).

2 See Deanna Campbell Robinson et al., *Music at the Margins: Popular Music and Global Cultural Diversity* (London: Sage, 1991), ch. 2.

3 See *Saturday Review*, 14 July 1956.

4 See Reebee Garofalo, *Rockin' Out: Popular Music in the USA* (Upper Saddle River NJ: Prentice Hall, 2002), p. 47.

5 See Andy Bennett, *Popular Music and Youth Culture* (London: Palgrave, 2000), ch. 2.

6 See Reebee Garofalo, *Rockin' Out: Popular Music in the USA* (Upper Saddle Rivers NJ: Prentice Hall, 2002).

7 For an excellent account of MTV's commercial practices, see Jack Banks, *Monopoly Television: MTV's Quest to Control the Music* (New York: Westview, 1996). For MTV's ideological critics, see Rosalind Williams, "The Dream World of Mass Consumption," in C. Mukerji and M. Schudson (eds.), *Rethinking Popular Culture* (Berkeley: University of California Press, 1991); and Simon Philo, "MTV's Global Footprint" in R. Browne and M. Fishwick (eds.) *The Global Village: Dead or Alive?* (Bowling Green: Bowling Green University Press, 1999).

8 See "Labels Limit Videos on Black Artists," *Variety*, 15 December 1982.

9 See Corinna Sturmer, "MTV's Europe: An Imaginary Continent?" in Tony Dowmunt (ed.) *Channels of Resistance: Global Television and Local Empowerment* (London: British Film Institute, 1993).

10 Elizabeth Brown, "MTV's Cultural Colonialism," *Christian Science Monitor*, 6 August 1991.

11 See Timothy Taylor, *Global Pop: World Music, World Markets* (London: Routledge, 1997), p. 201.

12 Bruce Orwall, "Latin Translation: Colombian Pop Star Taps American Taste in Repackaged Imports," *Wall Street Journal*, 13 February 2001.

13 "Asian Operation Built on Location," *Variety*, 8 October 2001.

14 See Peter Manuel, *Cassette Culture: Popular Music and Technology in North India* (Chicago: University of Chicago Press, 1993).

15 See Andy Bennett, *Popular Music and Youth Culture* (Basingstoke: Palgrave, 2000), ch. 5.

16 "India's Youth," *Business Week*, 11 October 1999.

17 See Tim Brace and Paul Freidlander, "Rock and Roll in the New Long March," in Reebee Garofalo (ed.) *Rockin' the Boat* (Boston: South End Press, 1992).

18 See Douglas McGray, "Japan's Gross National Cool," *Foreign Policy*, May–June 2002.

19 Steve Silberman, "Recombinant De-Re-Mi," *Wired*, 29 October 1997.

four

Fast Food: Coca-Colonization and McDomination

1 Mark Pendergrast, *For God, Country, and Coca Cola* (New York: Simon & Schuster, 1993), p. 203.

2 See Richard Kuisel, *Seducing the French: The Dilemma of Americanization* (Berkeley: University of California Press, 1993), p. 41.

3 Jean-Noël Jeanneney, "Coca-Cola: le sens d'un écho," *Le Monde*, 28 June 1999.

4 See Frederick Allen, *Secret Formula: How Brilliant Marketers and Relentless Salesmanship Made Coca-Cola the Best-Known Product in the World* (New York: HarperCollins, 1995), p. 11.

5 See Mark Pendergrast's history of Coca-Cola, *For God, Country, and Coca Cola*, ch. 14.

6 Mark Pendergrast, *For God, Country, and Coca Cola* (New York: Simon & Schuster, 1993), p. 288.

7 David Greising, *I'd Like to Buy the World a Coke: The Life and Leadership of Robert Goizueta* (New York: John Wiley & Sons, 1997) p. 287.

8 See, Betsy McKay, "Coca-Cola's CEO Woos Europe with New Formula for Success," *Wall Street Journal*, 23 June 2000. See also Constance Hays, "Learning to Think Smaller at Coke," *New York Times*, 6 February 2000.

9 See Walter LaFeber, *Michael Jordan and the New Global Capitalism* (New York: W.W. Norton & Company, 1999), p. 117.

10 See *Business Week*, "The Stars of Europe" (international edition), 12 June 2000. See also Suzanne Daley, "French See a Hero in War on 'McDomination,'" *New York Times*, 12 October 1999; and Jacqueline Friedrich, "From Small French Farmer to Big World Player," *Wall Street Journal*, 22 December 1999.

[11] Alison Maitland, "McDonald's responds to anti-capitalist grilling," *Financial Times*, 15 April 2002.

[12] Shirley Leung, "Armchairs, TVs, and Expresso—Is it McDonald's?" *Wall Street Journal*, 30 August 2002.

[13] See Gorbachev's foreword in George Cohon, *To Russia with Fries* (Toronto: McClelland & Stewart, 1999).

[14] See James L. Watson (ed.), *Golden Arches East: McDonald's in East Asia* (Stanford: Stanford University Press, 1997), ch. 1.

[15] For this view, see Ziauddin Sardar and Merryl Wyn Davies, *Why Do People Hate America?* (Cambridge UK: Icon Books, 2002), p. 130.

[16] Thomas L. Friedman, *The Lexus and the Olive Tree* (New York: Farrar Straus Giroux, 1999), ch. 10.

Conclusion

[1] See a book prepared by RAND for the U.S. Defense Department, John Arquilla and David Ronfeldt, *In Athena's Camp: Preparing for Conflict in the Information Age* (Washington: RAND, 1997). See also "Technology and International Policy," *Journal of International Affairs*, Spring 1998.

[2] Niall Feguson, *Empire* (New York: Basic Books, 2002). See also an Anarcho-Marxist analysis from Michael Hardt and Antonio Negri, *Empire* (Cambridge: Harvard University Press, 2000). And see essays under the title "Empire?" *The National Interest*, Spring 2003.

[3] James Kurth, "Migration and the Dynamics of Empire," *The National Interest*, Spring 2003.

[4] Jeffrey E. Garten, "Cultural Imperialism is No Joke," *BusinessWeek*, 30 November 1998. See also a critique in *The Economist* of leftist anti-globalization activist Naomi Klein's book, *No Logo: Taking Aim at the Brand Bullies*: "Pro Logo: Why brands are good for you," *The Economist*, 8 September 2001.

[5] See Henry Kissinger, "America at the Apex: Empire or Leader?" *The National Interest*, no. 64, Summer 2001. The Kissinger essay is an excerpt from his book, *Does America Need a Foreign Policy?* (New York: Simon & Schuster, 2001). See also William Pfaff, "The Question of Hegemony," *Foreign Affairs*, January/February 2001; David Rothkopf, "In Praise of Cultural Imperialism," *Foreign Policy*, Summer 1997; and Charles Krauthammer, "The Bush Doctrine," *Time*, 5 March 2001.

[6] Lewis Lapham, "The American Rome," *Harper's*, August 2001.

[7] R.C. Longworth, "Like it or Not, U.S. in Charge," *Chicago Tribune*, 4 December 1998.

[8] See quote in Robert Kagan, "The Benevolent Empire," *Foreign Policy*, Summer 1998.

Selected Bibliography

Abel, Richard. *The Red Rooster Scare: Making Cinema American 1900–1910*. Los Angeles: University of California Press, 1999.

Allen, Frederick. *Secret Formula: How Brilliant Marketers and Relentless Salesmanship Made Coca-Cola the Best-Known Product in the World*. New York: HarperCollins, 1995.

Arquilla, John and Ronfeldt, David. *In Athena's Camp: Preparing for Conflict in the Information Age*. Washington: RAND, 1997.

Badie, Bertrand. *La fin des territoires*. Paris: Fayard, 1997.

Badie, Bertrand. *Un monde sans souveraineté*. Paris: Fayard, 1999.

Balio, Tino. *The American Film Industry*. Madison: University of Wisconsin Press, 1985.

Banks, Jack. *Monopoly Television: MTV's Quest to Control the Music*. New York: Westview, 1996.

Barber, Benjamin. *Jihad vs. McWorld: How Globalism and Tribalism are Reshaping the World*. New York: Ballantine Books, 1996.

Barnet, Richard and Cavanagh, John. *Global Dreams: Imperial Corporations and the New World Order*. New York: Simon and Schuster, 1994.

Bennett, Andy. *Popular Music and Youth Culture*. London: Palgrave, 2000.

Bordwell, David. *Planet Hong Kong: Popular Cinema and the Art of Entertainment*. Cambridge MA: Harvard University Press.

Brownstein, Ronald. *The Power and the Glitter: The Hollywood-Washington Connection*. New York: Pantheon Books, 1990.

Brzezinski, Zbigniew. *The Grand Chessboard*. New York: HarperCollins, 1998.

Byrne, Eleanor and McQuillan, Martin. *Deconstructing Disney*. London: Pluto Press, 1999.

Campbell Robinson, Deanna, et. al., *Music at the Margins: Popular Music and Global Cultural Diversity*. London: Sage, 1991.

Cohon, George. *To Russia With Fries*. Toronto: McClelland & Stewart, 1999.

Cowen, Tyler. *In Praise of Commercial Culture*. Cambridge MA: Harvard University Press, 1998.

Cowen, Tyler. *Creative Destruction: How Globalization is Changing the World's Culture.* Princeton: Princeton University Press, 2002.

Craig, Timothy (ed.). *Japan Pop!: Inside the World of Japanese Popular Culture.* New York: East Gate, 2000.

Crane, Rhonda. *The Politics of International Standards: France and the Color TV War.* Norwood NJ: Ablex, 1979.

Dowmunt, Tony (ed.). *Channels of Resistance: Global Television and Local Empowerment.* London: British Film Institute, 1993.

Doyle, Michael. *Empires.* Ithica NY: Cornell University Press, 1986.

Eisner, Michael. *Work in Progress.* New York: Random House, 1998.

El-Nawawy, Mohammed and Iskandar, Adel. *Al-Jazeera: How the Free Arab News Network Scooped the World and Changed the Middle East.* Cambridge MA: Westview, 2000.

Ferguson, Niall. *Empire.* New York: Basic Books, 2002.

Friedman, Thomas. *The Lexus and the Olive Tree.* New York: Farrar Straus Giroux, 1999.

Garofalo, Reebee. *Rockin' Out: Popular Music in the USA.* Upper Saddle River NJ: Prentice Hall, 2002.

Gibbon, Edward. *The Decline and Fall of the Roman Empire.* New York: Heritage Press, 1946.

Greising, David. *I'd Like to Buy the World a Coke: The Life and Leadership of Robert Goizueta.* New York: John Wiley & Sons, 1997.

Gress, David. *From Plato to NATO: The Idea of the West and Its Opponents.* New York: The Free Press, 1998.

Hammono, Stefan. *Hollywood East: Hong Kong Movies and the People Who Make Them.* Chicago: Contemporary Books, 2000.

Hardt, Michael and Negri, Antonio. *Empire.* Cambridge MA: Harvard University Press, 2000.

Held, David, *et. al. Global Transformations: Politics, Economics and Culture.* Stanford: Stanford University Press, 1999.

Held, David and McGrew, Anthony (eds.). The *Global Transformations Reader.* Cambridge: Polity, 2000.

Huntington, Samuel. *Clash of Civilizations and the Remaking of World Order.* New York: Simon and Schuster, 1996.

Jarvie, Ian. *Hollywood's Overseas Campaign.* Cambridge: University of Cambridge Press, 1992.

Kagan, Robert. *Of Paradise and Power: America and Europe in the New World Order.* New York: Alfred A. Knopf, 2003.

Kaplan, Robert. *The Coming Anarchy.* New York: Random House, 2000.

Kennedy, Paul. *The Rise and Fall of the Great Powers.* New York: Random House, 1988.

Krasner, Steven. *Sovereignty: Organized Hypocrisy.* Princeton: Princeton University Press, 1999.

Kuisel, Richard. *Seducing the French: The Dilemma of Americanization.* Berkeley: University of California Press, 1993.

LaFeber, Walter. *Michael Jordan and the New Global Capitalism.* New York: W.W. Norton & Company, 1999.

Lechner, Frank and Boli, John (eds.). *The Globalization Reader.* Oxford: Blackwell, 2000.

Lewis, Bernard. *What Went Wrong? Western Impact Middle Eastern Response.* New York: Oxford University Press, 2002.

Love, John. *McDonald's: Behind the Arches.* New York: Bantam, 1995.

McDougal, Dennis. *The Last Mogul: Lew Wasserman, MCA, and the Hidden History of Hollywood.* New York: Crown Publishers, 1998.

Minc, Alain. *Le Nouveau Moyen Age.* Paris: Gallimard, 1993.

Moran, Albert. *Copycat TV: Globalisation, Program Formats and Cultural Identity.* Luton: University of Luton Press, 1998.

Nau, Henry. *The Myth of America's Decline: Leading the World into the 1990s.* New York: Oxford University Press, 1990.

Nye, Joseph S. Jr. *Bound to Lead: The Changing Nature of American Power.* New York: Basic Books, 1990.

Nye, Joseph S. Jr. *The Paradox of American Power.* New York: Oxford University Press, 2002.

O'Donnell, Hugh. *Good Times, Bad Times: Soap Operas and Society in Western Europe.* London: Leicester University Press, 1999.

Pells, Richard. *Not Like Us: How Europeans Have Loved, Hated, and Transformed American Culture Since World War II.* New York: Basic Books, 1997.

Pendergrast, Mark. *For God, Country, and Coca Cola.* New York: Simon & Schuster, 1993.

Puttnam, David. *Movies and Money.* New York: Alfred A. Knopf, 1998.

Richards, Jeffrey. *Imperialism and Music: Britain 1876-1953.* Manchester: Manchester University Press, 2001.

Rosenberg, Emily. *Spreading the American Dream: American Economic and Cultural Expansion 1890–1945.* New York: Hill and Wang, 1982.

Said, Edward. *Culture and Imperialism.* New York: Vintage, 1993.

Seagrave, Kerry. *American Films Abroad: Hollywood's Domination of the World's Movie Screens.* Jefferson: McFarland & Company, 1997.

Seagrave, Kerry. *American Television Abroad: Hollywood's Attempt to Dominate World Television.* Jefferson: McFarland & Company, 1998.

Smoodin, Eric (ed.). *Disney Discourse: Producing the Magic Kingdom.* New York: Routledge, 1994.

Suid, Lawrence. *Guts and Glory: The Making of the American Military Image in Film.* Louisville: University Press of Kentucky, 2002.

Swann, Paul. *The Hollywood Feature Film in Postwar Britain.* London: Croom Helm, 1987.

Taylor, Timothy. *Global Pop: World Music, World Markets.* London: Routledge, 1997.

Tomlinson, John. *Cultural Imperialism.* London: Pinter, 1991.

Watson, James (ed.) *Golden Arches East: McDonald's in East Asia.* Stanford: Stanford University Press, 1997.

Watts, Steven. *The Magic Kingdom: Walt Disney and the American Way of Life.* New York: Houghton Mifflin, 1997.

Zakaria, Fareed. *From Wealth to Power: The Unusual Origins of America's World Role.* Princeton: Princeton University Press, 1998.

Index